MARCIA LANGTON
WITH NINA FITZGERALD AND AMBA-ROSE ATKINSON

WELCOME TO COUNTRY

A Travel Guide to Indigenous Australia

hardie grant travel

FOREWORD

For years I lived far from my country. I found new homes. New smells, sights and sounds slowly erased the memories of my country.

But then I would fly home. I could feel Australia before I'd even seen it. I would often wake over the Red Centre, looking down on an earth like no other. Like a dot painting it revealed itself: a mosaic of brush and spinifex and red dirt cut with creeks and flat plains and hills.

This country does talk to me. It talks in a language as old as humanity. This is a language that lives in art and music and story. If we open ourselves up, it will speak to us all.

That is what Welcome to Country does, it speaks from somewhere deep inside our land to something deep inside all of us.

Marcia Langton takes us on a journey through this continent. We meet the keepers of sacred places; those who carry

the traditions of care for country. They have held it for time immemorial just for us; all of us, no matter where our ancestral journeys may have begun.

It is a story of place and a story of people. It is our relationship to land and our relationship to each other. My blood is buried deep in this place; my kinship winds back thousands of generations and it blends with those who have come here from other lands.

Marcia tells us that kinship matters; culture matters; stories matter. She tells us too that law matters; Indigenous law and the fight to have our place recognised in a country that denied us for too long.

This is an ancient book and a modern book. We live in a globalised world, we are a touch away from anyone anywhere. This is a book of song lines and trade routes; it is also a book of modern tourism in a global economy.

I live now in Sydney, but my real home lies six hours' drive away. I often take that trip, slowly I leave the noise of the city behind and the land opens up to me. There is a place on the Hume Highway where the road rises and dips. Off to my side is a valley leading to the Murrumbidgee River. I come alive here; nothing on earth feels like this.

This is my country. Welcome to country.

STAN GRANT

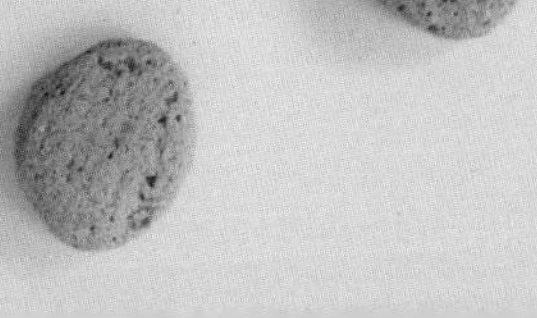

CONTENTS

1 **PART ONE: INTRODUCING INDIGENOUS CULTURES**

2 1. Introduction
6 2. Prehistory
11 3. Cultures and Languages
16 4. Kinship
20 5. Art
29 6. Performance
34 7. Storytelling
38 8. Native Title
43 9. The Stolen Generations
48 10. What if Your Guide is not Indigenous?
54 11. NAIDOC Week
56 12. Business and Tourism
64 13. Cultural Awareness for Visitors
72 14. Glossary
74 15. Endnotes

79 **PART TWO: EXPLORING INDIGENOUS AUSTRALIA**

80 1. Northern Territory
137 2. Western Australia
156 3. New South Wales
173 4. Victoria
184 5. South Australia
195 6. Queensland
211 7. Tasmania
217 8. Australian Capital Territory
222 9. Torres Strait Islands

226 Index
233 About the Author

PART ONE

INTRODUCING INDIGENOUS CULTURES

1

INTRODUCTION

Australia is alive with the long history of the Indigenous people, our culture and our presence. Nowhere else in the world can you see and experience the oldest living cultures of humankind. There are two distinctive Indigenous cultural groupings in Australia: Aboriginal peoples on the mainland and most islands; and the Torres Strait Islanders, whose homelands are in the Torres Strait between the northern tip of Queensland and Papua New Guinea. People are believed to have settled on these islands about 20000 years ago. Aboriginal peoples have been living on the mainland for more than 60000 years; archaeologists have uncovered evidence of people living in Arnhem Land in the Northern Territory 65000 years ago.

The Indigenous footprint can be found across the Australian continent and its islands, but it is often invisible until it is pointed out. Once you see the evidence of Aboriginal life, a whole new world opens up. You begin to see the country around you differently. Keen to share their cultural riches, hundreds of Aboriginal people have found ways to invite tourists into their lives, even briefly, to enjoy the experience of being in Aboriginal country with the people who know it best: the Traditional Owners. With a deep knowledge of the natural world, they are the ideal guides to show you the extraordinary range of environments across the country. For over 200 years, Indigenous Australians have hosted and guided scientists, scientific expeditions, and explorers seeking to understand the environments, flora, fauna and climate of this continent, as well as the cultures of the Indigenous people themselves. This has resulted in a vast literature on Australian life, but until recently much of it was read only by the experts. A growing number of writers, both Indigenous and other Australians, are now publishing more accessible books to show the wonders of this rich heritage to the world.

The opportunity for Indigenous Australians to share their experiences and knowledge with tourists opened up when land rights were recognised and Indigenous people became joint managers of large swathes of our country. Now there are visitors' centres, art and cultural centres, museums and festivals in even the most remote places, showcasing the fascinating history and cultures of Indigenous societies.

When you are travelling around Indigenous Australia, you will find yourself in extraordinary situations with extraordinary people, whether you are exploring by foot, vehicle, boat, horse or camel; in semi-arid areas such as the Central Desert or the Western Desert; savanna country across north Australia with its many dramatic rock outcrops, escarpments and gorges; or the wet rainforests where fast flowing rivers cascade over mountain ranges; the temperate-zone coastal and riverine plains; the forests; the Great Dividing Range in its many forms; or on the beaches, islands and reefs.

Indigenous people have established cultural and natural tourism businesses and opened up their country for tourists with great energy, determination and a love of sharing the beauty of their culture and heritage. Also, the benefits of tourism to local Indigenous people are many. In large parts of Indigenous Australia, where there are few other economic opportunities, tourism businesses are a pathway for local families to enjoy the benefits of their unparalleled ancestral heritage. With their own tourism projects, local people have the opportunity to work on their country with their family members. They can also teach their own young people as well as tourists about their culture, history and heritage because Indigenous tourism preserves traditional knowledge and involves the younger generations in its continuation. There are surprises, too, for even the most knowledgeable Traditional Owner. While visiting remote parts of their old estates, where threatened populations were protected from introduced predators and land clearance, Traditional Owners have discovered new species of flora and fauna, and surviving pockets of species thought to be extinct.

The Aboriginal domain was reduced to segregated reserves during and after colonisation and the spread of British settlers and their land clearing for farming and grazing across the continent.

Top: Indigenous man and woman photographed by explorer Sir George Hubert Wilkins ca. 1923–1925, during his expedition to northern Australia to document native flora and fauna for the British Museum

Bottom: An Indigenous guide leads a Dreamtime Southern X tour around The Rocks, Sydney, New South Wales

Top: Magnificent views to be had from Nadab Lookout, Ubirr Rock, Northern Territory

Bottom: Heritage tour run by Dreamtime Southern X, Sydney, New South Wales

The growth of Indigenous rights over the last fifty years has resulted in the return of land areas to the Traditional Owners and resumption of the Aboriginal traditions of management. Free once again to steward the land, Aboriginal people are protecting the biodiversity of the country with a range of strategies. Tourism is one of them, and often it is the Aboriginal rangers who take on the task of conserving the environment as well as working as guides for visitors.

Over the last century, Aboriginal and Torres Strait Islander people, like other Australians, have been attracted to the cities and towns from the rural and remote areas. Today, the majority of Indigenous people live in towns and cities. The remainder mainly live in small towns and Aboriginal settlements and communities scattered across the country. Even in the largest cities, such as Sydney and Melbourne, Aboriginal people have retained their traditional ownership customs and established tourism ventures to guide visitors across their land and waters and to understand their culture and history.

The best way to see the Sydney Harbour, for example, is aboard the *Mari Nawi*, or Big Canoe, operated by Tribal Warrior Cultural Cruises. The cruise is hosted by local Aboriginal people who tell the stories of the Gadigal, Guringai, Wagal, Gammeraigal and Wallumedegal people of the area as you tour Sydney Harbour. They take visitors ashore at Be-lang-le-wool (Clark Island) to show you their coastal way of life, traditional fishing methods, food gathering techniques, and a cultural performance.

In Melbourne, I recommend a walking tour of the city with Wemba Wemba-Wergaia man Dean Stewart and his people, who point out the Aboriginal places that remain despite the growth of this city, and explain their history, names and meanings. Dean's knowledge of Aboriginal Melbourne is encyclopaedic, based in both Aboriginal oral history and the records of the colony and the city. The most popular walks are the Aboriginal Yarra River tour: Walkin' Country, Walkin' Birrarung and Ngargee to Nerm Cultural tour: from Ancient Tree to Ancient Sea, which goes from a 600-year-old river red gum in St Kilda to the Albert Park grasslands. Dean has guided thousands of students from high school to university level, as well as tourists, around Aboriginal Melbourne and is a regular contributor to classes at the University of Melbourne.

These are two of the hundreds of attractions run by or with Indigenous people that you will read about in the pages of this book.

Tribal Warrior: tribalwarrior.org
Dean Stewart Aboriginal Tours and Education Melbourne: ATAEM@optusnet.com.au

2

PREHISTORY

Some archaeologists believe that humans were living on this continent before the last Ice Age, perhaps as far back as 125 000 years ago. That staggering thought is a key to understanding the global attraction to the Aboriginal world. Art collectors and galleries in the United Kingdom, Europe and North America have large collections of Aboriginal art, accumulated since French explorer Thomas Nicolas Baudin's expedition to Australia from 1801 to 1803. His collection in France includes the first musical annotation of an Aboriginal song, 'Coo-ee', as well as various rare objects. First collected by Francis Barrallier, a French settler in the colony at Port Jackson, the song 'Coo-ee' was set to music by Pierre-Francois Bernier (1779–1803), astronomer to the Baudin expedition (1800–1804).[1] This practice of acquiring Australian Aboriginal art is an aspect of the fascination people around the world have with the most ancient continuous culture. By exploring this culture we are also, in a way, exploring the nature of our humanity.

Art is central to Aboriginal life, identity and culture. One of the results of this unimaginably long period of human endeavour is the vast array of rock art that can be found in most parts of Australia. Captured in this ancient art are many of the totemic icons and visual design – or the 'Dreaming' elements – that appear in modern Aboriginal art and material culture, dance and storytelling. More than art alone, these are the signs of a great human migration across the oceans and the archipelago to our north, and across this vast continent. The remains of ancient Aboriginal life are to be found scattered across landscapes everywhere. For example, the stone walls of houses in south-west Victoria, the engraved trees on the inland plains of New South Wales and Victoria, the engraved concentric rings in rock faces that signal water sources in the arid areas, and stone tool-making sites.

Painting and engraving rock faces enabled people to write, read and, through time, negotiate the land's cultural meaning. The experience of standing in a rock-art gallery gazing at ancient paintings of people and times long gone is spine chilling. I have stood on sand in a sandstone escarpment shelter where people had camped tens of thousands of years ago. Gazing up at their paintings, some of them gigantic and elaborate, is a kind of time travel. The paintings seem to resonate with the spirit of the people who made them. The hand stencils made by groups of Aboriginal people record their visits to these rock galleries. Each man, woman and child in the group held their hand

Top: Rock art in Mount Borradaile, Arnhem Land, Northern Territory

Bottom: An engraving of Aboriginal tombs on Maria Island in Tasmania, ca. 1801–1803. Illustration published in 1895 in François Péron's account of a French cartographic expedition to Australia led by Thomas Nicholas Baudin in 1800–1804

Top: Mungo National Park, New South Wales, was a lake until approximately 15 000 years ago

Bottom: Burning country near Katiti Waterhole, Northern Territory

continent on Earth, and required adaptation to vastly different flora and fauna.'[2, 3]

These small populations arrived at different times, and their different physical attributes are well known to the historians who studied the small people in the Lake Mungo burials dated at 35 000 years ago and the more robust people at Kow Swamp, Victoria. The Smithsonian Human Origins study tells us that 'the oldest known human skeletal remains in Australia are about 40 000 years old. This 13 000- to 9000-year-old *Homo sapiens* skull from Kow Swamp has a more rugged build than earlier skulls.'[4] This diversity is evident in the many Aboriginal populations across Australia today.

Some archaeologists believe that humans arrived by sea craft on the northern shores of the continent. From there they moved along the coastlines and reached the southern shores about 35 000 years ago. Writing about 'Humans, water, and the colonisation of Australia', Michael I. Bird, from James Cook University in Cairns, and his colleagues used satellite imagery and their knowledge of prehistoric waterscapes to show that the migration route most likely followed the 'well-watered routes from northern Australia, through the eastern semiarid and arid zone, to southeastern Australia and into the rocky arid center of the continent'.[5]

This fascinating history of the world's driest inhabited continent is one of great human ingenuity in the face of unknown lands. With people arriving here before the last Ice Age this was the first southern-most human population on the globe.

The ancient peoples left traces of their lives in the rocks and on the rock faces everywhere they went. Perhaps their greatest legacy is to be found in the vegetation patterns and other evidence of their 'continent-wide Aboriginal management regime', as Bill Gammage put it. His book, *The Biggest Estate on Earth: How Aborigines made Australia*, is a eulogy for that world before the British colonisers arrived. Gammage scoured through historical and scientific research and wrote this extraordinary history of an entire continent and its islands. In it he details his epiphany about the role of a continent-wide Aboriginal management regime that made Australian landscapes and vegetation communities as they were found by Europeans in 1788.

Gammage sounds a note of sadness for what was: 'People made the land beautiful, but settlers took it because it was useful... The more carefully they made the land, the more likely the settlers were to take it.'[6] His thorough investigation of the records led him to many detailed conclusions about the Aboriginal land management system. He wrote, 'In 1788 people used almost every plant in some way.'

Further, 'In 1788 more water softened drought, spread resources, and let people walk easily over more of Australia. Even in arid regions they could expect to care for all their country, and think its plants and animals always sustainable.'

One of the seasonal Aboriginal tools for shaping their environment was fire. While scientists have written in detail about this, Bill Gammage's historical study is an accessible synopsis of the science: 'most fires were managed. Understanding fire locally made management possible.' He also found in the records what Aboriginal people know: 'Two dominant Australians, acacias and eucalypts, illustrate challenges and opportunities people faced in 1788...People could manage plants with fire...Most wattles regenerate densely after fire...Eucalypts and fire formed an ancient alliance, which people joined.' It pays to know something of this grand history of the evolution of our forests, scrub and grasslands. Many people think naively that it all 'looks the same' but when your eyes are opened to the sometimes dramatic, sometimes subtle shifts in vegetation types, the detail becomes evident, and all manner of flora and fauna and their habits can be better understood.

Australian vegetation communities in the wild have been shaped by fire and the Aboriginal fire management regime over millennia.

There is no one better to explain this practice than the Aboriginal rangers who work across thousands of square kilometres and continue to burn the small, cool fires in the vast grass and spinifex plains and the savanna forests. They are continuing this ancient tradition of using fire against fire, working with the fire-dependent species, such as eucalypts, to protect the vulnerable communities, including vine forests and ti-tree forests. These men and women in their distinctive ranger uniforms with their clan and totem emblems are the most knowledgeable guides across the country. Often they will be your guides when you visit Australia's many stunning national parks.

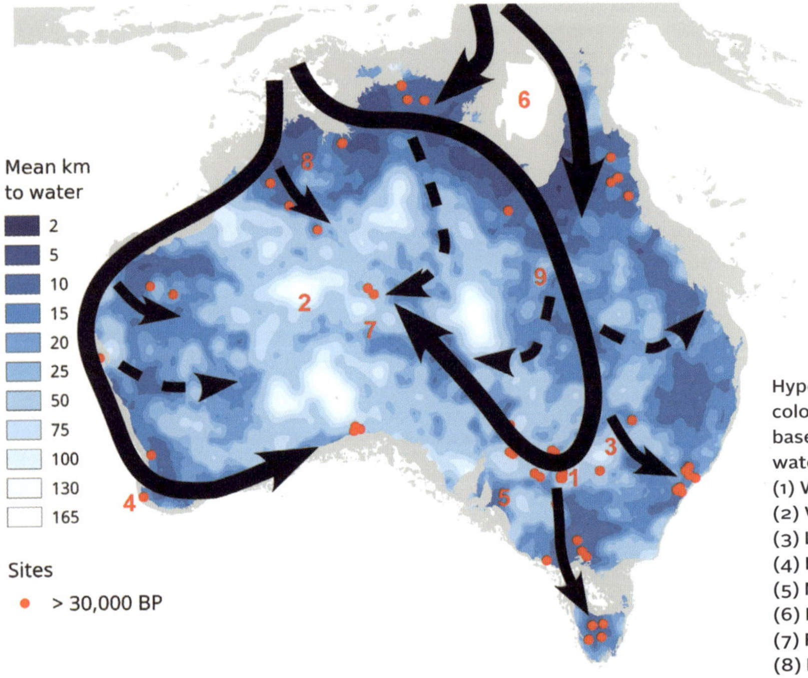

Hypothesised pathways for colonisation of Australia based on the distance to water. Places marked: (1) Willandra Lakes; (2) Western Desert; (3) Lachlan River; (4) Devils Lair; (5) Murray–Darling River; (6) Lake Carpentaria; (7) Finke River; (8) Kimberley; and (9) Channel Country.[7]

3

CULTURES AND LANGUAGES

Aboriginal peoples around Australia follow various traditions and carry out important rites and rituals that mark the sacred in everyday life. This way, they transform states of being, people, animals, and places from mundane to sacred.

The feature of Aboriginal life that most powerfully demonstrates the social effect of the sacred is the regard for ancestors and supernatural beings believed to have played a part in the creation of the world during a time called 'The Dreaming' or 'The Dreamtime'. These great spiritual beings are recorded in the rock art and are celebrated in songs and ceremonies today. They are revered as the 'Old People', as sources of great power. Sometimes it is dangerous power that must be mediated by the Elders, who guide their charges through the landscape where the Old People reside spiritually. Because the sacred past resonates in particular places, Indigenous owners follow traditions that will give safe passage to visitors. Hence, the custodians will carry out smoking or water blessing rituals. These rites of mediation are often called 'welcome to country' ceremonies. In many places, Elders introduce visitors to the ancestors, because driving or walking towards a place where they reside eternally without the permission of Traditional Owners can invite their anger. Traditional Owners perform welcome ceremonies in many different ways. Some groups light smoky fires with wet eucalyptus or paperbark leaves so that the smoke wraps around the visitors and makes them one with the place. Another ceremony involves throwing water on visitors; while another involves having the sweat of an Elder wiped on the face so that visitors smell like the Traditional Owner. One rite is the taboo on saying the names of the deceased and instead referring to the deceased with a substitute name. The deceased are memorialised in various ways – with special words, in designs in visual art, sculptures, funerary objects, songs and dances.

The idea of 'Old People' corresponds to the perception of stars as being representations of the past. The Old People are encountered in the landscape, just as we see stars when we gaze at the night sky. We know that stars are what can still be seen now of some cataclysmic event in the universe many thousands of light years ago. That is, the light of the explosion emanating through time and visible to our eyes in the present. Likewise, Aboriginal people perceive the spiritual presence of Elders in the landscape as what has emanated through time since the ancestor died.

There are hundreds of Indigenous cultures and their customs, and they vary greatly across the country. There are many Aboriginal peoples and many languages, despite the practices of banning and discouraging the use of Indigenous languages since colonisation. While there were more than 250 Indigenous language groups before British settlement, those practices were so destructive that it is remarkable that 120 of those languages are still spoken. Many are at risk as the speakers pass away, but some groups are reviving their languages by working with linguists to write and record their languages and teach them to younger people.[8] The will for Indigenous people to maintain their traditions grew out of millennia of life on this continent. Although they have adopted many of the ways of life of settler Australia, these peoples are the custodians of ancient cultural and natural resources that are uniquely Australian.

While it is almost impossible to map every known Indigenous Australian language, the Australian Institute of Aboriginal and Torres Strait Islander Studies (AIATSIS) has published a useful and important map, created by David Horton and based on data collected by AIATSIS, Aboriginal Studies Press and others. It depicts the linguistic and cultural riches of our country and it is available on the web or to purchase: aiatsis.gov.au/explore/articles/aiatsis-map-indigenous-australia

The team at AIATSIS also produced the *The Encyclopaedia of Aboriginal Australia: Aboriginal and Torres Strait Islander history, society and culture*.[9] I recommend it as a resource if you want to read more about Aboriginal Australia.

Visitors who want to hear an Indigenous language being spoken can watch one of my favourite films, *Ten Canoes*, directed by Rolf de Heer and Peter Djigirr, and released in 2006. The actors speak entirely in their language, Ganalbingu, but the narrative is easy to follow with some subtitles and the narration by the award-winning actor, David Gulpilil. This is a story of events that took place in the distant past among the Yolŋu or Yolngu peoples of the Arafura wetlands region in Arnhem Land in the Northern Territory. It involves stolen wives, revenge and war, and while it is a dark comedy, the storyline is carried by the superb acting of local people recreating a Dreaming story within a Dreaming story.[10] As a lesson in the customs and traditions from one area of Australia, this is a magnificent example.

Many Indigenous musicians sing in both English and their own languages. My favourite band, Yothu Yindi, cut several beautiful tracks in the Gumatj tongue of the Yolŋu Matha languages. Their song 'Tribal Voice' is the best example. Several of their most popular hits, such as 'Djapana: Sunset Dreaming', had fans around the world singing in an Aboriginal language. It is a *manikay* style song from the Yolŋu musical traditions, and concerns, among other things, the sacred sunset. Sunset is the divide between night and day, and is regarded, like dawn, as a sacred event. The term *djapana* refers equally to the yellow colour of clouds at sunset, the particular clans that are linked by the *waŋarr* (ancestral beings) and their journeys, and other matters. The colour yellow is one emblem of the Gumatj clan, of which Dr M. Yunupingu, the late lead singer of Yothu Yindi, is a famous son. Sunset is when the wind blows through the forest, the leaves rattle, white cockatoos swoop

AIATSIS map of Indigenous Australia, created by David R. Horton in 1996. This map attempts to represent the language, social or nation groups of Indigenous Australia.[11] To view details close up visit: aiatsis.gov.au/explore/articles/aiatsis-map-indigenous-australia

down to their roosts in the branches, and the inflamed sky darkens. It is customary for ceremonies to begin sometime just before sunset, and even if the ritual itself is delayed, people gather at this time on such occasions.

At a more prosaic level, every time you say the word 'kangaroo' you are speaking an Aboriginal language. Captain James Cook wrote down this word at the Endeavour River, where he moored to undertake repairs on his ship. Cook and his men encountered Guugu Yimithirr speakers, who told them their name for this marsupial that is now on Australia's coat of arms. Hundreds of Aboriginal words have entered modern Australian English, although some have changed from the original: koala, coo-ee, kookaburra, wallaby, billabong, dingo and wombat, are just a few examples.[12]

Kriol refers to the language spoken across much of northern Australia by perhaps 4000 people, according to one estimate from the 2011 census but that is most likely an under-representation. Linguist Dr Greg Dickson writes that, 'Linguists put the number of Kriol speakers closer to 20000, knowing that census data struggles to accurately capture high levels of multilingualism in remote Aboriginal communities.'[13] He also tells us that: 'Creole, as a linguistic term, is a type of language typically born out of abrupt and often brutal colonisation processes. Creoles are generally based on the dominant language of the colonisers'.

In the Torres Strait, as well as the two native languages and their variants, Torres Strait Kriol, Creole or *Broken*, is widely spoken as a very distinctive form of creole.[14]

As well as the various styles of Creole, linguists also recognise Aboriginal English,

Top: Man in ceremonial body paint at the Tiwi Islands Football Grand Final and Art Sale

Bottom: Smoking ceremony in Mossman Gorge, Daintree National Park, Queensland

defined by Dr Diana Eades from the University of New England as 'the name given to dialects of English which are spoken by Aboriginal people and which differ from Standard Australian English in systematic ways'.[15] Dr Eades points out that 'Aboriginal people in areas where there was no pidgin language made English into an Aboriginal English by bringing into it accents, grammar and ways of speaking from their traditional languages.'[16] Many people assume that speakers of Aboriginal English have not learnt Standard English adequately and therefore are poor speakers of English. This is not the case as Aboriginal English is a dialect of Standard English in its own right. Speakers of Aboriginal English can also learn Standard English and switch between the two depending on the circumstance. Among other Aboriginal people, instead of saying, 'You are very well dressed,' I would say 'You too flash,' or 'You lookin' deadly.'

A handy summary of the languages of the Torres Strait Islands is provided by the State Library of Queensland, see below.[17] This text reveals the great language complexity in just one region of Northern Australia. The eastern languages of the Torres Strait Islands are not related to the Aboriginal or, properly speaking, the Australian languages of the mainland, while the western and central languages are.

There are two traditional languages of the Torres Strait Islands, Miriam Mir and Kala Lagaw Ya.

Meriam Mir *(also written as Miriam Mer) is the language of the Eastern Islands of the Torres Strait. Linguistically, it is connected to the Papuan languages of the Austronesian family of languages. There are two regional dialects:*

Mer dialect *– Mer (Murray), Waier, Dauar.*

Erub dialect *– Erub (Darnley) and Ugar (Stephen).*

Kala Lagaw Ya *(also written as Kalaw Lagaw Ya) is the traditional language owned by the Western and Central islands of the Torres Strait. It is linguistically connected to the Aboriginal languages of the Australian mainland and has four distinct regional dialects derived from this language:*

Mabuyag *– The dialect of Mabuiag, Badu and St Paul's Village.*

Kalaw Kawaw Ya *– The dialect of the top western islands of Saibai, Dauan and Malu Ki'ai.*

Kawrareg *– The dialect of the south western islands of Kubin, Kaiwalagal, Muralag (Prince of Wales), Nurupai (Horn), Giralag (Friday), Waiben (Thursday Island), Keriri (Hammond), Maurura (Wednesday), Moa (Banks). It is also known as Kawalgau Ya.*

Kulkalgau Ya *– The dialect of the central islands of Aurid (Aureed), Damut (Dalrymple), Iama (Yam or Turtle-backed), Masig (Yorke), Mauar (Rennel), Naghir (Mount Earnest), Poruma (Coconut) and Warraber (Sue).*

The dialects are determined geographically and developed over time with influences by traditional trade, visits, inter-marriage and kinship ties.

Torres Strait Creole

The contact with missionaries and others since the 1800s has led to the development of Torres Strait Creole; it has developed from a Pidgin and now has its own distinctive sound system, grammar, vocabulary, usage and meaning. Torres Strait Creole (also known as Ailan Tok or Yumplatok) is spoken by most Torres Strait Islanders and is a mixture of Standard Australian English and traditional languages. It is an English-based creole; however each island has its' own version of creole.

4

KINSHIP

The hottest topic in Aboriginal get-togethers is often kinship – how people are related to each – and determining this by exploring personal histories is regarded as a matter of utmost importance. If a biological kinship link cannot be identified, there are ways to create kinship relationships that are often just as meaningful as close family ties. Many Aboriginal and Torres Strait Islander people follow ancient kinship rules in their everyday relations with others. They believe that these kinship rules are laws left by the sacred ancestors who created the living environment and its people.

There are several different types of Aboriginal and Torres Strait Islander kinship systems operating across Australia. They are far more complex than English or European systems of kinship and recognise many more types of kinfolk. Most Aboriginal systems recognise twenty-eight types of kin roles. In the Aboriginal world, everyone is kin, either close or distant. But all relationships, whether or not people are biologically related, are determined by kinship and classification laws. In addition to kinship systems that name kin roles such as mother and father, brother and sister, son and daughter, wife and husband, and so on, there are classifications, such as moieties and 'skin systems'. These classification systems operate in conjunction with the kinship system, binding everyone into a world of relatedness and principles of behaviour.

When no kinship link can be identified, an outsider is allocated to a kinship role or a 'skin' in a kind of adoption, and a kinship relationship is established and sanctioned. A local woman will declare to another woman who is visiting, 'You are my sister,' and the rules of behaviour among sisters will be explained. The husband of this woman becomes the brother-in-law of this newly acquired sister, and her sisters and brothers, and her children will call her 'mother' in the local language. Where these traditional kinship systems are followed, people often do not refer to each other by their personal names, but by kinship terms, as this is considered polite and proper. Through my associations with Yolŋu people from north-east Arnhem Land, I refer to my sisters as yapa and my brothers as wäwa, and their mothers and their mother's sisters as my mother or ŋän<u>d</u>i.

There is much more to a kinship system than human relationships. In the Yolŋu-Matha, the languages of the Yolŋu, the term for kinship is gurru<u>t</u>u but it has a much broader set of meanings, taking in relationships with traditional land estates, ancestral beings and all things associated with them, the division of all named entities in the world into the binary classification of either Dhuwa or Yirritja, and the spiritual meanings that attend to these myriad relationships. Important relationships are paired in ways that apply not just to people but to the land estates. From a female perspective, yothu–yindi means child–mother and gutharra–märi means daughter's child–mother's mother, yet these terms also express people's relationships to places and are loaded with spiritual meanings.

Clan groupings are the major form of social organisation in Yolŋu society. They are determined by descent from a male apical ancestor, and operate as the corporation that owns the clan's land estate and other property both spiritual and physical.

My friends and colleagues, ethnomusicologist Aaron Corn and the late Yolŋu elder and scholar Joe Gumbula, worked closely together to describe gurruṯu through various lenses.[18]

They write that Yolŋu society is an expansive network of more than sixty clans or mala who own numerous homelands in north-east Arnhem Land. Children are born into the clans of their fathers, and share in hereditary ownership of the fathers' homelands. All Yolŋu people, clans, homelands, ancestors and bodies of law are classified as being either Dhuwa or Yirritja.

The Yolŋu understand themselves to be 'direct descendants of the waŋarr (ancestral progenitors) who originally shaped, named and populated north-east Arnhem Land, and remain sentient and ever-present in its lands and waters'.[19] These sacred ancestral entities are further said to inform the souls of all living Yolŋu upon conception, and travel through ancestral waters back to their spiritual homes following death. Through this sacred birthright, all Yolŋu are born as owners or wäŋa-waṯaŋu (country-holders) of their clan's homelands, and rom-waṯaŋu (law-holders) in associated canons of names, songs, dances and designs that prove their clan's ownership of its homelands under ancestral law.[20]

Marriage rules are laws in all Aboriginal kinship and classification systems. As shown in this diagram based on an original painting by Joe Gumbula,[21] in the Yolŋu system, a person born into a Dhuwa clan must marry a spouse from a Yirritja clan, and vice versa.

Marriage must be between a person from a Dhuwa clan and a person from a Yirritja clan in Yolŋu law

As shown in the next diagram, in addition to being born into one's father's clan (o), Yolŋu people, whether Dhuwa or Yirritja, also use the gurruṯu system to trace their relationships to other clans through the mother's lineage.

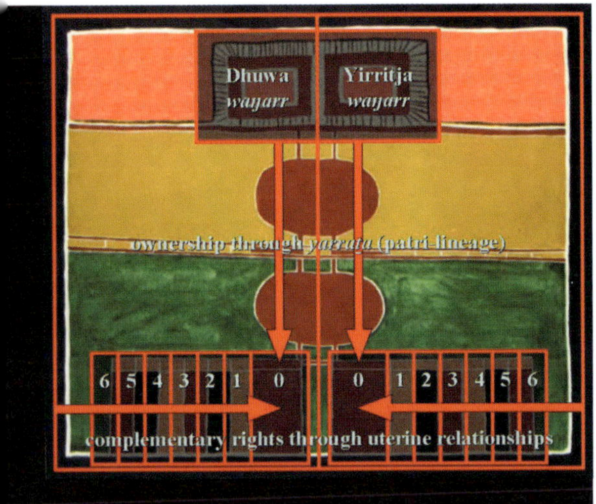

Top: Relationships through the mother's lineage as recognised in Yolŋu gurruṯu

Bottom: Yothu–yindi relationships between selected Yolŋu clans and homelands

In this way, a Yolŋu person will also identify strongly with the clans of people from whom they descend and who are descended from them in the relationships of mother (1), mother's mother (2), mother's mother's mother or woman's child (3), and mother's mother's mother's mother or sister (4). A Yolŋu person will also recognise the importance for their father's full female lineage and the complete female lineages of the children of each clan's men.

The next diagram by Aaron Corn shows how the Yolŋu recognise such chains of yothu–yindi (child–mother) in relationships between different clans (in red text) and homelands (in black Roman text).[22] These homelands include tracts of sea (in black italic text), which is a distinctive feature of the Yolŋu land tenure system in this rich coastal landscape. Hereditary knowledge of how the ancestral entities associated with each of these clans passed through each other's homelands are commonly said to bind these clans together in yothu–yindi relationships today.

The Yolŋu place great emphasis on their binary Dhuwa and Yirritja classifications, and less emphasis on their 'skin' system. By contrast, desert peoples, such as the Arrernte and Warlpiri, place much greater emphasis on 'skin' systems in which each person in society is born with a standard 'skin' name that marks their various kinds of relationships with everyone else. 'Skin' systems present another means of linking people in family relationships. The following diagram drawn from Aaron Corn's writing with the Warlpiri artist and scholar, Steven Wanta Jampijinpa Patrick,[23] shows the ideal Warlpiri system for relationships through marriage and descent for people distributed within four greater ceremonial groups (represented by circles) across sixteen different 'skin' names (represented by horseshoes). All 'skin' names inherited by females start with 'N', while all borne by males start with 'J'. The single-headed arrows show mother-to-child relationships, while the double-headed arrows indicate pairs of 'skin' names that permit their bearers to join in marriage.

Marriage and descent in the Warlpiri skin system

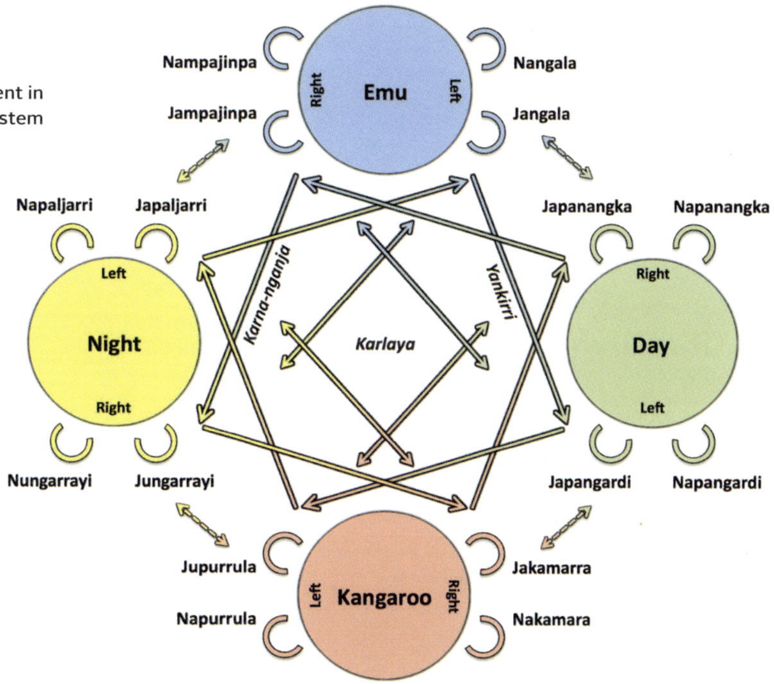

5 ART

Australian Indigenous artists are acclaimed around the world and their works are held in the major public and private galleries locally and internationally. The diversity of artistic styles of Indigenous Australia grows each year as communities, clans and families venture into the art market with renditions of their visual traditions. So too, the media and materials used by the artists expands from bark painting and canvas and acrylic formats, to encompass fabric and fibre weaving, screen-printing, linocut prints, metal sculptures, multimedia presentations using communications technology and computer imagery, photomedia and sound. There are many more styles of Indigenous art than is generally understood. They range from adaptations of traditional ritual and rock art to the full gamut of modernist and post-modernist.

When art collectors first approached Aboriginal painters to buy their work, there was no Indigenous art market as we know it today. Very little had been written about Aboriginal design traditions and material culture, and the standard view was that only European works could be considered as art. The work of other 'races' was generally seen as merely primitive mark making. Paintings on bark and various funerary sculptures were collected as exotica for anthropological study and exhibition, or by Christian missionaries who attempted to establish a cottage art industry to financially support their endeavours.

Explorers in the eighteenth and nineteenth century collected objects and material culture as exotic trophies and evidence of their travels. Also, some came across rock paintings and revealed them to the world. Sir George Grey, later appointed governor of South Australia, happened on the Wandjina paintings on sandstone escarpments in the Kimberley region during his exploration of the area in 1838. The Wandjina is the Rain Maker spirit and is often painted with headdresses that represent thunder and lightning. In 1891, pastoralist Joseph Bradshaw saw ancient rock paintings in the north-west Kimberley region. They are now known as the 'Bradshaws', but more correctly should be called by their Aboriginal names, which include *Gwion Gwion* and *Giro Giro*. These are finely detailed paintings of figures, and still the subject of research today.

Top: Rock art in Mount Borradaile, Arnhem Land, Northern Territory

Bottom: Indigenous painter creating artworks at Maruku Arts, Uluru, Northern Territory

Art historian Andrew Sayers surveyed nineteenth-century Aboriginal artists and their relationships with the European artists they encountered.[24] He found that in the colonies of New South Wales and Victoria, European artists gave Aboriginal artists paint and other materials, and the Aboriginal men observed the painting styles of the newcomers. The result is a body of drawings and paintings that departs from the men's symbolic traditions. Adopting to some degree the representational styles of the European artists they met, they painted and sketched detailed representations of the rapidly changing world around them. Sayers documented drawings by a man called Black Johnny, which resulted from his meeting with Austrian artist Eugene von Guérard in Victoria's Western District in 1855. Sayers also studied works by William Barak of Corranderk in Victoria, Tommy McRae of the Upper Murray River district of Victoria, and Mickey of Ulladulla in New South Wales. Sayers wrote that the work of these Aboriginal artists had two major themes: ceremonies, and traditional hunting and food gathering. Other subjects included encounters with Europeans, such as William Buckley, the 'wild white man', squatters – both sober and inebriated, Chinese men being chased by Aboriginal men, and sailing ships.

In the first half of the twentieth century, Ronald M. Berndt and Catherine H. Berndt documented Aboriginal societies in Western Australia and the Northern Territory, and they also worked briefly in South Australia. During 1947 they lived in Yirrkala in Arnhem Land in the Northern Territory, and gave some Yolŋu people there brown paper and crayons and asked them to depict their world. The works these people produced represent a turning point in the understanding of Aboriginal art. They are brightly coloured renditions of

Top: The Aboriginal Memorial of 200 hollow-log coffins at the National Gallery of Australia, Canberra

Bottom: Indigenous artworks on display as part of the Desert Mob Art Fair, Alice Springs, Northern Territory

traditional ceremonial and body painting, with some variation from the classical forms. Ronald Berndt documented their subjects in detail, and this extraordinary collection is now registered with the Australian Memory of the World Register, a project of the UNESCO Memory of the World Register.[25]

In June 1956, the Czech artist Karel Kupka arrived at Milingimbi in Arnhem Land with the intention of finding Aboriginal bark paintings as examples of the work of 'early man'. Basel Museum had commissioned him to bring back works to add to their small collection. Milingimbi, long the homeland of the Gupapuyngu people, had become the location of a mission settlement established by the Methodist Overseas Mission, and here Kupka developed a friendship with artists Tom Djawa and Dawidi Birritjama to understand their art. He travelled to other communities as well. The result of his collecting and studying was a short book that shone little light on these great traditions. Translated into English as *Dawn of Art*, its original title, *Un Art a l'État Brut (Art of a Brutish State),* says a great deal about attitudes to Aboriginal people in the 1950s.[26]

I have mentioned only a few of the encounters with Aboriginal artists before the 1960s and 1970s when radical changes took place in the world of Aboriginal art and a refined art audience and market developed. In 1971, Geoffrey Bardon, a school teacher stationed at the government settlement of Papunya in Central Australia, invited some of the men in the community to paint a blank school wall. The men took a great interest in this startling transference of their ceremonial sand-sculpture designs to modern materials, and Bardon supplied them with acrylic paint and encouraged them to paint on boards. Soon their works were being exhibited to great acclaim. In 1972, the artists successfully established their own company, which continues today as Papunya Tula Pty Ltd. This famous art cooperative brought the art traditions of a small group in the arid zone of Australia to the world. Their style came to be synonymous with Aboriginal art, despite the long history of many other regional styles.

Exhibitions in Paris and the United Kingdom, principally of the Papunya style of art with the distinctive lines and dots that appear to depict a bird's eye view of landscapes, excited the art world and a new interest developed. Soon, paintings began to sell for high prices as collectors competed for the rare pieces that reached the northern hemisphere.

Today, as I have mentioned, a wide range of styles are represented in all major public galleries in Australia. Each capital city has a public art gallery with significant Aboriginal and Torres Strait Islander collections. There are also collections exhibited in many major international collecting institutions, such as the British Museum, the Musée du quai Branly–Jacques Chirac and the Kluge-Ruhe Collection at the University of Virginia in the United States.

Visitors to Australia have a wide choice for sourcing Aboriginal art. The best places to buy authentic art are the Aboriginal communities that have their own art cooperatives, such as Papunya Tula and also the Buku-Larrnggay Mulka Centre in Yirrkala. As well, there are important art fairs that specialise in Aboriginal art, presenting hundreds of works by established and emerging artists working in all the local and regional styles. In Alice Springs in Central Australia, Desart, an Aboriginal art organisation representing the community art centres, hosts the Desert Mob art fair at the Araluen Arts Centre each year. It opens in early September and closes in late October or early November. In Darwin, the capital of the Northern Territory, the Darwin Art Fair exhibits works from over sixty Aboriginal and Torres Strait Islander art centres at its annual event, held for two weeks in early August. The Cairns Indigenous Art Fair, held in early July each year, is also a spectacular event showcasing the artworks of the many Indigenous cultures of Queensland.

The Cairns Indigenous Art Fair is the best venue for buying works by Torres Strait Islander artists. Some of the local galleries mount special exhibitions during the art fair and provide a window on the leading artists and the innovations from this remarkable archipelago. Look out for screen-print and linocut works by Brian Robinson, works in various media by Ellen Jose, and the fascinating sculptures modelled on traditional headdresses by Ken Thaiday Sr, and others.[27] Their works are collected by major institutions such as the Queensland Art Gallery, the National Gallery of Australia in Canberra, and the Art Gallery of New South Wales.

Many artists are represented by galleries in the major cities, and their works can be searched online. If you are interested in modernist, post-modernist and conceptual artists, such as Tracey Moffatt, who represented Australia at the Venice Biennale in 2017; Brook Andrew, whose work has been shown in galleries in Europe and Asia; and Warwick Thornton, whose work has been shown at Documenta, you can see their work in private galleries in Sydney and Melbourne. Check these artists' websites for details of their exhibitions.

Traditional ownership of inherited styles

Establishing the authenticity of an artwork is important for both the Aboriginal and Torres Strait Islander artists and the purchasers of their art. All reputable and ethical commercial galleries and art cooperatives document each piece and the artist, and provide certificates of authenticity. Even so, fraudsters have copied works or made works in the style of famous artists and sold them to naive buyers. The art cooperatives represented at the Indigenous art fairs are backed by groups such as Desart and the Association of Northern, Kimberley and Arnhem Aboriginal Artists, which are governed by elected councils of Aboriginal artists and advocate for their members. Protection of Aboriginal artists' rights has been the subject of government inquiries, court cases and campaigns over several decades.

Crudely manufactured goods made in China or Indonesia, and sold to tourists as 'Aboriginal art', 'boomerangs' and 'didgeridoos' fill souvenir shops and galleries in the tourist precincts of Australia. This trade causes immense harm to Indigenous artists and their families, and brings Indigenous art into disrepute. After several copyright cases in the courts, it was a fraud case in Victoria in 2007 that finally delivered justice to the Aboriginal artists whose works had been copied. In the first successful prosecution of art fraud, Pamela Yvonne Liberto and her husband Ivan Liberto were found guilty by a county court jury. They had conned the major art auction houses into selling fraudulent copies. It was reported in the *Age* newspaper in 2007 that 'The Libertos received more than $300 000

Top: Explaining traditional artworks to visitors at the Buku-Larrnggay Mulka Centre, Yirrkala, Northern Territory

Bottom: A bush birds weaving workshop at Godinymayin Yijard Rivers Arts and Cultural Centre, Katherine, Northern Territory

Top: Performers wearing contemporary designs at the Cairns Indigenous Art Fair, Queensland

Bottom: Rock art in the Flinders Ranges, South Australia

after forging and selling four paintings, supposedly by renowned artist Rover Thomas, whose work is keenly sought by collectors across the world and attracted a record price when the National Gallery of Australia purchased *All That Big Rain Coming from Top Side* for $778 000 in 2001.' Scientific examination of the paint and materials to date the works, carried out by the University of Melbourne Centre for Cultural Materials Conservation, provided the evidence of fraud.

Fraud leads to financial losses for the artists and their families, and the artists themselves often feel that their soul has been stolen. Some artists have refused to work again after they discovered copies of their works sold under their name. Clans or traditional land-owning groups own their traditional designs, and often one person in the group is authorised by their father or mother, or grandparent to execute the designs of their people. These designs are inherited, and even though the work of art is intended for the market, the artist feels that they are offering it to the world as a gift with the spirit of their ancestry and special places. Also, the traditional works often depict religious content. In further copyright cases in the 1980s and 1990s, aggrieved artists gave evidence to this effect but these cases did little to protect their rights.[28]

Advice on buying authentic art

It is the work of the catalogue writers and art historians, who meticulously document the art styles and the artists' biographies, that offers the best protection for the buyer. To verify authenticity it is possible to find examples of artists' works, their representatives, and the explanations of their works in galleries, published in books, and in catalogues online.

The Art Galleries Association of Australia and the Australia Commercial Galleries Association have websites that list their members.

Reputable galleries subscribe to the Code of Ethics of the National Association for the Visual Arts.[29]

Indigenous Art Code (indigenousartcode.org) was set up in 2010 to preserve and promote ethical trading in Indigenous art. Articles on its website discuss buying art ethically, and the harm caused to artists when people buy fakes.

The official Tourism Australia website, www.australia.com, offers the following advice on buying authentic Indigenous art.[30]

Develop an idea of which style of Indigenous art you like
Visit the Indigenous collections at Australia's major museums to educate yourself about the different styles of art

Make sure it's authentic
As with any art form, Indigenous art has authentic works and imitations. It gets more complicated when you learn that the majority of Indigenous works are not signed. You can, however, be assured that works are authentic if you buy from members of the Aboriginal Art Association of Australia, the Australian Commercial Galleries Association or the Indigenous Art Code. Those are the blue chip industry bodies that provide authentication and pay artists fair commissions. High profile auction houses such as Sotheby's, Christie's and Lawson-Menzies are also sources of reputable Indigenous art.

Explaining artwork to visitors at Narana Aboriginal Cultural Centre, Geelong, Victoria

Browse at commercial galleries
A number of exceptional commercial galleries across the country have knowledgeable staff that can give professional advice on what to purchase given your interests and budget.

Travel to remote Indigenous art centres
There are dozens of community-based Aboriginal art centres, many in remote areas, all over Australia. These centres organise the delivery of supplies to artists and market their art nationally and internationally, often online. Two key umbrella organisations are Desart, which represents 30 Aboriginal art and craft centres in Central Australia, and the Association of Northern and Kimberley Aboriginal Artists of Australia (ANKAAA), which is the peak advocacy and support agency for Aboriginal artists working individually or through 48 remote art centres spread across one million square kilometres (390,000 square miles) in Arnhem Land, Darwin/Katherine, the Kimberley and the Tiwi Islands. Key art centres include Warmun, Waringarri and Mowanjum, in the Kimberley, Buku Larnggay at Yirrkala in Arnhem Land, Balgo in Western Australia, Maruku near Uluṟu and Tiwi Designs on Bathurst Island. The first art centre in Australia using modern acrylics and canvas was Papunya Tula in the Western Desert. You can buy work at its gallery in Alice Springs. If you would like to visit remote art centres, Palya offers art tours by small plane.

6
PERFORMANCE

Music

Singing, composing, dancing and making music are at the core of Indigenous cultures in Australia. The styles and genre are many, and Aboriginal and Torres Strait Islander musicians have also adopted all manner of musical instruments and techniques from around the world. The traditional ways of making music include singing, percussion with various styles of clapping, keeping the rhythm and beat with clap sticks, instruments such as the *yidarki* (commonly called the didgeridoo), and in the Torres Straits, various styles of drums are used. For non-traditional performances, Indigenous musicians use guitars, including electric guitars, ukuleles, pianos, most of the orchestral instruments such as brass instruments, modern drums, percussion instruments, and even gum leaves.

The traditional styles of music and performance are now endangered, but rescue programs and festivals are working to preserve these musical forms, which are the oldest in the world. Responding to their vulnerability, Yolŋu musicians, ethnomusicologists and scholars joined forces to stop their decline, forming the National Recording Project for Indigenous Performance in Australia. The Project's 'Garma Statement on Indigenous Music and Dance' of 2002 tells us:

Songs, dances and ceremonial performances form the core of Yolŋu and other Indigenous cultures in Australia. It is through song, dance and associated ceremony that Indigenous people sustain their cultures and maintain the Law and a sense of self within the world.

Performance traditions are the foundation of social and personal wellbeing, and with the ever-increasing loss of these traditions, the toll grows every year. The preservation of performance traditions is therefore one of the highest priorities for Indigenous people.

Indigenous songs should also be a deeply valued part of the Australian cultural heritage. They represent the great classical music of this land.

These ancient musical traditions were once everywhere in Australia, and now survive as living traditions only in several regions. Many of these are now in danger of being lost forever.

Indigenous performances are one of our most rich and beautiful forms of artistic expression, and yet they remain unheard and invisible within the national cultural heritage. Without immediate action many Indigenous music and dance traditions are in danger of extinction with potentially destructive consequences for the fabric of Indigenous society and culture.

The recording and documenting of the remaining traditions is a matter of the highest priority both for Indigenous and non-Indigenous Australians. Many of our foremost composers and singers have already passed away leaving little or no record.[31]

In northern and central Australia, traditional songs are generally sung in cycles. Each song is short but can be combined with others and repeated and performed throughout a ceremony. When singing the cycles, men usually have two lead singers and a chorus, and a *yidarki* player. Each singer uses clap sticks to keep the rhythm. Women sing in a variety of styles. For example, following a death a senior woman will lead the keening or high-pitched singing. In the desert, groups of women sing the cycles, led by one or two lead singers, and clap to keep the beat.

The singing style made popular by bands such as Soft Sands, Yothu Yindi, East Journey, and many others from Arnhem Land is called *manikay*. Ethnomusicologist Aaron Corn explains the powerful force of *manikay* in Yolŋu society in the touching tribute he wrote in September 2017 to singer, composer, elder and scholar, the late Dr Gumbula. Describing them as 'singing ancestral records' he said:

whenever people sing Manikay, their voices are not their own, but rather mingle with those of the ancestors themselves – all those who have gone before and all those who are yet to be. The Manikay tradition codifies all the observations and strategies for living given to the Yolŋu by the original ancestors who originally named, shaped and populated their myriad homelands in northeast Arnhem Land.[32]

Dr Gumbula's band, Soft Sands, started in the 1970s and led the way for Aboriginal

Top: Christine Anu performs at National Reconciliation Week, 2016

Bottom: East Journey performing live at the National Indigenous Music Awards, Darwin, Northern Territory

Opposite page: Yothu Yindi performing live in 1991

musicians to experiment, fusing introduced and Aboriginal styles and instrumentation, particularly rock music. It was followed by Yothu Yindi, formed in 1986. Yothu Yindi became the most successful and internationally recognised Aboriginal band in that decade. Warumpi Band, with its mix of Arnhem Land and Warlpiri style with rock, also became successful, touring with Midnight Oil. In South Australia, Us Mob and No Fixed Address became popular and toured with several hit songs in Australia and the Pacific.

Torres Strait Islander music is called *Ilan* style, and combines traditional singing with a variety of introduced styles, particularly hymnal music and songs shared by sailors whose ships stopped in the islands. Predominantly vocal with drum and other percussion accompaniment, the songs celebrate living with the sea, love and adventure. Island songs are performed in two or three-part harmony, and are improvised by the singers. The best example of modern Torres Strait music is that of Seaman Dan, whose work is produced by Karl Neuenfeldt. Born in 1929, he was seventy years old when he began to sing publicly, going on to release five albums of traditional music and his signature *Ilan* style blues and jazz. In his biography, *Steady Steady: The Life and Music of Seaman Dan,* Uncle Seaman tells stories of his life in the islands pearl diving and his development as a professional singer and musician.[33]

ARIA award-winning singer Christine Anu also hails from the Torres Strait. She has had success with a number of albums and film appearances, as well as singing at the closing ceremony of the 2000 Sydney Olympics.

If you happen to be in Darwin in August, you should go to the National Indigenous Music Awards where Indigenous musicians, many of whom sing in their native languages as well as English, compete for the honour of being named the best in their category or genre, from traditional to heavy metal. Emerging artists, such as Gawurra, Apakatjah, Electric Fields, Emily Wurramara, Tia Gostelow and Yirrmal, have had their careers launched at this prestigious event. In 2017, one of my favourite dance troupes, and a favourite of anyone who has seen them, the Numbulwar Red Flag Dancers, won in the traditional music category with their CD complete set. See: nima.musicnt.com.au

Top: Dancers decorated in traditional paint at the Laura Aboriginal Dance Festival, Laura, Queensland

Bottom: Young boys celebrating their heritage at the Laura Aboriginal Dance Festival

Dance

Traditional Aboriginal religion is organised in ceremonial forms, and usually involves dance performances and singing that bring the ancestors to life, and also bring the ancestral stories into the lives of Aboriginal families. Some ceremonies are for man-making, or initiation, while others celebrate particular ancestors. Funeral ceremonies are often celebrations of the ancestral connections of the deceased. These ceremonies are often now mixed with Christian traditions, and sometimes have other cultural influences as well. Dance performances are also staged for storytelling and for pure entertainment.

One spectacular feature of Aboriginal dances at ceremonies is body painting, and each of the designs painted onto the skin has a meaning. Men adorn themselves with colourful cloth wrapped around their bodies, feather headdresses, gum-leaf anklets, and other decorations to indicate their clan and various affiliations. Women wear swaying skirts and when topless, they paint their bodies with ochre. Both men and women paint their faces with clan emblems. There are ceremonial dance performances that involve men and women, and others that are performed by men only, or by women only. In public forms of ceremony, children are included. Dancers are barefoot and kick up the sand they are dancing on as a part of the performance.

The best example of the mix of traditional and modern performance is Bangarra, a dance company formed in 1989. American dancer Carole J. Johnson was a founding director of NAISDA (National Aboriginal Islander Skills Development Association) Dance College and with NAISDA graduates, Rob Bryant and Cheryl Stone, she went on to found Bangarra Dance Theatre.

Artistic Director Stephen Page has led Bangarra for many years, and in this time it has become one of the most successful performing arts companies in Australian history. Performing nationally and internationally, the company's dancers are professionally trained, and each has an Aboriginal and/or Torres Strait Islander background. Indigenous choreographers and musicians collaborate with the dancers to create works that are both contemporary and draw on 40 000 years of stories and culture.

Bangarra performances can be seen during their annual national tour of the leading art centres in Australia's capital cities, and often in venues in America and Europe. See: www.bangarra.com.au

7 STORYTELLING

It must be said that for a people on the verge of extinction in the early twentieth century, the resilience shown by the Indigenous cultural warriors who paint, sing, write and tell stories is a testament to the power of our culture. Storytelling and oratory continue in much the same forms as before European contact, and storytellers can be heard at Indigenous festivals and writers' festivals around the country. Storytelling is the original classroom where history, morality and knowledge about people, places and the world are relayed to each new generation. Many collectors of Aboriginal stories are surprised at how little they have changed through the generations of telling. There are stories that tell of the rising of the oceans around 7000 years ago, erupting volcanoes 20 000 years ago, and the very different climate and landscapes of the long distant past. Storytelling is also entertainment, bringing people together to laugh about life, adventures, love, travelling and mishaps. When the best storytellers are in charge, humour and tragedy bring stories to life. Stories can be told through song and dance, and a traditional performance is often a form of theatre.

The new storytellers are the film and television makers who are bringing ancient and contemporary stories to the screen. A great example of a modern Aboriginal story is told in the film *The Sapphires*, written by Yorta Yorta man Tony Briggs. It received standing ovations at its premiere at the Cannes Film Festival in 2012. The British newspaper, *The Times*, described it as 'the kind of film that makes you want to leap from your seat and shout for joy'. This feature-length film, directed by Indigenous director and actor, Wayne Blair, tells the story of four Yorta Yorta sisters who took their soul music act to Vietnam in 1968 to entertain the troops. Its cast includes Jessica Mauboy, a singing sensation from Darwin, and Irish actor Chris O'Dowd. It is an adventure story, a love story, and a musical with its historical basis in the Aboriginal community at Cummeragunga on the Murray River that forms the border of Victoria and New South Wales.

Follow The Rabbit Proof Fence was written by Doris Pilkington Garimara and published in 1996. It is a true, powerful and heart-breaking account of how Doris' mother, Molly, Doris' aunt, Daisy, and Molly's cousin Gracie – all Martutjarra girls – were forcibly removed from their families in the East Pilbara in Western Australia in 1931, under the 'assimilation' policy. Molly (aged fourteen), Daisy (eleven) and Gracie

Top left: Leah Purcell with her award for Best New Australian Work during the 2017 Helpmann Awards

Top right: Ellen van Neerven, author of *Heat and Light* (2014)

Bottom: Cast of *The Sapphires* on the red carpet in New York, 2013 (left to right: Shari Sebbens, Miranda Tapsell, Deborah Mailman and Jessica Mauboy)

(eight) escaped from the Moore River Native Settlement, where they had been taken, and were pursued by an Aboriginal tracker. The girls walked for some 1600 kilometres using the rabbit-proof fence that runs north-south through Western Australia as their guide. Historian Doris Pilkington Garimara used archival evidence and interviews with her mother and her Aunty Daisy to write the story. Scriptwriter Christine Olsen obtained the film rights and convinced Australian director Phil Noyce to direct the film. It is gripping viewing, with David Gulpilil in the role of the tracker and Kenneth Branagh in the role of A.O. Neville, the 'chief protector of Aborigines' who ordered the forced removal of Aboriginal children in Western Australia. The film won many awards and was shown worldwide. This story about members of the Stolen Generations helped Australians to understand the suffering that has been caused to thousands of families. Eventually the sentiment around the country led to the National Apology to the Stolen Generations, delivered by then prime minister Kevin Rudd in 2008.[34]

Indigenous writers

Aboriginal poets, playwrights and authors of novels, histories and memoirs continue the tradition of storytelling that has preserved the history and myths of our peoples for thousands of years. Their works have won national and international awards, and hold a highly respected place in Australian literature.

There are many recommendations of works by Indigenous writers and works by non-Indigenous writers about Indigenous writers. Here is my own list of the best books by Aboriginal authors, poets and playwrights. This short list is a good starting point.

Kim Scott is an award-winning Noongar author of novels, a children's book, short stories and other works. His major novels are:

- *True Country*, Fremantle Arts Centre Press, 1993
- *Benang: From the Heart*, Fremantle Arts Centre Press, 1999
- *That Deadman Dance*, Picador, 2010
- *Taboo*, Picador, 2017

Scott's oral-history account of his family, who are Noongar people from the south coast of Western Australia, *Kayang and Me* (2005), was written in collaboration with his aunt, Noongar Elder Hazel Brown.

Bruce Pascoe has won many literary awards for his novels, non-fiction and children's books. He is from the Bunurong clan in Victoria and has worked as a teacher, farmer, a fisherman and an Aboriginal-language researcher. Now Pascoe is the Director of the Commonwealth Australian Studies Project. Some of his works are:

- *Night Animals*, Penguin Books, 1986
- *Fox*, McPhee Gribble/Penguin books, 1988
- *Shark*, Magabala Books, 1999
- *Nightjar*, Seaglass Books, 2000
- *Ocean*, Bruce Sims Books, 2002
- *Convincing Ground: Learning to Fall in Love with Your Country*, Aboriginal Studies Press, 2007
- *Bloke*, Penguin Books 2009
- *Fog a Dox*, Magabala Books, 2014
- *Dark Emu: Black Seeds: Agriculture Or Accident?*, Magabala Books, 2014

Tony Birch, a Melbourne Koori, is an award-winning writer, academic and activist. In 2003, Birch's PhD thesis won the Chancellor's Prize for Excellence at the University of Melbourne, where he lectured for many years. He is currently the inaugural recipient of the Dr Bruce McGuinness Indigenous Research Fellowship at Victoria University. Here are some of his novels and short-story collections:

- *Blood*, University of Queensland Press, 2011
- *Ghost River*, University of Queensland Press, 2015
- *Shadowboxing*, Scribe Publications, 2006
- *Father's Day*, Hunter Publishers, 2009
- *The Promise: Stories*, University of Queensland Press, 2014

Leah Purcell is an award-winning author, playwright and actor. Her play, *The Drover's Wife*, a radical re-interpretation of Henry Lawson's short story of the same name, won the Book of the Year Award in the NSW Premier's Literary Prize in 2017. Her works include:

- *Box the Pony* (playscript), Hodder Headline, 1999
- *Black Chicks Talking*, Hodder Headline, 2002
- *The Drover's Wife*, Currency Press, 2016.

Alexis Wright is an award-winning novelist and writer, and member of the Waanyi nation of the Gulf of Carpentaria. She has written widely on Indigenous rights. Her major novels are:

- *Plains of Promise*, University of Queensland Press, 1997. It was shortlisted for the Commonwealth Prize and published in France as *Les Plaines de L'Espoir*.
- *Carpentaria*, Giramondo Publishing, 2006. It won five national literary awards in 2007, including the ASAL Gold Medal and the Miles Franklin Award.
- *The Swan Book*, Giramondo Publishing, 2013
- *Tracker*, Giramondo Publishing, 2017
- Her other books are: *Grog War*, Magabala Books, 1997, a study of alcohol abuse in Tennant Creek; and as editor, *Take Power, Like this old man here*, IAD, 1998, a collection of essays and stories celebrating twenty years of land rights in Central Australia.

I also recommend these writers: Tara June Winch, author of *Swallow the Air*, 2006, and *After the Carnage*, 2016, both published by University of Queensland Press. Ellen van Neerven, author of *Heat and Light*, University of Queensland Press, 2014. And Dr Anita Heiss, who is the author of poetry, non-fiction and fiction, including commercial women's fiction.

My two favourite Indigenous poets are Yvette Holt, *Anonymous Premonition*, University of Queensland Press, 2008; and Lionel Fogarty, *Yerrabilela Jimbelung: Poems about Friends and Family*, Keeaira Press, 2008.

8

NATIVE TITLE

Eddie Koiki Mabo, born on the Island of Mer in the Torres Strait in 1935, had an impact on Australian life that was profound and life-changing for thousands of Torres Strait Islanders and Aboriginal people across the nation. In 1974, he was working as a gardener at the James Cook University in Townsville. There he met historians Henry Reynolds and Noel Loos, and the three men became friends. For so long, writers and historians had ignored the history of Indigenous Australia, but both Henry and Noel wrote ground-breaking books about Indigenous people in North Queensland that placed Indigenous people at the centre of Australian history.

Through Noel and Henry, Koiki found out that he did not own his traditional land: that it had been annexed by the state of Queensland. Koiki began teaching, lecturing and writing about his culture and his ties to his land, and wrote about the land ownership and inheritance system on Murray Island. In 1982, he met with a group of lawyers in Townsville to begin his legal challenge to the Queensland land laws. He simply did not accept that the land his grandfather had bequeathed to him did not belong to him by law.[35] That year the case was lodged in the High Court. Koiki was the leading plaintiff and he was joined by fellow traditional owners of Mer as plaintiffs: Father Dave Passi, Mr James Rice, and for a time, Mrs Celuia Mapo Salee, until she passed away.

Central to the case was the evidence, written and oral, that the people of Mer had their own laws that were given to them by their god, Malo, who is often represented as an octopus. The plaintiffs challenged the idea that the entire continent and islands of Australia were ceded to the British upon 'discovery' on the grounds that the inhabitants had no system of governance and laws that could be recognised. This idea is called *terra nullius* or 'land belonging to no one'.

Their path was not easy. The Queensland government passed the *Queensland Coast Islands Declaratory Act 1985* in an attempt to negate any claims Torres Strait Islanders may have had to the land. The Act declared that when the Queensland government annexed the Torres Strait Islands under the Coast Island Act in 1879, title to the islands was transferred to the state of Queensland and could not be subject to other claims. The plaintiffs from Mer appealed to the High Court, which found the *Queensland Coast Islands Declaratory Act 1985* contravened section 10 of the *Racial Discrimination Act 1975*, and was therefore invalid. In the decision of the judges, it was argued that if Native

Top: Protestors campaigning for recognition of Aboriginal land rights on Bicentennial Day, 1988, Sydney, New South Wales

Bottom: Aboriginal activists rally on 1 May 2015 against forced closure of remote Aboriginal communities

Title rights did exist, they should be viewed as part of the human right to own and inherit property. On those grounds, the Coast Islands Act unfairly compromised the property rights of people in the Torres Strait.

On 3 June 1992, ten years after Koiki, Passi, Rice and Mrs Mapo Salee lodged their case, the High Court of Australia handed down its decision, upholding by a six to one majority the claim for the Miriam people of Mer Island to have their native title recognised at law.[36] In this case, called Mabo No 2, the High Court overturned 200 years of the 'legal fiction' of *terra nullius* and established that customary rights to land had pre-existed and, under certain conditions, survived British sovereignty. Koiki Mabo did not live to see his victory in court.

Following this judgement, a bitter national debate on the impact of this case on Australian land tenure ensued. After more than a year of difficult negotiations involving Aboriginal leaders and industry representatives from the farming, grazing and mining industries, on 16 November 1993, the *Native Title Act of 1993* was passed into Australian law. In the second reading speech of the Native Title Bill, former prime minister Paul Keating outlined the intention of the legislation: '[to] make the Mabo decision an historic turning point: the basis of a new relationship between Indigenous and other Australians'.[37]

The terms of this Act regulate the circumstances in which Native Title can be recognised and the restricted circumstances in which Native Title over land survives.

Sign carried by protestor at an Australia Day rally organised by Aboriginal rights activists on 26 January 2017 in Melbourne, Victoria

In many cases these terms have led to bitter disappointment for the Traditional Owners. Courts have dismissed claims when groups of people have been unable to prove their connection to land through an unbroken line of descent to a time before British annexation because of the lack of historical records. The Yorta Yorta case in northern Victoria was such a case.

On 12 December 2002, the High Court handed down its decision in the case of the *Members of the Yorta Yorta Aboriginal Community v State of Victoria and Others*.[38] The Yorta Yorta people claimed their traditional rights in land and waters covering 2000 square kilometres along and around the Murray and Goulburn rivers. They sought to be recognised as the peoples belonging, by tradition, to that country. Justice Olney of the Federal Court found that before the end of the nineteenth century the Yorta Yorta people had ceased to occupy their traditional lands 'in accordance with their traditional laws and customs', and relied on a phrase in the Mabo No 2 judgement of the High Court: 'the tide of history'. Justice Olney wrote, 'the tide of history has indeed washed away any real acknowledgement of their traditional laws and any real observance of their traditional customs'. The Yorta Yorta plaintiffs appealed to a majority of the Full Court of the Federal Court, which upheld Justice Olney findings. They then appealed to the High Court, which also confirmed Olney findings.[39]

This case was widely debated because the courts' findings seemed unjust and discriminatory. Legal scholars[40] turned to arguments about 'tradition', noting the findings of the Chief Justice of the Federal Court, Justice Michael Black, who was in the minority: 'far from being concerned with what is static, the very notion of "tradition" as involving the transmission from generation to generation of statements, beliefs, legends and customs orally or by practice implies recognition of the possibility of change'.[41] With such a long and brutal colonial history of land dispossession and incarceration in reserves, Aboriginal groups, including the Yorta Yorta people, understandably felt that another great injustice had been done in their Native Title case.

Native Title has had little impact on the lives of most Australians and the fears of enormous damage to the economy expressed by opponents of Aboriginal rights after the High Court's findings in the Mabo case have failed to materialise. This may be because it is such a weak title as compared with the usual freehold title that homeowners have, with its exclusive possession and far greater protection at law. There are several types of Native Title claims, but for Aboriginal or Torres Strait Islander Traditional Owners, the usual path is the claimant makes an application to the Native Title Tribunal. The Tribunal defines it in this way:

A claimant application is made by a group of people, a native title claim group, who declare they hold rights and interests in an area of land and/or water according to their traditional laws and customs.

The members of the native title claim group are seeking a decision from the Court that native title exists, so their rights and interests are recognised by the common law of Australia. This is called a native title determination. A determination is a decision by the Federal Court or High Court of Australia, or a recognised body, that native title either does or does not exist in relation to a particular area of land or waters.

If the Court finds that native title rights and interests exist, the group must set up a prescribed body corporate to hold the rights and interests, as an agent, or in trust, for the group.[42]

Many claims have been successful, but usually in the remote areas, such as in the Western Desert, which covers a vast area of Western Australia. In that state, the Aboriginal population is large, and while 90 per cent of the state has been claimed, the registered and determined Native Title claims over land, intertidal and sea areas, do not affect the rights of other land owners.

Australia, unlike other former British colonies, has no treaty with its Indigenous people. Customary systems of law pre-date the arrival of the British by many thousands of years and survive, often in highly adapted forms, in many parts of postcolonial Australia. Native title recognition in Australia is only twenty-five years old. This is in contrast to other common law jurisdictions such as New Zealand and Canada where native title has been recognised for at least 150 years. These countries have superior legal and political regimes for recognising and dealing with Indigenous systems of law and governance than the Australian jurisdiction, in part because of the treaty rights negotiated in their colonial period.

For more than a decade, Indigenous leaders have sought the agreement of successive governments to hold a referendum to change the Australian Constitution to recognise Aboriginal and Torres Strait Islander people and their cultures. Their consultations and research resulted in an elegant statement agreed to by a unanimous vote of 250 Indigenous leaders at Uluṟu, one of the most sacred and iconic places in Aboriginal Australia. The National Indigenous Constitutional Convention agreed on their approach to being included in the nation in an honourable way, and set this out in The Uluṟu Statement from the Heart. The Australian government did not agree to this approach, issuing a cursory statement in November 2017. This rejection is just another in a long history of disappointments, but the Indigenous leaders are committed to pursuing their goal, just as their forebears did. Understanding of the cultural foundations of the Indigenous world is difficult to achieve, but as you will see, as you are hosted by Aboriginal and Torres Strait Islander people, the riches of Indigenous culture are a window onto a long human relationship with a beautiful continent and its islands.

9 THE STOLEN GENERATIONS

The term 'Stolen Generations' refers to the Aboriginal children who were forcibly removed from their families by the state, territory and federal governments of Australia from 1788 onwards. The children were placed in controlled institutions, or from a young age were made to work without pay in the homes of white people, or adopted or fostered into white families. Most were never able to find their birth families again. This had terrible consequences for the mental and physical health of the children and their parents throughout their lives, and for Indigenous people down through the generations. It also resulted in cultural loss on a nationwide scale for the affected families.

The intention of the policies and laws that led to children being taken from their parents was to 'assimilate' part-Aboriginal people into the general Australian population, leaving the 'full bloods', as these people were called, separated and incarcerated on Aboriginal reserves. Governments regarded 'miscegenation', as mixed racial descent was known as, to be a danger to the 'racial hygiene' and health of white Australian society.

For much of the twentieth century, most Australians had no qualms about this cruel practice or were unaware of it. In the 1980s, victims began to challenge the status quo by telling their stories and looking for their birth families. Their efforts led to the revelation that perhaps tens of thousands of children had been removed from their families. Growing evidence from the survivors, who numbered about 13000, told of the sometimes extreme physical and sexual abuse they suffered at the hands of adoptive and foster families and employers (to whom some were indentured or enslaved). Aboriginal organisations called for a national inquiry.

Eventually, in 1995, the federal Attorney-General established the National Inquiry into the Separation of Aboriginal and Torres Strait Island Children from their Families. Two special commissioners were appointed, Sir Ronald Wilson QC, President of the Human Rights and Equal Opportunity Commission, and Professor Mick Dodson, the Aboriginal and Torres Strait Islander Social Justice Commissioner.

After taking evidence from across the entire country, the commissioners presented *Bringing them home: The 'Stolen Children' report* to the Australian Parliament in 1997. Professor Dodson and Sir Wilson found that the race-based child-removal policies were a special instance of genocide under the definition in the United Nations Convention on the Prevention and Punishment of the Crime of Genocide. This was clearly the case in Western Australia, for example, where the instructions and justification were aimed at eliminating the entire 'race'. This incited a national debate among many Australians, and in May 1998 the first National Sorry Day was held, one year after the tabling of the report. On Sorry Day, 28 May 2000, around 300 000 people walked across the Sydney Harbour Bridge in the Walk for Reconciliation, and all around the country Australians were demanding a national apology to the Stolen Generations.

From 1996 until it lost the election in 2007, the federal government led by Prime Minister John Howard, refused to apologise. It was claimed that an apology would establish the grounds for financial compensation. In the Northern Territory and South Australia survivors went to court to seek justice. The Cubillo and Gunner cases were unsuccessful, but a case in 2007 brought by Bruce Trevorrow in South Australia resulted in him being awarded $500 000 compensation. Mr Trevorrow died before the compensation was paid.

At that time the nationwide campaign for an apology was growing. Tens of thousands of people signed 'Sorry' books to register their own apology and to demand an apology from the Australian government.

On 13 February 2008, then prime minister Kevin Rudd gave an apology in federal Parliament to the Stolen Generations. Here is the parliamentary transcript of his speech:

The Speaker: Prime Minister.

Prime Minister (Hon Kevin Rudd MP): Mr Speaker, I move:

That today we honour the Indigenous peoples of this land, the oldest continuing cultures in human history.

We reflect on their past mistreatment.

We reflect in particular on the

Top: Marita Ah Chee, taken from her family in 1947, points to a photo of herself at the Garden Point Mission on Melvin Island as a young girl

Bottom: An Indigenous woman overcome with emotion while watching former prime minister Kevin Rudd deliver his National Apology speech in federal Parliament during the Sorry Day proceedings on 13 February 2008

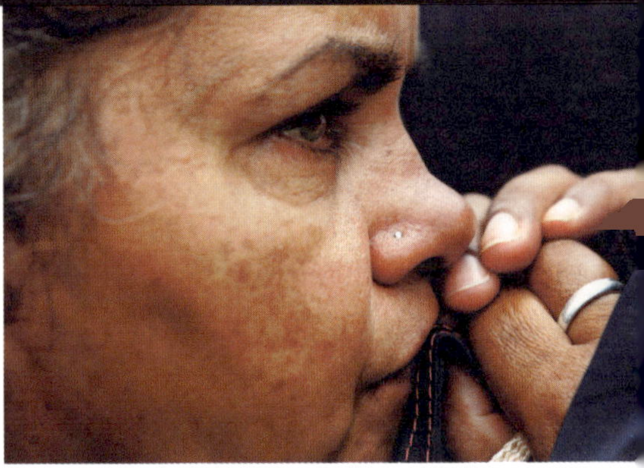

mistreatment of those who were Stolen Generations – this blemished chapter in our nation's history.

The time has now come for the nation to turn a new page in Australia's history by righting the wrongs of the past and so moving forward with confidence to the future.

We apologise for the laws and policies of successive Parliaments and governments that have inflicted profound grief, suffering and loss on these our fellow Australians.

We apologise especially for the removal of Aboriginal and Torres Strait Islander children from their families, their communities and their country.

For the pain, suffering and hurt of these Stolen Generations, their descendants and for their families left behind, we say sorry.

To the mothers and the fathers, the brothers and the sisters, for the breaking up of families and communities, we say sorry.

And for the indignity and degradation thus inflicted on a proud people and a proud culture, we say sorry.

We the Parliament of Australia respectfully request that this apology be received in the spirit in which it is offered as part of the healing of the nation.

For the future we take heart; resolving that this new page in the history of our great continent can now be written.

We today take this first step by acknowledging the past and laying claim to a future that embraces all Australians.

A future where this Parliament resolves that the injustices of the past must never, never happen again.

A future where we harness the determination of all Australians, Indigenous and non-Indigenous, to close the gap that lies between us in life expectancy, educational achievement and economic opportunity.

A future where we embrace the possibility of new solutions to enduring problems where old approaches have failed.

A future based on mutual respect, mutual resolve and mutual responsibility.

A future where all Australians, whatever their origins, are truly equal partners, with equal opportunities and with an equal stake in shaping the next chapter in the history of this great country, Australia.[43]

The cruel legacy of the policies of removing Aboriginal children from their families has been felt for generations. Even now there would not be an Aboriginal person alive today who has not been tragically touched in some way, directly or indirectly, by the impact of these policies.

Apologising to the victims of the historical policies of Aboriginal child removal achieved at least two important goals. First, it helped to restore the sense of dignity and legitimacy that the victims ought to feel but were denied. Secondly, it was a national acknowledgement of the wrong and harm done by previous governments to generations of people on the grounds of race-hate, an acknowledgement that should state explicitly that this should never occur again. The victims' inheritance has been denied by their removal. The denial of that inheritance is the key to their suffering and the correct grounds for compensating them: they were denied their family lines and their links to a family past and legacy, their material inheritance, their culture and history, and most importantly, a sense of self shaped by the people who brought them into the world.

The primary significance of an apology must be for the victims of the policies of removing Aboriginal children from their families. But almost as significant is the effect of a formal apology on the citizens on whose behalf the apology was made.

In 2010, the Healing Foundation was established in Canberra to provide trauma support for the victims, assistance with commemorative events and to undertake research.[44] Also, several monuments have been erected around the country to remind us of this tragedy, and families visit them on National Sorry Day every year. As there are so many it is not possible to mention them all here, nor all the commemorative plaques. For example, the six plaques placed in culturally significant sites around Brisbane – King George Square, Teralba Park in Everton Park, Kalinga Park in Nundah, Orleigh Park in West End, Sherwood Arboretum, and the Wynnum foreshore. Instead I will focus on three of the monuments.

Stolen Generations Memorial

Reilly Lane, Sydenham Green, Sydney, New South Wales

The Stolen Generations Memorial at Reilly Lane, Sydenham Green, is a sandstone sculpture by Aboriginal artist Joe Hirst. Its inscription is taken from Link-Up, the organisation established by victims to find their families.

We may go home, but we cannot relive our childhoods.
We may reunite with our mothers, fathers, sisters, brothers, aunties, uncles, communities, but we cannot
re-live the 20, 30, 40 years that we spent without their
love and care, and they cannot undo the grief and mourning they felt when we separated from them.
We can go home to ourselves as Aboriginals, but this
does not erase the attacks inflicted on our hearts, minds, and bodies by caretakers who thought their mission was to eliminate us as Aboriginals.

Link-Up (New South Wales)[45]

Stolen Generations Memorial

Phillip Creek Native Settlement, Manga Marda Waterhole, Tennant Creek, Northern Territory

In 1946, sixteen 'part Aboriginal' children were moved from the Phillip Creek Native Settlement at the Manga Manda waterhole, to the notorious Retta Dixon Home in Darwin. This kidnapping was authorised by the Native Affairs Department of the Northern Territory government. In 2004, eleven survivors of the group taken from the Phillip Creek mission returned to the place where they were abducted to dedicate a memorial at the long-abandoned settlement. They used the dedication ceremony as a time to distance themselves from their shocking experiences at the Retta Dixon Home and rebuild their ties with their own families. The Phillip Creek mission was opened in 1945 as an interim ration depot for Aboriginal people. They had been displaced from their land after gold was discovered in the Tennant Creek region in the 1930s. By 1956, the mission was abandoned and a permanent site was established at Warrabri.[46]

Stolen Generations Memorial Garden

Beinda Street, Bomaderry, New South Wales

This garden, created on the site of the Bomaderry United Aboriginal Mission (UAM), was dedicated on 21 October 2001. The mission was established in 1908, a year before the enactment of the *Aboriginal Protection Act of 1909*, and became the destination for many of the children in New South Wales who were taken from their families.

Top: Indigenous women demonstrating for the Stolen Generations, Darwin, Northern Territory

Bottom: Kevin Rudd hugs a member of the Stolen Generations after delivering the National Apology in Canberra on 13 February 2008

The inscription on the plaque at the garden reads:

This PLAQUE and MEMORIAL GARDEN
Is Dedicated To
'ALL' THE ABORIGINAL CHILDREN
Of The 'STOLEN GENERATION'
Who Were Residents Here At
BOMADERRY, The Former
'UNITED ABORIGINES MISSION'
(U.A.M.). Also To Honour and Respect The
Children Who Are Now Deceased
This Site Is The BIRTHPLACE Of The
'STOLEN GENERATION'
Here In New South Wales[47]

10

WHAT IF YOUR GUIDE IS NOT INDIGENOUS?

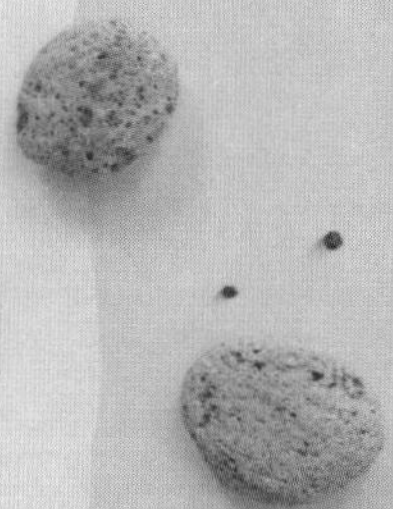

Aboriginal and Torres Strait Islander guides are employed at many places, especially in national parks that have joint management schemes with the Traditional Owners, such as Kakadu National Park and the Uluṟu–Kata Tjuṯu National Park, and at experiences offered by Indigenous-owned companies. However, it is unlikely that you will have an Indigenous guide at most popular tourist attractions. Instead, your guide will usually be a young white Australian. Also, it is sometimes the case that the guides will not mention Aboriginal history and culture at all, or, if they do, they sometimes repeat degrading stereotypes.

In 1996, two Hawai'ian women visited Australia. One was Mahealani Kahau, an important Hawai'ian cultural leader, who came to attend the Australian Reconciliation Council in Melbourne, and the other was her sister. Mahealani told me that her sister had taken a bus to northern Australia because she wanted to meet Aboriginal people in communities there. She was deeply shocked by what she saw, Mahealani said, but even more so when the bus driver who acted as a guide repeatedly made extremely racist statements throughout the trip. When she objected, the driver threw her off the bus and she had to find other means to return to Melbourne.

When I worked in Central Australia in the 1980s, visitors told me that tour guides would tell 'jokes' about the 'inferior' status of Aboriginal people. Here's one: 'How do you make a gin squash? You run her over with your road train.' For those initiated into Australian everyday racism, 'gin' is a racist term for an Aboriginal woman. A road train is a truck towing one or more trailers, and used in rural and remote areas of Australia to transport goods. Other jokes are too crude to retell here.

These stories are not common now. The Australia reconciliation movement has changed attitudes and many racist ideas and habits are being recognised as such and are no longer tolerated. Whereas in the past, Aboriginal people were despised and discriminated against, and excluded from Australian society, reconciliation has enabled Australians to accept Aboriginal people as a part of Australian life without the fear and anger that typified earlier attitudes – at least for many Australians. Indigenous events, art exhibitions, films and television programs, as well as the National Indigenous Television service, and tourism experiences have led to greater understanding and awareness of Aboriginal and Torres Strait Islander cultures.

In some parts of Australia, however, rather than the experience of Mahealani's sister, you may find that there is absolutely no information available for tourists about Aboriginal and Torres Strait Islander cultures and history. In 2017, I received an email from an Australian woman who visited Tasmania. That is the island state across the Bass Strait, which is infamous because of the vicious campaign by British troops from 1824 to 1831, called the Black Wars in some history books,[48] aimed at eradicating Tasmania's entire Indigenous population. They almost succeeded, but of this you will hear nothing from a guide in Tasmania. Historians still debate whether the Black Wars should be defined as an act of genocide. Governor Arthur formed 'roving parties' of civilians to capture Tasmanian Aborigines, offering them a reward of five pounds for each adult and two pounds for each child. The resistance was awe-inspiring. In April 1828, Governor Arthur was forced to defend his colony against the silent guerrillas who attacked the settlers ruthlessly and without warning. He declared martial law and made it illegal for Aboriginal people to go into any British settlement. Seventy years after the arrival of the British, the bloody wars came to an end in 1873. By that time, the sealers and whalers from the northern hemisphere, many from Cornwall, had already wreaked murderous havoc especially on the smaller islands.[49]

My correspondent wrote this to me:

I am currently holidaying in Tasmania for the first time (I live in mainland Australia), and am visiting many iconic historical and wilderness areas, on occasions on guided tours. What has appalled me is the (almost all) negation in tourist booklets and from tour guides, of information regarding Aboriginal Australians during first contact and beyond.

Top: Painting of Captain Phillip declaring British possession of New South Wales at Sydney Cove, January 1788, by Algernon Talmage, 1939

Bottom: Illustration of the arrival of Captain Cook in Adventure Bay, Tasmania, November 1777, by R. Caton Woodville

Although I have questioned tour guides about specific areas relating to the first peoples and their experiences, I have been stonewalled and in one instance told...you do not want to know. Actually, I did want to know and responded accordingly. In another instance on the former penal colony of Sara Island, I was informed that the experiences of Aboriginal peoples during that time could not be spoken about, however there were places on this island that were restricted due to significant cultural Aboriginal heritage (good, re the latter).

Whilst I have furthered my knowledge about the experiences of convicts and their colonial masters, I remain frustrated at the omissions, bordering on negation of the real history of contact, by the rhetoric of the tourist industry.

What has been alluded to in rhetoric, is that contact history stories, are not to be told by non-Aboriginal people. Is this the case? If so, why doesn't the government allocate funding to have Aboriginal Australian guides contest and enrich the rhetoric, with Aboriginal truths?

I feel very uncomfortable in Tasmania because of the complete suppression of this history by the settlers. My limited access to the responses of the Palewa – or Tasmanian Aboriginal people – is via Palewa artists and academics. Photographer Ricky Maynard, artists and academics Julie Gough and Greg Lehman, and medical leader Ian Anderson have educated me about lives lived in the shadow of their terrible history with dignity and intellectual vigour.

This is too often the challenge of travelling through Indigenous Australia: deciphering the deceit and outright lies about the Aboriginal presence and absence, and seeking out Indigenous people for the story. Occasionally,

Top: Photograph of Indigenous people from Tasmania, including Truganini (far right), a well-known Tasmanian Aboriginal woman who assisted European settlers in an attempt to protect her people

Bottom: Indigenous girls and women at the Hermannsburg mission photographed with the wife of the missionary, taken around 1900 by German visitors

I have met locals from the settler population who will talk about the history of their area, but the norm is the triumphalist colonial history about 'brave white pioneers'. The fate of Aboriginal people is rarely mentioned, and if it is, the accounts are often brief and inaccurate.

It is best to read the histories on these matters. Robert Hughes' *The Fatal Shore: The Epic of Australia's Founding*,[50] published in 1987, is a robust account of Australia's penal settlement origins and its convicts, but it records very little about the fate of the Aboriginal people during the early period of British rule. It was not until 1849 in New South Wales and Van Diemen's Land, as the colony in Tasmania was called, that transportation of convicts to Australia ended, following protests by the freed convicts and free settlers to 'felons' being sent to the colonies. Thomas Keneally's *The Commonwealth of Thieves: The Story of the Founding of Australia*, published much later in 2006, is detailed and fascinating, although just as trauma inducing. The historians who doggedly told the story of Aboriginal people have been persecuted and hounded for doing so. Henry Reynolds, Lyndall Ryan, and a growing body of scholars, persist, however. If you are not a reader, there are DVDs, and I highly recommend *First Australians*, an eight-episode series on the history of Aboriginal people since British occupation.

Our history: what you should know when visiting Australia

I have explained that Aboriginal people were the first humans to colonise the southern most parts of the planet. Aboriginal people came from what is now Asia and moved across the whole continent before the last Ice Age.

When the British arrived in force in 1788 with eleven ships under the command of Captain Arthur Phillip, and established the first British settlement at Port Jackson on the shores of Eora country in what is now Sydney, the world of Indigenous peoples across the continent and islands was fated. At the time the penal colony was set up at Port Jackson, the British were losing the War of Independence in North America. The Native Americans were offered treaties, many of which remain legally binding today. After Independence, the British were no longer permitted to send convicts to America. As The United States of America became independent, the British sent eleven ships to Port Jackson to establish a penal colony.

The Colony of New South Wales was the first colony, and Arthur Phillip became its first governor, in charge from 1788 to 1792. Governor Phillip and the governors who followed him all failed to control the violence of the frontier. Eventually, six colonies were established, each with its own history of attempts to exterminate Aboriginal people. Unknown numbers of Aboriginal people died in the wake of the frontier, the population falling from an estimated one million at first settlement to less than 50 000 in the early twentieth century.

These colonial beginnings of the nation are a hotly debated issue in Australia, especially on each Australia Day on 26 January.[51] Indigenous people hold their own events, such as the Yabun Festival in Sydney, and in 2017 some local councils voted to celebrate the nation on a different day.

The history of twentieth century Australia was also brutal. So brutal that in many parts of the country, as I have explained, the historical facts have been suppressed and contested, and many still deny the terrible treatment that Indigenous people experienced.

As the settlers spread out across the lands of Aboriginal peoples, they seized control, assisted by the British troops. Missionaries followed, and Aboriginal people were eventually rounded up and placed in missions and government administered settlements. When people today refer to an Aboriginal community, they are often unaware of the history of these places.

In 1901, Australia became a nation when the six English colonies of Queensland, New South Wales, Victoria, Tasmania, South Australian and Western Australia formed the Commonwealth of Australia under a new constitution.
Aboriginal and Torres Strait Islander people were not citizens after the constitution was enacted. At best, they were treated as wards of the state under acts of parliament in each state and territory that set out the laws for Aboriginal labour, confining Aboriginal people to reserves, and many other rules. In the constitutional referendum of 1967, Australians were asked to vote on whether the Commonwealth Parliament should be able to make laws for Aborigines, and whether Aboriginal people should be counted in the Australian census.
After the referendum's success – a resounding 'yes' vote – all the states and the Northern Territory permitted Aboriginal people to vote.

A change of the federal government in 1975 brought about sudden policy changes, including the recognition of Aboriginal land rights, the recognition of distinctive Aboriginal cultures, and the need for Aboriginal organisations. A new Prime Minister, Gough Whitlam, initiated the legal recognition of Aboriginal land rights by handing over a land lease to the Gurinjdi people at Wattie Creek, now called by its proper Aboriginal name, Daguragu, in the Northern Territory. Whitlam appointed Justice Woodward to the Aboriginal Land Rights Commission of Inquiry and, in 1976, the Commonwealth Parliament enacted his principles in the *Aboriginal Land Rights (Northern Territory) Act*.

As the century proceeded, the impact of colonisation on Aboriginal people became a major human rights issue. The stealing and removal of thousands of Aboriginal children, incarcerating them in institutions throughout the twentieth century under the so-called 'assimilation' policy, became the subject of a human rights inquiry, as discussed in the previous chapter. The late Sir Ronald Wilson and Mick Dodson presented their national report, *Bringing them home*, to Parliament in 1997 at the same time as the National Reconciliation Convention. Eventually these Stolen Generations were the subject of the government apology delivered in 2008.

The practice of jailing Aboriginal people in such numbers that in parts of Australia the imprisonment rate was the highest recorded in the world became another human rights issue. The Royal Commission into Aboriginal Deaths in Custody was established in 1987, and the final report of the commission, published in 1991, remains the most comprehensive survey of Indigenous law and justice issues and of the underlying causes that bring Aboriginal people into excessive contact with the justice system. Despite the Royal Commission's 339 recommendations, Indigenous people are still fourteen times more likely to be imprisoned than non-Indigenous Australians. The Royal Commission recommended a reconciliation process and the Council for Aboriginal Reconciliation was formed, consisting of both Indigenous and non-Indigenous members who initiated programs leading to many changes in attitude and practice.

National institutions, such as the National Museum of Australia, the Australian Museum, the Australian Institute of Aboriginal and Torres Strait Islander Studies, the Australian Broadcasting Commission, and the Australian Human Rights and Equal Opportunity Commission, have produced timelines of the many events in Australian history that are significant to Aboriginal and Torres Strait Islander people in remembering their past, and increasingly to more Australians as historians reveal this past.

These websites are a good guide to the history of Australia since 1788:

www.nma.gov.au/exhibitions/lag_meta_aus/timeline

australianmuseum.net.au/indigenous-australia-timeline-1901-to-1969

www.50yearjourney.aiatsis.gov.au/

www.abc.net.au/news/2015-07-06/indigenous-recognition-timeline-of-australian-history/6586176

www.humanrights.gov.au/timeline-history-separation-aboriginal-and-torres-strait-islander-children-their-families-text

Top: Hermannsburg is said to have been the first Aboriginal mission in the Northern Territory

Bottom: Rally to support the Black Lives Matter movement and highlight Indigenous Australian deaths in custody on 17 July 2016 in Melbourne, Victoria

11
NAIDOC WEEK

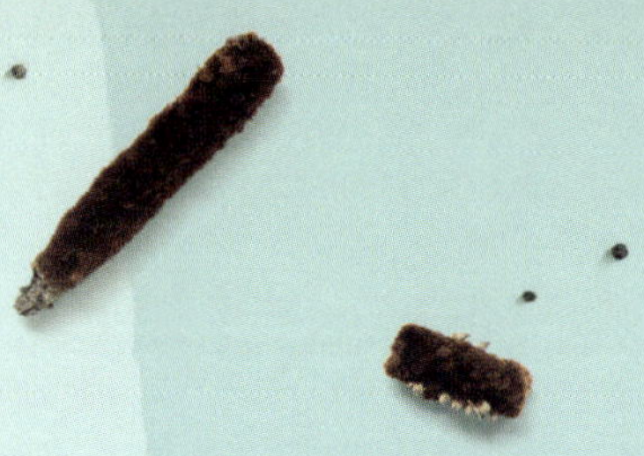

Held annually in the first week of July, NAIDOC Week is a national celebration of Aboriginal and Torres Strait Islander cultures, achievements and history. Originally the acronym NAIDOC stood for 'National Aborigines and Islanders Day Observance Committee', which would organise the activities. Now Aboriginal and Torres Strait Islander people in communities and urban areas, as well as government agencies, local councils, schools and workplaces organise events in towns, cities, and rural and remote areas around the country. The celebrations include ceremonies, dancing, singing, storytelling and other events. Everyone – Indigenous and non-Indigenous – is welcome to join in.[52]

Started over forty years ago, the celebrations have grown to become a part of Australian life. Awards ceremonies are held in each state and territory to choose outstanding achievers, young and old, from a wide range of fields. The week culminates in the National NAIDOC Awards Ceremony, hosted by a city chosen each year.

During NAIDOC Week, the Aboriginal and Torres Strait Islander flags are flown across the nation, on buildings, schools and on flagpoles lining avenues and streets. Permission is not required to fly either the Aboriginal or Torres Strait Islander flag. However it is essential to apply for permission if you want to reproduce the flags in some form.

A different theme for NAIDOC Week is announced each year. In 2017, the theme was 'Our Languages Matter' to 'emphasise and celebrate the unique and essential role that Indigenous languages play in cultural identity, linking people to their land and water and in the transmission of Aboriginal and Torres Strait Islander history, spirituality and rites, through story and song'.[53]

To see the NAIDOC Week events calendar visit: www.naidoc.org.au/naidoc-events

Top: Natarsha Bamblett was awarded the Miss NAIDOC title at NAIDOC Week in Melbourne, 2017

Bottom: Performers at 'NAIDOC in the City' in Sydney, 2017

12

BUSINESS AND TOURISM

Travellers coming to Australia fifty years ago would have found it almost impossible to visit Aboriginal and Torres Strait Islander communities and lands. Only the most determined adventurers succeeded in obtaining access at that time when government policies of racial segregation and exclusion kept most Indigenous people apart from the rest of Australia. Over the past thirty years, the Indigenous tourism industry has grown from a tiny number to hundreds of businesses today.

Tourists are now able to visit easily. But the opportunities for Indigenous people to build tourist facilities on their lands and in their communities did not come about so easily. The key industries in rural and remote Australia are mining, pastoralism and tourism – all land-based. As peoples with profound attachments to their land, a large part of the Indigenous population has sought to become involved in these industries. About a quarter of Australia's land mass is Aboriginal-owned and this preference for investment in their own assets and regions is a rational choice. However, to make this happen successfully it was necessary to change the models of economic development that were available to Indigenous communities. A radical overhaul was designed to address the legacy of underdevelopment and exclusion of the previous two centuries.

Business

Changes in attitudes towards Indigenous business came slowly. First the iron-ore miners, then many of the top 200 Australian corporations, and now the commonwealth government have created an Indigenous supply chain by procuring goods and services from Indigenous businesses. The growth in the number of these businesses is a core achievement of a new approach to engaging with Indigenous Australians, and all Australians benefit from the outcomes. In 2007, the ANZ Banking Group collaborated with Reconciliation Australia and was the first major private sector company to develop a Reconciliation Action Plan (RAP).

Reconciliation Australia is a non-government body that advises Australians on ways to improve relationships with Aboriginal and Torres Strait Islander people and create opportunities for them. Launched in 2006, Reconciliation Australia's strategy has been enormously successful and resulted in more than 300 Reconciliation Action

Plans with many more in development. It assists companies, government and non-government entities, educational institutions and other bodies to develop RAPs as frameworks to realise their vision for reconciliation. They are practical plans: 'RAPs create social change and economic opportunities for Aboriginal and Torres Strait Islander Australians'.[54] In an evaluation report of their effectiveness by AusPoll in 2012, the RAPs are described as: 'plans that organisations can make to identify clear actions with realistic targets that they can take to improve the relationship between Indigenous people and other Australians both within the organisation and more widely'.[55]

Many major Australian corporations have adopted RAPs and this action has accelerated opportunities for Indigenous businesses as well as encouraging the acceptance of Aboriginal and Torres Strait Islander people in workplaces and recruitment strategies. During the mining boom, companies moved quickly to develop Indigenous business opportunities to demonstrate their commitment to the local Traditional Owners of land where they operated. The results were outstanding. In 2011, Fortescue Metals Group announced its Billion Opportunities program 'to generate business opportunities for Aboriginal people' and to recognise that 'economic opportunity and participation is the key benefit to flow from Native Title agreements'.[56] Since then, the company has awarded 244 contracts and sub-contracts valued close to $2 billion to 105 Aboriginal-owned businesses and joint ventures. Other companies such as Rio Tinto have achieved similar results. In the last decade, Australian governments have caught up with the private sector and developed Indigenous business policies and programs.

Indigenous entrepreneur Michael McLeod and his non-Indigenous business partner Dug Russell were inspired by the National Minority Supplier Development Council in the USA. They developed the idea of creating the Australian Indigenous Minority Supplier Council to achieve parity in procurement of Indigenous goods and services, and made a submission to the inquiry by Australian Parliament's Standing Committee on Aboriginal and Torres Strait Islander Affairs in 2008. Their submission outlined the creation of the council and focused on the development of Indigenous enterprises in Australia. One year later, the government announced it would invest $3 million to pilot AIMSC over three years. It was launched on 15 September 2009 at Parliament House in Canberra. In 2013, after successfully completing the pilot phase, AIMSC rebranded to become Supply Nation and has developed the largest membership in Australia of corporate, government and non-profit organisations committed to supplier diversity and Indigenous business development. It certifies Indigenous suppliers and registered businesses in every state and territory. Then it partners these businesses with companies and governments seeking to buy Indigenous goods and services. Through the work of Supply Nation, private sector expenditure on Indigenous business services has grown dramatically.

In 2015, the Australian government recognised that Indigenous businesses had been largely excluded from its enormous purchasing power and announced a revised and improved Indigenous procurement policy. This led to the increase in federal government spending on Indigenous goods and services from $6 million in 2014 to $594 million in 2017, with the awarding of 4880 contracts to 956 Indigenous-owned businesses with a total value in two years.[57] There is great interest in these developments because Indigenous businesses employ Indigenous people at far higher rates than other companies, as much as 100 times more, according to the Forrest Review of Indigenous Employment and Training, undertaken by Andrew Forrest, former CEO of Fortescue Metals Group, for the Australian government. Estimates are that there are between 3000 and 5000 Indigenous businesses nationally.

In 2015, the Community Development Program or CDP, a work-for-the-dole scheme, supported 37 000 people across 1000 communities. More than 80 per cent of the participants were Indigenous. This program had had several name changes in just a few years and many rule changes, none of which have improved the situation. The government's work-for-the-dole scheme applied in Aboriginal Australia has had a success rate of transitioning its participants to jobs of only 2 per cent. According to Andrew Forrest's report, 'an additional 188 000 Indigenous Australians will have to find work in the next five years if we are to achieve parity. This will require a doubling of the current number of working Indigenous Australians'.[58]

Indigenous Business Month is held annually in October throughout Australia (follow the Twitter account @IndigBizMonth) and events are held nationally to raise awareness of the Indigenous business sector.

The Indigenous tourism sector

The Indigenous tourism sector is small and faces great challenges. For the foreseeable future, it will remain small-scale and attract smaller numbers than the most popular mainstream attractions. It appeals mainly to visitors seeking boutique experiences in art, adventure and environmental experiences. 'There is low awareness amongst the domestic market that Indigenous tourism experiences are available in Australia,' says a research report, *Demand and Supply Issues in Indigenous Tourism,* by Dr Lisa Ruhanen and her colleagues, published in 2013. The situation has not improved since then. Only 5 per cent of international tourists cite Indigenous experiences as an activity they want to take part in while in Australia. Most want to stay on the eastern seaboard, especially in Sydney. According to the researchers who found this to be the case by interviewing tourists, 'less than 25 per cent for domestic respondents and less than 20 per cent for international respondents' are aware of Indigenous tourism experiences available to them. 'Preferences for Indigenous tourism experiences declined to 12 per cent and intention/visit to 2 per cent'. Also, the researchers found that domestic visitors have little interest in Indigenous tourism.[59] I hope that readers will see from this book that Indigenous tourism offers opportunities to learn about another side of Australia, away from the mainstream attractions, and to have great fun in the process.

The report was commissioned in 2012 by the Indigenous Business Australia (IBA), the federal Department of Resources, Energy and Tourism and the Indigenous Tourism Working Group. Academics from the University of Queensland and Griffith University were engaged to investigate the supply of and demand for Indigenous cultural tourism in Australia. Released in early 2013, *Demand and Supply Issues in Indigenous Tourism* was based on interviews with more than 1300 international and domestic tourists and more than thirty Indigenous tourism operators. It revealed significant opportunities and challenges for the sector.

It is important to consider what tourists are looking for. Some people want short, relatively inexpensive, urban activities. This applies particularly to mainstream tour groups. Other types of tourism, such as adventure, art, cultural and environmental tourism attract far smaller numbers of visitors but these are the types of tourist attractions run by Indigenous operators. The researchers found that businesses can tailor their tour to suit particular groups. For instance, if an Indigenous tourism business wants to be included in a Chinese tour company's itinerary, the operators should produce an 'Aboriginal cultural show; bush tucker/story telling; guided nature/ environment tours with Indigenous guide'. The researchers also advised that the venues should be 'located in close proximity to major cities/urban areas, have a brochure and interpretation provided in Chinese', and offer souvenir and shopping opportunities. Many Indigenous operators in rural and remote areas would find it impossible to achieve all of the points suggested in the report.

IBA is using the information contained in this important report to inform its engagement with Indigenous tourism operators and the advice it provides on product development, particularly to assist potential tourism operators to better understand the domestic and international tourism market. The full report is available from the IBA website at www.iba.gov.au.

The research by Dr Lisa Ruhanen and her colleagues has also had an impact on improving government support for the Indigenous tourism sector. IBA, a government statutory body set up with the purpose of investing in Indigenous businesses, improved its Indigenous Tourism Champions Program thanks, in part, to the report. In 2013, it linked more Indigenous tourism operators to tourism industry expert mentors – from fifteen businesses in 2011–2012 to thirty-seven in 2012–2013. It also provided matched funding so Indigenous tourism operators can participate in trade events and access marketing and other business development services. Although these steps are small, they are essential if Indigenous tourism ventures are to achieve greater success in the future.

Gourmet food and culinary tourism

The high quality of Australian produce makes gourmet tourism experiences very appealing. Mr Mark Olive, aka The Black Olive, was one of the first people to make it easy for tourists to sample and enjoy Indigenous food. This Bundjalung man is Australia's most famous Indigenous chef, and his cooking is highly regarded nationally. His television programs and corporate catering experiences introduced Australians and visitors to the world of wild bush foods and the experience of bush foods in gourmet cooking. Mark's company, Black Olive Catering based in Melbourne, is sought out for major events all around the country and his series *The Outback Cafe* is watched around the world. In his role as the Outback Academy Ambassador – Hospitality

Top left: Modern Indigenous-inspired cuisine at Charcoal Lane, Fitzroy, Victoria

Top right: Josh 'Koomal' Whiteland leads coastal foraging tours in south-west Western Australia

Bottom: Restaurateur Mark Olive with his students at the Garma Festival, Arnhem Land, Northern Territory

Programs, Mark has helped many Indigenous people to train as chefs and he has attracted chefs from around the world to experience Australian wild, or bush, food. Chefs looking for exciting new ingredients were not disappointed. Even Heston Blumenthal has experienced Indigenous wild food.

Another Indigenous chef is Clayton Donovan, the only hatted Indigenous chef. He is the star of his *Wild Kitchen* television program. Clayton lives in the Nambucca Valley, northern New South Wales, and brings Indigenous ingredients, both foraged and farmed, to a wide audience at festivals and events.

Mark Olive: www.blackolive.net.au

Clayton Donovan's 'Wild Kitchen', ABC Television: www.abc.net.au/tv/programs/wild-kitchen-with-clayton-donovan/

Charcoal Lane (p. 182)

Charcoal Lane is named after the ballad by Aboriginal singer Archie Roach, and the laneway he made famous. It is one of the most popular restaurants offering Indigenous foods. Located in the inner-Melbourne suburb of Fitzroy, it has a contemporary menu with the best of Australia's native foods. Mission Australia operates Charcoal Lane as social enterprise that provides hospitality training, guidance and opportunities for young people, many of whom are Aboriginal, and in need of a fresh start in life.

136 Gertrude St, Fitzroy, Victoria
www.charcoallane.com.au

Roelands Village (p. 155)

Mark Olive, The Black Olive, has worked with the Indigenous bush foods farm Roelands Village in the south-west of Western Australia, to bring their produce to a wide market. Roelands Village is a working farm, producing native bush foods, and a nationally significant heritage site set in a majestic environment surrounded by the rolling Seven Hills. It has accommodation, conference and catering facilities, and is a great food and wine destination. Formerly known as Roelands Mission, it was an institution for the Stolen Generations. From the 1940s to the 1970s, around 500 Aboriginal children were taken to the mission. Now some of those people are transforming Roelands Village into a place of social business, education and healing. In 2004, the Indigenous Land Corporation bought the property on behalf of Woolkabunning Kiaka Incorporated, representing the former residents, and its purpose now is to promote the overall development of the community.

575 Seven Hills Rd, Roelands, Western Australia
www.roelandsvillage.com.au

Koomal Dreaming (p. 146)

Josh 'Koomal' Whiteland, a Wadandi man, operates Koomal Dreaming at Yallingup, west of Dunsborough in the south-west of Western Australia. Josh offers cultural tours and gives visitors the opportunity to taste native foods, learn about bush medicine and explore the beautiful Margaret River region, three hours south-west of Perth. Sampling the fresh wild food from the sea and the land that Josh knows so much about, as well as swimming at the pristine beaches and walking through the natural environment makes Koomal Dreaming a special experience. Josh took part in the first Margaret River Gourmet Escape in November 2012, along with some internationally renowned Australian chefs. He introduced the chefs and other visitors to the Nyoongar people's calendar of six seasons and the abundant wild food of the area, including edible flora, kangaroo, emu, abalone and squid. This major annual food festival is a popular attraction for gourmands.

Yallingup Caves Rd, Yallingup, Western Australia
www.koomaldreaming.com.au

Margaret River Gourmet Escape:
gourmetescape.com.au

Immersive cultural experiences

The Garma Festival (p. 80)

The Garma Festival has been listed in the top ten festivals in the world. It offers a unique combination of traditional Yolŋu ceremonies, held every afternoon, and a forum that attracts a gathering of 2500 political and business leaders from across the globe to share Yolŋu knowledge and culture and to discuss the most pressing issues facing Indigenous Australians. Coordinated and programed by the Yothu Yindi Foundation (YYF), the proceeds are used to improve the lives of Yolŋu people in northeast Arnhem Land through education and community development programs. Garma incorporates visual art, ancient storytelling, dance – including the famous nightly *bunggul* or ceremony– and music. As well, important forums are held and education and training programs relevant to cultural tourism, craft, governance and youth leadership are run during the festival. Garma is presented by the YYF in early August each year. YYF is a not-for-profit Aboriginal corporation with tax deductibility gift recipient status. Read more about the Garma Festival in the Northern Territory chapter of this book.

Gulkula, north-east Arnhem Land, Northern Territory
www.yyf.com.au/

Tourism in the outback: the landscapes of Indigenous Australia

Brambuk National Park and Cultural Centre, Grampians National Park (p. 177)

The ancient landforms in the Gariwerd Grampians National Park date from the Gondwana period, and it shows. These mountains and valleys look and feel old. And they are: about 180 million years old. This is a unique place because of its geological history and also because it is rich in Aboriginal history and culture. The Traditional Owners are the Jardwadjali and Djab Wurrung peoples. The majority of the rock-art sites in Victoria are in the Gariwerd, with some dating back 22 000 years. Their Traditional Owners are still involved in Gariwerd and maintain the culture and the stories of the land. Like other Aboriginal groups, the Jardwadjali and Djab Wurrung peoples have six distinct seasons that have an impact on the times when plants flower and fruit, and on animal behavioural patterns.

The Brambuk Cultural Centre is located in the town of Halls Gap in the Gariwerd or Grampians National Park. Its film, photographic and cultural presentations are windows into the cultures, geology and history of this awe-inspiring mountain range and its valleys.

The Centre has cultural activities and activities for school groups, guided walks, and the Bushfoods Cafe. I always go there before heading off on a walk or a swim in a lake in the national park. The waterfalls are beautiful after rain, and the forests and vegetation are endlessly fascinating and full of birdlife. The walks in the Gariwerd range from easy to challenging. The Gariwerd ancestral story involves twins who rest eternally in the two southernmost mountains of the ranges, Mount Sturgeon and Mount Abrupt. From the tops of these mountains the views are spectacular.

Gariwerd Grampians National Park: parkweb.vic.gov.au/explore/parks/grampians-national-park
Brambuk Cutlrual Centre: www.brambuk.com.au/about.htm

You will find information about many other national parks, Indigenous tours and events in the state and territory chapters in this book.

Top left: Women performing at the nightly bunggul (ceremony) at the Garma Festival, Arnhem Land, Northern Territory

Top right: Men performing traditional dance at the Garma Festival

Bottom: Teaching visitors about local cultures at the Brambuk Cultural Centre in the Grampians, Victoria

13 CULTURAL AWARENESS FOR VISITORS

The Aboriginal way of welcoming visitors to their homelands is often a very simple affair, with just a few words of welcome, sometimes in the local language and in English. Some groups light a fire, wetting special leaves such as ti-tree or gum to make a fine smoke and ask visitors to walk through the smoke, while others splash water on their guests. Occasionally, more elaborate ceremonies are held, which involve singing traditional songs. Participating in these rituals is the best way of showing respect for Aboriginal and Torres Strait Islander hosts and guides. Showing respect for Aboriginal and Torres Strait Islander people is often explained in unnecessarily complicated language in cross-cultural awareness programs. As travellers you will probably have met people from many different cultures and usually you will find that it is easy to talk to people in a normal tone of voice and say the usual greetings, such as, 'Good morning. How are you?' Or, 'Hello, my name is...' Also, you will learn a great deal by listening to and observing what your hosts and guides say and do.

In most of Indigenous Australia, English or a form of English is spoken. So there is no need to buy a phrase book that provides translations of everyday expressions such as 'hello' and 'where does the bus leave from?' – if, indeed, a phrase books for travellers in Indigenous languages is even available. I think it is more fun to get to know people and ask them questions such as, 'How do you say "hello" in your language?'

As I have explained, there are about 120 Indigenous languages still spoken in Australia. This astonishing diversity of languages is one reason why there aren't many, if any, language books for travellers or many other books and guides about Indigenous languages for the general reader.

Many Indigenous people were prevented from speaking their mother tongues during the assimilation period, and were often punished for doing so. That history combined with residual racism has resulted in a great reticence on the part of Indigenous Australians to speak their languages except in their own social settings. Fortunately, there are many grammars and dictionaries published by linguists and language revival programs, but this does not make it any easier for the visitor to engage in basic conversations in local languages.

Showing respect for your host is as simple as trying to say some words in that person's language, if you meet an Indigenous person who is willing to share their language. Speaking a few words of an Australian language is a great way to make friends, too. Your teacher will want to share more if you show a keen interest. Increasingly, many Indigenous tour guides are very proud and happy to share words about the flora and fauna and their traditional environmental knowledge, such as the names of seasons and weather patterns, and the behaviour of plants and animals during those times. The training provided by Indigenous ranger programs has enabled people to discuss their traditional knowledge openly and without fear.

Top: Showing visitors a smoking ceremony at Uptuyu Aboriginal Adventures, Western Australia

Bottom: An Indigenous artist running a Dot Painting Workshop at the Maruku Art Gallery, Uluru, Northern Territory

Questions

You need to know that not all questions are welcome, even if you are sincerely interested in finding out more about a place or a cultural point. In some areas of Australia, Aboriginal people will not respond to questions. Either the question makes no sense culturally, or it breaches local customs. Often an Aboriginal person – whether a man or a woman – is not permitted to discuss local customs without the permission of their group or clan. Instead of saying, 'I am not authorised to answer that question,' an Aboriginal person will remain silent or answer another question. This is still the Aboriginal way in many areas today. Asking too many questions can be seen as intrusive, even though meant with goodwill. Some trained guides and rangers are accustomed to the inquisitive visitor and deal with questions in a way that the visitor expects of a commercial guide. Aboriginal hosts are not always trained, and even if they are, will not bend their local rules. A good way to get a conversation going is with an observation about what you are being shown. By example, if you are walking by a forest at sunset and the trees are alive with flying foxes, or bats, you might say, 'That's a lot of bats. I have never seen so many.' This might start a discussion about the bats, the forest they live in, the season, and local customs. Or not, but you if you are in a different culture, such differences are to be expected.

When to use names of people and places and when not to

Visitors using Aboriginal and Torres Strait Islander names of people and places is not a problem when it is clear that this is allowed because your host has used the names or they appear on signs. Some Aboriginal and Torres Strait Islander names are difficult to pronounce, but it is always worth trying. You may get it right, and no one will be offended if you tried and didn't say it correctly. There are rules about names that cannot be used, but this practice is usually confined to the members of an Aboriginal society. Visitors are not expected to follow these rules, unless the hosts have explained that particular names may not be spoken.

In many areas, when a person dies, the name and images of that person cannot be used at all until the family of the deceased makes a public declaration that the taboo has been lifted. In the case of famous Aboriginal people, it may be some years before this happens. For famous Aboriginal musicians, an elliptical way of referring to the deceased will be used, such as 'that lead singer of the Yothu Yindi band'.

Top: A tour guide at Top Didj Cultural Experience and Art Gallery, Katherine, Northern Territory

Bottom: Photo of Johnny Mullagh, who lead the 1868 Aboriginal cricket tour of England, from the Harrow Discovery Centre, Victoria

Example of warnings displayed in respect for Aboriginal and Torres Strait Islander peoples

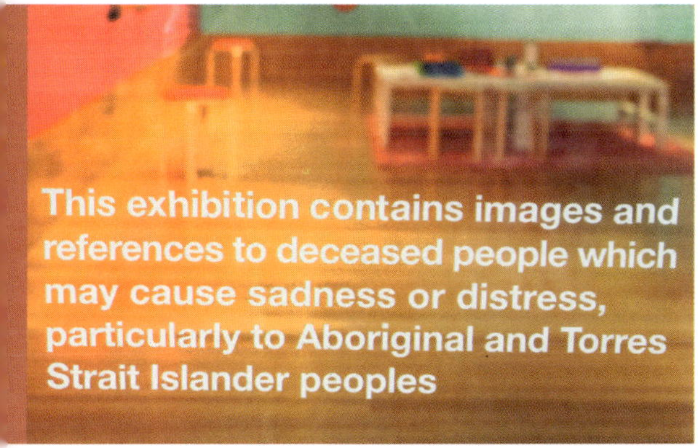

Place names that are the same as, or similar to a deceased person's name will not be used by Aboriginal people in the areas where these traditions are followed. For some years, Alice Springs was referred to as *Kumunjayi* by local people because of the death of a woman with the same first name as the town. Television stations and websites in Australia that broadcast or publish photographs and videos of Aboriginal people provide warnings at the beginning of the content so that Aboriginal and Torres Strait Islander people will be aware that they are likely to see images of deceased people. These practices have been in place for the last two decades and are commonplace. They show respect for the cultural protocols of the First Australians, and help other Australians to understand these cultural differences.

Language rules

In every language in the world there are rules about what is appropriate to say in public. Aboriginal groups may have words that only women are permitted to use, or that only men are permitted to use. There are words that are not allowed to be spoken in public but are confined to ceremonies. The esoteric languages of many Aboriginal societies are used only in ceremonial or ritual contexts. Visitors may have read in books by anthropologists about Aboriginal cultural practices such as rituals. In many cases, it is not polite or acceptable to speak about these matters in public. When in doubt, don't ask questions about anything that you think might be sensitive, and do not share what you have read in an obscure anthropological text.

I was in Paris many years ago at an international conference on Indigenous cultures when it was the fashion in French universities for students to interpret the 'meanings' of Aboriginal rock art through the lens of European psychological theories about sexual deviation. On a table in the foyer of the conference centre were piles of various documents published by a local publisher. I flipped through a few and my skin crawled. The texts bore no resemblance whatsoever to the meanings of the rock art as explained by the Traditional Owners. One of these texts stated that the art referred to a particular sexual deviation, when in fact the rock art represented a Lightning Ancestor who rouses the world during the monsoon season with thunder and flashes of light. None of the students had been to Australia, and clearly there was a theoretical formula imposed by a Freudian anthropologist in a faraway Parisian classroom. My advice: Don't try out European theories on Aboriginal people.

Photographs and videos

You must ask permission before filming or taking photographs of people, especially children. Aboriginal and Torres Strait Islander people do not feel comfortable with visitors taking photographs or videos of them or their family members without explicit permission. Aboriginal hosts at public events and tourist events will make it clear if photography is permitted. There have been a number of legal cases involving unauthorised photography, commercial use of photographs in publications without permission, and the distribution of photographs and videos. The use of unauthorised photography and video on social media platforms is also becoming a problem, and complaints from Aboriginal people have been acted on by police.

Signs and published cultural rules and protocols

Because of the great diversity, culturally and linguistically, in Indigenous Australia, many groups publish their own rules and protocols. A good example is the 'Behaviour protocols' published on the website of the Garma Festival hosted by the Yolŋu people of north-east Arnhem Land in the Northern Territory.[60] It is a thorough and useful guide to the rules and protocols in the area. There are some differences from area to area so keep in mind that something that is acceptable in one area or at one event might not be elsewhere.

At Garma, you are requested to observe and work within Yolŋu protocols.

Remember you are on Yolŋu land and entering Yolŋu time. Yolŋu perceptions, priorities and preoccupations are different from those of mainstream Australia. Be patient, and try to leave at home your expectations of how things are learnt, and how events should run. Traditionally Yolŋu learn by observation, by looking and listening. Asking too many questions can be inappropriate. So, when you have questions, choose them carefully and thoughtfully.

Respect Yolŋu people's personal space, particularly in the camping areas and each individual guest's tent. Sticking to the walking paths provided is important to ensure you're not stumbling across cultural space.

Avoid strolling around and visiting Yolŋu campsites unless specifically invited and accompanied by Yolŋu.

Please exercise courtesy and sensitivity when taking photographs – seek the permission of the Yothu Yindi Foundation and the subjects if taking close-ups, or photographs of small groups, particularly in the women's programs and men's programs cultural and health sessions. The Yothu Yindi Foundation has enforced strict Intellectual Property policies that safe guard both individuals and Yolŋu families when posting Garma to social media channels. You are reminded that we are working in a realistic environment of high mortality. Cultural protocols are strict for that matter and we ask guests to respect this process. If you wish to use Garma imagery, you will need to seek approval from our Director of Media media@yyf.com.au.

Visitors should NOT leave the Gulkula site on their own and should only walk along specifically marked Festival trails. This is about showing respect for land and is also a safety issue. Wild buffalo wander this country and organisers spend considerable effort in monitoring their trails prior to Garma each year. Please ensure someone knows your travel plans.

Treat the old people with the greatest of respect – they hold the knowledge and the power.

Please be conscious that dress standards may often vary from what is considered acceptable at your home. By dressing conservatively you will avoid the possibility of causing offence. Too much skin on display draws inadvertent attention not appropriate for this event. Schools attending the festival should advise their students of this policy. Our dress standards also protect our participants from sunburn, sunstroke and dehydration. Plan a sensible wardrobe, practical and covered shoes and include a hat to protect you from the elements.

You might wonder how practical advice about wearing hats and covered shoes might be cultural protocols. This is a good question. Aboriginal people become very upset if their visitors are injured or become sick while visiting their homeland because they feel a great sense of responsibility for visitors. They might think that they have not done their job well as responsible Traditional Landowners by reassuring the spirits of the land about their visitors. Other Traditional Owners may blame them for not paying attention if someone becomes sick or injured while visiting. The cultural belief in the power of the spirits in places is still very strong in many parts of Australia. An example of this is the ongoing argument about whether visitors should be allowed to climb Uluṟu.

A sign at the base of Uluṟu, erected by the Aṉangu people, states:

Please don't climb.

We, the Aṉangu traditional owners, have this to say

Top: Tourists ignoring the 'no photos' sign next to them

Bottom: Sign erected at Tjukatjapi, Uluṟu, Northern Territory

Uluṟu is sacred in our culture. It is a place of great knowledge.

Under our traditional law climbing is not permitted.

This is our home.

As custodians, we are responsible for your safety and behaviour.

Too many people do not listen to our message.

Too many people have died or been hurt causing great sadness.

We worry about you and we worry about your family.

Please don't climb.

We invite you to walk around the base and discover a deeper understanding of this place.

Along with the sacred nature of Uluṟu, Traditional Owners are troubled by the number of visitors who have died while climbing this great rock. Since 1958, thirty-six people are reported to have died from heart attacks and heat exhaustion. The rock is 348 metres high and subject to strong winds. The climb is steep and the temperature on the rock face is much higher than on the ground. Many non-Indigenous tourist operators will not explain these issues to their groups. Visitors are asked to make up their own minds, and having travelled so far to see this iconic feature of the Australian landscape, many still feel that the experience of climbing the rock must be ticked off their list of things to do.[61] It is hard to fathom the willingness of the tourist industry to continue to allow the desecration of this sacred place and the discomfort caused to the Traditional Owners by visitors climbing their sacred Uluṟu.

In October 2017, just as I finished writing this introduction to the marvels of the Australian Indigenous peoples and their cultures for this book, the members of the Uluṟu–Kata Tjuṯa National Park Board decided unanimously to ban tourists from walking on Uluṟu, starting in 2019. The eight Traditional Owners and three national parks representatives, which make up the Board, consulted the Aṉangu people, who were overwhelming in support of banning the climbing of Uluṟu by tourists. The chairperson, Sammy Wilson, stated in his speech on the matter that this place is of deep cultural significance and not a 'theme park like Disneyland'. The ban will take effect on 26 October 2019, to coincide with the 34th anniversary of the return of Uluṟu and Kata Tjuṯa to the Traditional Owners under a Commonwealth law.[62]

Rarely do Aboriginal Traditional Owners have the opportunity to set out their protocols as clearly as the Yolŋu in their Garma protocols or the Aṉangu in their statement asking visitors not to climb Uluṟu. In some places the Traditional Owners assert their rights to state what should and should not happen on their land, which they own under Australian law. In other areas, even when the Traditional Owners legally own the land, they might not have the means to erect signage about their protocols.

In many places there are hidden dangers that Traditional Owners and custodians know about, but non-Indigenous guides are unaware of. So when rules and protocols are explained in signs and publications everyone should observe them for their own safety.

In most national parks and conservation areas, government authorities install signage for visitors' safety. In north Australia, for example, there are the ubiquitous signs warning about crocodiles and the dangers of swimming as sharks, stingray, stone fish, gropers, fresh and saltwater crocodiles, sea snakes, eels, poisonous jellyfish, 'stingers'

Signs throughout the Northern Territory warn visitors about the dangers of crocodiles, such as this one at South Alligator River, Kakadu National Park, Northern Territory

and other dangerous creatures inhabit the seas, rivers and waterholes. In other parts of Australia, Aboriginal custodians and government authorities are particularly concerned about the dangers of drowning, people being washed out to sea and bites or injuries from the many dangerous creatures. In view of these and other hazards, signs warning against swimming are common in some areas and should always be taken seriously.

There are many protocols that are not mentioned in tourist guides. I have learnt about fishing protocols, for instance, from Traditional Owners. In northern Australia, when Traditional Owners have taken me on fishing trips, they would speak to the ancestral spirits or hold the fishing line over a smoky fire, and tell me a few rules. It is forbidden to gut fish near water and leave the entrails near bodies of water or on beaches. Clearly this is a practical safety rule because of the constant presence of saltwater crocodiles and wild boar. The smell of fish entrails will attract them very quickly and present an immediate danger. I never sleep or camp near water for the same reason. There are religious rules about this practice as well: it is an offence to the ancestral spirits to leave the remains of fish or other animals near water bodies. There is the constant concern of Traditional Owners that fresh water should not be contaminated, and the traditional way to drink from scarce fresh water sources, especially in arid areas, is to kneel at the edge of the water and sip it, or carefully fill a container without contaminating the water. Most visitors will not encounter these situations, but if you are travelling in the outback, it is good to know the basic Aboriginal rules, for your own safety as well as out of respect for the Aboriginal custodians.

In all cases right around Australia, my advice is: Do not ignore the safety signs.

14 GLOSSARY

Aboriginal people, Torres Strait Islander people, Indigenous people, First Australians, First Nations peoples, or First People: These terms are all generally acceptable when referring to the Aboriginal and Torres Strait Islander people of Australia. Despite much political correctness and nitpicking, none of these terms is offensive. Confusion arises among non-Indigenous people because of the long history of race hate towards Aboriginal people. Colonial and early twentieth-century laws used terms such as 'natives', 'aborigines', 'full-bloods', 'half-castes', and others. These terms are offensive because of their expression of racial supremacy and grading of people according to discredited race theories. With the advent of international human rights laws and standards, the term 'indigenous' came to be used in two ways: first, to refer in international law to those peoples who predate colonising peoples, such as Aboriginal people in Australia, Native Americans in the USA, and Maori in New Zealand; and, second, with a capital 'I' to refer to Aboriginal and Torres Strait Islander people.

Country: This is a Kriol term (Kriol is a modern, post-contact Aboriginal language) that has been universally adopted by Aboriginal people. It refers to their traditional land estates inherited from their forebears as a matter of custom and according to traditional land tenure laws of each people or society.

Language: All human groups have one or more languages, and the estimate by *Ethnologue* is that the number of languages spoken in the world today is 7099. This number is constantly in flux as we 'learn more about the world's languages every day'[63] A third of those languages are now endangered, many of which are Australian Aboriginal languages. Also, with the dominance of English and other languages that travelled with colonising powers, more than half the world's population now speak just twenty-three languages. The languages of Australia that predate colonisation and that are still spoken number about 120. Estimates differ but the consensus is that before colonisation there were between 250 and 500 languages in Australia.

Welcome to country: This is a custom among many Aboriginal groups to ensure the safe passage of visitors through their country. It is now extended to include Traditional Owners giving a welcome at the start of a speech or an event.

Basket weaving at Pudakul Aboriginal Cultural Tours, Northern Territory

Acknowledgement of country: Anyone – Indigenous and non-Indigenous – can acknowledge the Traditional Owners of the land at the start of a speech or an event.

Land rights and Native Title: These are legal concepts that developed with the advent of human rights law in Australia. They mean different things by law but both refer to legal recognition of Aboriginal rights to land.

Native Title is the legal doctrine that includes the recognition of Aboriginal and Torres Strait Islander rights to land and water according to tradition – Aboriginal and Torres Strait Islander traditions of owning land that predate colonisation, and are inherited from forebears according to local descent principles. These rights have been recognised under the Native Title Act in limited circumstances, such as where no title has been issued by an Australian government or colony.

Land rights are recognised under some laws that apply in the Northern Territory under a commonwealth act, and in some states, such as South Australia and New South Wales. Land rights laws usually grant title to Aboriginal groups to be held in trust.

A comprehensive glossary of terms that are used to apply to Australian Indigenous people, events, laws and so on, is provided by the Agreements, Treaties and Negotiated Settlements project at: atns.net.au/glossary.asp

The Australian Institute of Aboriginal and Torres Strait Islander Studies provides a searchable engine called the Pathways Thesauri for places, languages and subject at: aiatsis.gov.au/publications/products/pathways-thesauri

15
ENDNOTES

1 State Library of New South Wales. 'French in Australia', retrieved 10 January 2018, from: www.sl.nsw.gov.au/stories/diplomatic-relations-explorers-tourists-and-consuls

2 C. Clarkson, et al, 'Buried tools and pigments tell a new history of humans in Australia for 65,000 years', *The Conversation*, 20 July 2017; theconversation.com/buried-tools-and-pigments-tell-a-new-history-of-humans-in-australia-for-65-000-years-81021

3 C. Clarkson, et al, 'Human occupation of northern Australia by 65,000 years ago', *Nature*, vol. 547, pp. 306–10, 20 July 2017; www.nature.com/nature/journal/v547/n7663/full/nature22968.html?foxtrotcallback=true

4 The Smithsonian Institute; humanorigins.si.edu/evidence/human-fossils/fossils/kow-swamp

5 Michael I. Bird, et al, *Proceedings of the National Academy of the Sciences of the United States of America*, vol. 113, no. 41: 11477–11482; www.pnas.org/content/113/41/11477

6 Bill Gammage, *The Biggest Estate on Earth*, Allen & Unwin, Sydney, 2011, p. 95.

7 Michael I. Bird, et al, *op. cit*.

8 Australian Institute of Aboriginal and Torres Strait Islander Studies. Indigenous Australian Languages; aiatsis.gov.au/explore/articles/indigenous-australian-languages

9 David R. Horton (ed.), *The Encyclopaedia of Aboriginal Australia: Aboriginal and Torres Strait Islander history, society and culture*, Aboriginal Studies Press, Canberra, ACT, 1994.

10 Australian Screen. 2006. *Ten Canoes*. Synopsis: aso.gov.au/titles/features/ten-canoes/notes/

11 David R. Horton (creator), AIATSIS map of Indigenous Australia, Aboriginal Studies Press, AIATSIS, and Auslig/Sinclair, Knight, Merz, 1996

12 Australian National Dictionary Centre, ANU, *Borrowings from Australian Aboriginal Languages*; andc.anu.edu.au/australian-words/vocabulary/borrowings-from-australian-aboriginal-languages

13 Greg Dickson, 'Explainer: The largest language spoken exclusively in Australia – Kriol', *The Conversation*, 26 April 2016; theconversation.com/explainer-the-largest-language-spoken-exclusively-in-australia-kriol-56286

14 *Ibid.*

15 Diana Eades, 'Aboriginal English', *Pen 93*, Primary English Teaching Association, 1993, reprinted 2000, p. 2; www.naclc.org.au/cb_pages/files/Aboriginal%20English%20in%20the%20Legal%20System%20-%20Diane%20Eades.pdf

16 *Ibid.*

17 State Library of Queensland, 'Languages of the Torres Strait Islands'; www.slq.qld.gov.au/resources/atsi/languages/torres-strait

18 Aaron Corn and [Joe] Neparrna Gumbula, 'Rom and the Academy Repositioned: Binary Models in Yolnu Intellectual Traditions and their Application to Wider Intercultural Dialogues', in L. Russell (ed.), Boundary Writing: An Exploration of Race, Culture and Gender Binaries in Contemporary Australia, University of Hawai'i Press, Honolulu, 2006, pp. 170–97.

19 *Ibid.*, pp. 174–75.

20 *Ibid.*, pp. 178–79.

21 *Ibid.*, pp. 176–81.

22 Aaron Corn, 'Dreamtime Wisdom, Modern Time Vision: Tradition and Innovation in the Popular Band Movement of Arnhem Land, Australia', PhD thesis, The University of Melbourne, 2002, p. 219.

23 Aaron Corn and [Steven] Wantarri Jampijinpa Patrick, 'Pulyaranyi: New Educational Contexts for Transferring Warlpiri Knowledge,' UNESCO Observatory Multi-disciplinary Journal in the Arts, 4.2, 2005: 11.

24 Andrew Sayers, *Aboriginal Artists of the 19th Century*, Oxford University Press in association with National Gallery of Australia, Melbourne, 1994.

25 Australian Memory of the World Committee, Ronald M. Berndt Collection of Crayon Drawings on Brown Paper from Yirrkala, Northern Territory; www.amw.org.au/about-australian-memory-world-program

26 Karel Kupka, *Dawn of Art: Painting and Sculpture of Australian Aborigines*, Angus & Robertson, Sydney, 1965.

27 A good summary of the art history of this island region is 'Art Sets. Art of the Torres Strait Islands' on the website of the Art Gallery of New South Wales: www.artgallery.nsw.gov.au/artsets/hav5uo

28 Colin Golvan, 'Aboriginal Art and Copyright. An overview and commentary of recent developments', *Media Arts Law Review*, vol, 1, September 1996, pp 151–154; www.colingolvan.com.au/downloads/law-articles-essays/aboriginal-art-copyright-overview-commentary.pdf

29 See National Association for the Visual Arts, Code of Ethics: visualarts.net.au/media/uploads/files/Code_of_Ethics.pdf

30 Tourism Australia, 'Locals' Tips for Buying Aboriginal Art'; www.australia.com/en/things-to-do/aboriginal-australia/tips-for-buying-aboriginal-art.html

31 The Garma Statement on Indigenous Music and Dance: www.aboriginalartists.com.au/NRP_statement.htm

32 Aaron Corn, 'Friday essay: Dr Joe Gumbula, the ancestral chorus, and how we value Indigenous knowledges', *The Conversation*, 29 September 2017; theconversation.com/friday-essay-dr-joe-gumbula-the-ancestral-chorus-and-how-we-value-indigenous-knowledges-84438

33 Henry Gibson Dan and Karl Neuenfeldt, *Steady, Steady: The Life and Music of Seaman Dan*, Aboriginal Studies Press, Canberra, 2013.

34 Australian Government. Apology to Australia's Indigenous Peoples; www.australia.gov.au/about-australia/our-country/our-people/apology-to-australias-indigenous-peoples

35 E. Mabo, 'Land Rights in the Torres Strait' in E. Olbrei (ed.), *Black Australians: The Prospects for Change*, Students Union, James Cook University, Townsville, 1982.

36 *Mabo v Queensland* [No 2] (1992) 175 CLR 1.

37 Prime Minister Paul Keating, Second Reading Speech to the Native Title Bill, Hansard, House of Representatives, 16 November 1993.

38 *Members of the Yorta Yorta Aboriginal Community v Victoria* [2002] HCA 58, 12 December 2002.

39 *Ibid.*

40 See, for instance, James Cockayne, 'Members of Yorta Yorta Aboriginal Community v Victoria; Indigenous and Colonial Traditions in Native Title', *Melbourne University Law Review* 25 (3), 786, 2001; www.austlii.edu.au/au/journals/MelbULawRw/2001/25.html

41 *Yorta Yorta* [2001] FCA 45; (2001) 180 ALR 655, 666.

42 National Native Title Tribunal, Native Title Claims; www.nntt.gov.au/nativetitleclaims/Pages/default.aspx

43 Australian Government. Apology to Australia's Indigenous Peoples, *op. cit.*

44 Healing Foundation; healingfoundation.org.au/about-us/

45 Monuments Australia. Stolen Generations Memorial; monumentaustralia.org.au/themes/culture/indigenous/display/23125-stolen-generations-memorial

46 Monuments Australia. Stolen Generations Memorial; http://monumentaustralia.

org.au/themes/culture/indigenous/display/80245-stolen-generations-memorial

47 Monuments Australia. Stolen Generations Memorial; http://monumentaustralia.org.au/themes/culture/indigenous/display/20437-stolen-generations-memorial

48 Henry Reynolds, *Fate of a Free People: The Classic Account of the Tasmanian Wars*, Penguin, Melbourne, 2004; L. Ryan, *The Aboriginal Tasmanians*, UQP, St Lucia, 1981.

49 N.J.B. Plomley, *The Sealers of Bass Strait and the Cape Barren Island Community*, Tasmanian Historical Research Assoc., Canberra, 1988.

50 Robert Hughes, *The Fatal Shore. The Epic of Australia's Founding*, Alfred A. Knopf, New York, 1987.

51 See for instance, *10 Things you should know about January 26*, by Luke Pearson, Sophie Verass; www.sbs.com.au/nitv/article/2017/01/18/10-things-you-should-know-about-january-26

52 NAIDOC website: www.naidoc.org.au/about

53 2017 NAIDOC Week theme: www.naidoc.org.au/2017-national-naidoc-theme

54 Reconciliation Australia, Rap Hub: www.reconciliation.org.au/raphub/

55 Reconciliation Australia and AusPoll, *Evaluating the effectiveness of Reconciliation Action Plans.* Report prepared by Auspoll, 2012; www.reconciliation.org.au/wp-content/uploads/2013/12/Auspolls-Evaluating-the-effectiveness-of-Reconciliation-Action-Plans-Overall-analysis.pdf

56 www.fmgl.com.au/workingresponsibly/creating-positive-social-change/creating-opportunities

57 Australian Government. Department of Prime Minister and Cabinet. Indigenous Procurement Policy; www.pmc.gov.au/indigenous-affairs/economic-development/indigenous-procurement-policy-ipp

58 www.pmc.gov.au/sites/default/files/publications/Forrest-Review.pdf

59 Dr Lisa Ruhanen, The University of Queensland, Dr Michelle Whitford & Dr Char-lee McLennan, Griffith University, *Demand and Supply Issues in Indigenous Tourism: A Gap Analysis.* Prepared for the Indigenous Business Australia & Department of Resources, Energy and Tourism, Indigenous Tourism Working Group, January 2013: www.iba.gov.au/wp-content/uploads/2013/03/20130304ResearchReport_Demand-and-Supply-Issues-in-Indigenous-Tourism-A-Gap-Analysis.pdf

60 Yothu Yindi Foundation, 'Garma Protocols and Conduct'; www.yyf.com.au

61 www.outback-australia-travel-secrets.com/climbing-ayers-rock-uluru.html

62 The ban was widely reported in the Australian and international media. See, for instance, www.abc.net.au/news/2017-11-01/uluru-climbs-banned-after-unanimous-board-decision/9103512

63 Ethnologue: www.ethnologue.com/guides/how-many-languages

Bangarra Dance Theatre perform *Bennelong* in 2017

PART TWO

EXPLORING INDIGENOUS AUSTRALIA

1

NORTHERN TERRITORY

FESTIVALS

Barunga Festival

First held in 1985, Barunga Festival is one of regional Australia's longest running community festivals. It showcases the Indigenous cultures and communities of the Katherine region. Today, about 4000 visitors descend on the small community of Barunga each June long weekend to participate in a 3-day program that is rich in traditional arts, cultural activities, music and sport. The festival provides an exceptional opportunity to engage with remote Indigenous community life.

WHERE: Barunga community is 80 km south-east of Katherine. The festival can be accessed by car.
WHEN: Queen's Birthday long weekend in June.
CAMPING AND ACCOMMODATION: Camping sites are available in Barunga, or hotel/motel accommodation in Katherine.
PERMITS: Guests do not require permits to enter the community as tickets enable access for the duration of the festival.
COST: Adult: $50; youth 12–17 years: $15; child 5–11 years: $5.
CONTACT: 08 8941 8066
www.barungafestival.com.au

Garma Festival

This world-renowned festival is an extraordinary cultural event. Over four days the Yolŋu people of North-East Arnhem Land share their knowledge and culture. Each year it attracts about 2500 people, including prominent political and business leaders, academics, intellectuals and journalists from around the globe. A celebration of visual art, dance, music and ancient storytelling, Garma aims to foster economic opportunities for the Yolŋu people through community development, education, self-governance, enterprise and youth leadership. It is now regarded as an Australian Aboriginal equivalent of the annual World Economic Forum in Switzerland. As well as discussing the challenges and solutions to economic issues faced by Aboriginal and Torres Strait Islander people, Garma also aims to strengthen, preserve and maintain ancient Aboriginal culture and foster a greater understanding between Aboriginal and non-Aboriginal Australians.

Festival features

THE KEY FORUM: Addresses a theme of national significance to Australian Indigenous people.

Top: Aboriginal dancers in traditional body paint at the Barunga Festival

Bottom: Guests to the Garma Festival can participate in spearfishing workshops

It combines the wisdom, experience and vision of Indigenous peoples from around the country with those of political leaders and policy makers. The local people and everyone taking part in the forum are committed to producing practical solutions to improve Aboriginal and Torres Strait Islander lives.
THE YOUTH FORUM: Aims to foster the leadership capacity of the next generation, both Indigenous and non-Indigenous. Workshops, art, music, film production and social media tasks are designed to educate the youth in the avenues available to improve the state of Aboriginal and Torres Strait Islander disadvantage. Students from 8–18 years of age participate in this forum, and all registered guests of Garma may attend and observe activities.
EVENING BUNGGUL DANCE: This is arguably Garma's major attraction. From 4 pm until sunset, significant traditional ceremonies are performed by men, women and children from the various clans of the Yolŋu people. The performances showcase the unique traditional ceremonies of North-East Arnhem Land and combine breathtaking song and dance.
CULTURAL WORKSHOPS: Designed to give attendees an experience of some unique Yolŋu cultural practices, these workshops are run by local Yolŋu hosts. Attendees can participate in workshops on a wide range of subjects including cultural education, traditional bush medicine, pandanus basket weaving and spear making.
LIVE MUSICAL PERFORMANCES: They provide the entertainment each evening. The list of performers is announced by June of each year.
GAPAN GALLERY: Works by highly respected Arnhem Land Yolŋu artists are exhibited in an open-air gallery in a grove of stringybark trees.
WHERE: Gulkula site, 30 minutes from Nhulunbuy on the Central Arnhem Hwy. Airnorth runs direct flights to Nhulunbuy from Darwin and Cairns. A shuttle service is provided from Nhulunbuy airport to the Gulkula site. Alternatively, hire car companies operate in Darwin and Nhulunbuy, including: Manny's Car Rentals: 08 8987 2300; Gove Rentals: 08 8987 1700; and Nhulunbuy Ute Hire: 08 8987 2872.
WHEN: Annually in August
PERMITS: The official Garma ticket becomes the permit to enter the traditional Yolŋu lands of the Gulkula site and the township of Nhulunbuy. In buying a ticket, all guests are permitted to enter these lands and no further permit application is required. However, permits are required for any side trips and are strictly regulated. These must be applied for separately.
COST: Adult: $1815; student or child: $1056. Tickets cover an all-inclusive package deal. For registered guests, airport shuttles, camping (with assembled tent, sleeping bag and air mattress), and all meals are provided, as well as access to basic tea and coffee making facilities.
CONTACT: Yothu Yindi Foundation: 08 8945 5055 www.yyf.com.au

Mahbilil Festival

The Mahbilil Festival celebrates the rich culture and community of Kakadu. *Mahbilil* is the name of the cooling afternoon breeze that occurs in Kakadu's Gurrung season. This is a time of regeneration and hence a perfect time to celebrate. Running from midday to midnight, the festival includes various activities, children's workshops, Indigenous art exhibitions, weaving and painting demonstrations, traditional dance performances, and much more. When the sun sets, the festival becomes a buzz of activity, with spectacular lightshows and a diverse program of music and dance. Food is a prominent feature of the festival, with bush food, such as buffalo, barramundi and the specialty of the region, magpie goose, which is cooked in large earth ovens for guests to sample. There is even a magpie goose cook-off.

WHERE: Jabiru, 300 km from Darwin along the sealed Arnhem Hwy. The town of Jabiru is the gateway to Kakadu. It is a fantastic base from which to explore the wonders of Kakadu National Park. There is a supermarket and other essential shops to stock up for camping trips.
WHEN: Annually in late August to early September.
CONTACT: info@mahbililfestival.com www.mahbililfestival.com

MUSIC

National Indigenous Music Awards (NIMAs)

The NIMAs are a platform for the rich musical talent of Aboriginal and Torres Strait Islander people from around Australia. They are a special celebration, and showcase up-and-coming artists alongside those who are internationally acclaimed, such as Archie Roach, Jessica Mauboy, Yothu Yindi and the late Dr G Yunupingu. The NIMAS have been running for twelve years and are held annually in the beautiful George Brown Darwin Botanic Gardens Amphitheatre beneath the stars. The night's electric atmosphere attracts audiences from all around Australia, and it is a must-see event for music lovers of all ages and cultures.

WHEN: Early August. The NIMAs normally coincide with the beginning of the Darwin Festival. This is the Dry season in Darwin. Evening temperatures are beautiful and cool and can drop to around 20°C.
COST: For ticket prices and other information, visit the NIMA website.
www.nima.musicnt.com.au

Top: Rock/reggae band East Journey performing at the National Indigenous Music Awards in Darwin

Bottom: Traditional painting at the Tiwi Islands Grand Final and Art Sale

SPORT

Tiwi Islands Grand Final and Art Sale

This unique sporting and cultural event attracts thousands of locals and tourists to Bathurst Island each year. The passion for football engulfs the entire community of the Tiwi Islands and the grand final is the highlight of the season. The day has moved beyond the football match alone and has become a celebration of Tiwi Islands' culture. The Jilamara Arts and Crafts Association is joined by smaller art centres from other communities on the islands to showcase the work of many local artists at the primary school. A large selection of paintings, prints, carvings and woven pieces is available for tourists to purchase at reasonable prices.

WHERE: Bathurst Island, about 80 km north of Darwin. SeaLink ferries run return trips to the Tiwi Islands: adults: $120; concession: $90; child: $65. The trip is just under 3 hours each way. For more information visit: www.sealinknt.com.au/ferry. Fly Tiwi charters light planes to Bathurst Island, which take 30 minutes each way.
WHEN: March. This is the end of the Wet season, so be prepared for rain.
www.northernterritory.com/darwin-and-surrounds/events/tiwi-islands-grand-final-and-art-sale

Top: Sweeping views of Judbarra–Gregory National Park

Bottom: Fishing on the Cobourg Peninsula, Garig Gunak Barlu National Park

NATIONAL PARKS

The NT government manages more than 90 parks and reserves in the Territory, which cover over 45000 sq km or approximately 3.5 per cent of the NT land mass. In addition to the ones included here, visitors can find out about the many other parks at: nt.gov.au/leisure/parks-reserves/find-a-park-to-visit

Garig Gunak Barlu

Covering the entire Cobourg Peninsula, the surrounding waters of the Arafura Sea and Van Diemen Gulf, as well as some neighbouring islands, this national park is one of northern Australia's most spectacular areas. The park lies within the traditional lands of the Iwaidja-speaking Arrarrkbi people of Western Arnhem Land. Four clans – the Agalda, Madjunbalmi, Muran and Ngaindjagar – share ownership of the area and engage in management of the land and sea through independent traditional management practices, and are also employed as park rangers. The Arrarrkbi people have proven links to the land and sea that date back 40 000 years. Numerous sacred sites and large middens testify to their long-term occupation. The remote and rugged lands of Garig Gunak Barlu are fringed by pristine beaches with brilliant white sand and sparkling turquoise waters.

The park is a fantastic location for camping, boating, bushwalking, observing wildlife and birdwatching. Barramundi and mangrove jack can be found in tidal creeks and estuaries, but blue water fishing is better known in the area.

Visit the Black Point Cultural Centre, within the Black Point Ranger Station, for an insight into the diverse history of the peninsula. As well as the Aboriginal people, the Macassan traders and European explorers also played a role in the area's history.

WHERE: On the Cobourg Peninsula about 570 km north-east of Darwin. Drive from Darwin via Arnhem Hwy through Kakadu, then through Arnhem Land via Oenpelli and Murgenella rds, 4WD only; the unsealed road is open only during the Dry season (May–October). You can also travel via air charter to Smith Point or via boat (2-day sail from Darwin).
PERMITS: Bookings are required in advance to travel through Arnhem Land and also to camp; for permit applications contact: Permits and Concessions Unit, GPO Box 1448, Darwin NT 0801; 08 8999 4814; pwpermits@nt.gov.au. Additional permits are required to travel further into Arnhem Land.
BEST TIME TO VISIT: May to August; roads open May to October only.
TIPS FOR VISITORS: **Limited bore water is available so take as much water as you can.**
CONTACT: www.nt.gov.au/leisure/parks-reserves/find-a-park-to-visit/garig-gunak-barlu-national-park

Judbarra–Gregory

Judbarra–Gregory National Park lies in the transitional zone between the tropical and semi-arid regions of the NT. Encompassing a huge 13 000 sq km area, the park includes soaring escarpments with spectacular range and gorge scenery, tropical woodlands and magnificent river systems. Within the national park there are significant Aboriginal sites, and evidence of European pastoral and exploration history.

ABORIGINAL CULTURAL HERITAGE: The land here is of high spiritual significance to the Traditional Owners and is still used for traditional ceremonies and rituals. Indigenous language groups associated with the park are the Wardaman, Ngariman, Ngaliwurri, Nungali, Jaminjung and Karrangpurra people. One of the largest rock-art sites in Australia is found here, and it depicts the ancient history of Aboriginal occupation in the park area. The most common motifs are human figures, which appear in a style unique to this particular region.

THINGS TO DO: Private tours of the Victoria River can be organised in Timber Creek and at the Victoria River Roadhouse. There are challenging and rewarding 4WD tracks and plenty of opportunities for bushwalking.
BUSHWALKING: Most walks in the park are well marked and start close to the Victoria Hwy.
FISHING: This is a popular activity in the park. Regulations do apply, so make sure you are familiar with them before trying any fishing.
WHERE: 160 km west of Katherine; 220 km east of Kununurra. From Katherine or Kununurra via the Victoria Hwy; from Halls Creek via the unsealed Buntine Hwy; from Top Springs via the unsealed Buntine Hwy or unsealed Buchanan Hwy and Victoria River Downs Station. From December to April, the Wet season rains may make all roads, including the Victoria Hwy, impassable. Road conditions should be checked before any travel.
CAMPING AND ACCOMMODATION: There are numerous campgrounds around the park. Most have basic facilities, including toilets, fire-places, and picnic tables. Sullivan Creek Campground is 17 km east of the Victoria River, on the banks of a permanent waterhole. Big Horse Creek campground is 10 km

west of Timber Creek and is popular with anglers for its boat ramp and accessible fishing areas. Limestone Gorge campground is well situated for access to the calcite flow walk, the Limestone Creek Billabong and fishing in the East Baines River. Bullita campground is 60 km south of Timber Creek, near the historic Bullita Homestead and close to the East Baines River. Accommodation is available at the Victoria River Roadhouse and Bullita Homestead.

PERMITS: Permits are required for overnight bushwalking and are available from Timber Creek or Bullita ranger stations.

BEST TIME TO VISIT: From May to August is the most comfortable time to visit, with temperatures ranging from 10–35°C. In November to April the weather is much warmer and wetter, however woodlands become lush, river systems surge and campgrounds are quiet. Take precautions and care in the wetter months.

TIPS FOR VISITORS: **Saltwater crocodiles inhabit the waterways in Judbarra–Gregory National Park. Do not swim and be croc-wise at all times.**

COST: A standard fee applies at all campgrounds. Near the entrance to the campgrounds there is a fee deposit box and envelopes provided. Fees are assigned based on the campground facilities. Check the website below for a list of fees.

CONTACT: Parks and Wildlife Commission of the Northern Territory (PWCNT). PWCNT Katherine: 08 8973 8888; Kununurra Visitor Centre: 08 9168 1177
www.nt.gov.au/leisure/parks-reserves/find-a-park-to-visit/judbarra-gregory-national-park

Kakadu

World Heritage listed Kakadu National Park is a landscape of unsurpassed beauty, with world-renowned wetlands attracting extraordinary numbers of birds, thundering waterfalls that plunge from towering escarpments into natural rock pools, and open woodlands that offer a refuge for a wide range of native animals. It is Australia's largest national park and has entire ecosystems within its extensive boundaries. More than one-third of Australia's bird species are found in Kakadu, along with hundreds of plant, animal and marine species that do not exist anywhere else on the planet. Kakadu is also a very spiritual place, with a rich cultural heritage that reflects the unique relationship between the Aboriginal Traditional Owners and the land itself.

ABORIGINAL CULTURAL HERITAGE: Kakadu is a landscape of living culture. Rock art of the region indicates Aboriginal people have occupied Kakadu for between 40 000 and 60 000 years, the longest record of continual human occupation of any area on Earth. The rock-art galleries show that early Indigenous groups had a strong culture based on deep spiritual beliefs. This spiritual connection to the land is recognised globally in the World Heritage status of Kakadu.

The name *Kakadu* comes from an Aboriginal language, Gagudju, spoken in the north of the park at the beginning of the 20th century. In 1978 the Gagudju people were granted title of their land, which they then leased for use as a national park. Kakadu is jointly managed by the Bininj/Mungguy people and Parks Australia. Although Gagudju is no longer spoken by Aboriginal people in the area, surviving dialects include Kunwinjku (in the north), Gundjeihmi (in the centre) and Jawoyn (in the south). Aboriginal people of the region know themselves as Bininj (pronounced Bin-ning). Languages, kinship, ceremonies and caring for country have been passed on through the generations from the time of Creation when important ancestral beings crossed the landscape and created the plants, animals, landforms, and the people who live there today.

A major creator acknowledged in the region is the Rainbow Serpent, which is known Australia-wide by various Aboriginal

Top: Peaceful waterholes are dotted throughout Kakadu National Park

Bottom: Gunlom Falls boast stunning views along with cool, refreshing waters

groups. As the Rainbow Serpent moved through the land she formed the features of the landscape in Kakadu, such as waterways, waterholes and hills. Her role in creating the cultural obligations of the Bininj/Mungguy people is very important, as is her creation of the plant and animal life cycles and the seasonal changes. In the Kakadu region she is also known as *Almudj* in Gundjeihmi, *Ngalyod* in Kunwinjku, *Nama'rdeedjurr* in Gagudju, *Bolung* in Jawoyn and *Lulydjudjan* in Limilngan. Other important ancestral beings that feature in creation stories and rock-art depictions include *Bula* (Jawoyn Ancestor), *Namarrgon* (Lightning Man) and *Warramurrungundji* (Earth Mother).

The main Aboriginal rock-art sites are at Ubirr and Burrungkuy (Nourlangie), while an excellent understanding of Kakadu's Aboriginal culture can be gained by visiting the Bowali Visitor Centre and Warradjan Cultural Centre.

THE SIX SEASONS OF KAKADU: The Bininj/Mungguy people divide the year into six seasons to account for the dramatic changes in weather in Kakadu.

- *Gudjewg*, from December to March, is the monsoon season or the true wet. There are thunderstorms, heavy rain and flooding, a vibrant growing season and abundant wildlife. Temperatures range from 24–34°C.
- *Bang Gerreng*, in April, is when the rain clouds disperse and the clear skies return. Floodwaters and streams recede and start to run clear again, and plants are fruiting. Windstorms occasionally occur early in the season, but otherwise the air is clear and the winds warm. It is a beautiful time to visit the park and is very popular among visitors. Temperatures range from 23–34°C.
- *Yegge*, from May to mid-June, is cooler with relatively low humidity. Waterlilies cover the wetlands and billabongs, and early morning mist hangs above the plains and waterholes. The Bininj/Mungguy start burning patches of land to encourage new growth. Temperatures range from 21–33°C and are perfect for visitors.
- *Wurrgeng* is the cold weather season, from mid-June to mid-August. Creeks stop flowing and floodplains dry up, and an abundance of water birds crowd shrinking billabongs. The Yellow Water Billabong is an explosion of activity. Controlled burning continues and birds of prey patrol fire lines in their hundreds, looking for small animals fleeing the flames. The humidity is low and temperatures range from 17–32°C.
- *Gurrung*, from mid-August to mid-October, is the hot dry season. The country has been cleansed from the burning and is now ready to regenerate. Magpie geese are still numerous, laying their eggs in the wetlands, but Bininj/Mungguy also hunt long-necked turtles and file snakes. Waterfalls have less water, and the drier heat is perfect for touring and trekking. Days are warm, but nights are still cool; temperatures range from 23–37°C.
- *Gunumeleng* is the pre-monsoon storm season. It generally runs from mid-October to late December, but exact dates vary each year. Humidity rises and scattered thunderstorms bring the flow of streams and the filling of floodplains. Traditionally Bininj/Mungguy had to move camp to the stone country, to shelter from the storms. With all the water, dramatic changes in the landscape occur across the park and it is a captivating time to visit. Temperatures at this time range from 24–37°C.

NATURAL FEATURES: The eastern boundary of the park follows the East Alligator River and the 140-million-year-old Arnhem Land escarpment, which is the western edge of the Arnhem Land Plateau, an imposing geological feature that stands some 300 m above the tropical woodland of the park and extends for more than 500 km.

The escarpment is the edge of the stone country of Arnhem Land and many rivers in the Top End have their headwaters here, including the East and South Alligator, which flow through the tropical woodland of Kakadu, across the floodplains and out to the Van Diemen Gulf. The plains are broken up by impressive rocky outcrops, or 'outliers'. Areas of the escarpment and massive rock formations, such as Burrungkuy, were shelters for Aboriginal people, who often used the rock walls and overhangs as a canvas on which to depict their daily lives and spiritual beliefs.

Compared to the escarpment, which dominates the landscape in the east of the park, the rivers and coastal areas are more modern formations, built up over thousands of years as silt was carried out of Arnhem Land. During the Wet season, rivers and creeks break their banks and flood the plains, creating Kakadu's famous wetlands that also include monsoonal rainforests, swamps and billabongs. It is these areas, rich in plant and insect life, which make Kakadu National Park one of the most abundant areas for wildlife in Australia. There are over 280 bird species, more than 50 fish species, over 120 reptile and amphibian species, 60 mammal species, 100 termite species and more than 300 ant species in the park. Also, biologists have recorded more than 2000 plant species in the area.

Things to do

BUSHWALKING: One of the best ways to experience Kakadu is on foot. Throughout the park there are various walks that cater to a wide variety of fitness levels and trip itineraries, including shorter day walks and more challenging full-day hikes. There are also overnight walks, which require high levels of experience and careful planning as you walk through unmarked and rugged country. Permits are required for all overnight walks.

BURRUNGKUY AREA: In this area is the picturesque Anbangbang Billabong and the renowned Burrungkuy Rock, a vast, ancient rock-art gallery and an inspirational place that projects a sense of how Indigenous people once lived. The turn-off to Burrungkuy is 19 km south of Bowali, on the Kakadu Hwy. A circular walk (1.5 km) winds through some of Australia's most spectacular art sites and ancient living areas. Other walking trails include Nawurlandja Lookout walk (1.2 km return, 40 minutes, medium difficulty), involving a moderate climb for views of the escarpment and Anbangbang Billabong; Nanguluwur Art Site walk (3.4 km return, 2 hours, easy), through open savannah woodlands to a secluded art gallery; Gubara walk (6 km return, 4 hours, easy) through woodlands and along a string of lovely forest-rimmed rock holes to interesting rock art; Bubba walk (3.5 km circuit, 2 hours, easy) starting at Muirella Park camping area and trailing through wetlands. A longer trail in the Burrungkuy area, Barrk walk (12 km loop, 6–8 hours, difficult), traverses the sandstone country, passing the Nanguluwur art site along the way.

JIM JIM FALLS AREA: This area is 43 km from Kakadu Hwy along a 4WD road and is only accessible during the Dry season. Jim Jim Plunge Pool, at the end of a 1 km walk from the carpark (1–2 hours return, medium difficulty – it involves some rock-hopping), is one of the most beautiful swimming areas in Kakadu. It is surrounded by 150 m-high cliffs and fed by a powerful waterfall that stops flowing during the Dry season. Nearby, Budjmi Lookout walk (1 km return, 45 minutes, medium difficulty) is a Dry-season trail that starts at Jim Jim camping area and involves a moderate-grade climb to the top of a rocky outcrop for expansive views of the Arnhem Land escarpment. Barrk Marlam walk (6 km return, 5–6 hours, difficult) is another Dry-season track that branches off the Jim Jim Plunge Pool track and goes through rugged sandstone country. 10 km further on from Jim Jim Falls is Twin Falls, where a spectacular waterfall feeds a beautiful rock hole, rimmed by a white sandy beach. Access is by a boat shuttle service. Swimming is not allowed because of saltwater crocodiles, but there is a lovely walk, Twin Falls Plateau Trail (6 km return, 5 hours, difficult), that climbs the cliffs above the falls.

MARY RIVER AREA: The belief of the Jawoyn Aboriginal people is that powerful creation ancestors rest here and should not be disturbed. Access to Gunlom is via a gravel road and an unsealed dirt road (check Wet-season access). The Gunlom plunge pool is wide, deep and scenic, and with its wispy Dry-season waterfall, this is the most popular place in the southern part of the park. A steep trail (2 km return, 1.5 hours, medium difficulty) leads to the top of the falls. Up here some beautiful rock pools, including an infinity pool, provide stunning views of the southern areas of Kakadu and are probably the safest places to swim in the park. The Yurmikmik walks are several separate, but interconnected, walks that provide a wonderful experience of the Kakadu.

SOUTH ALLIGATOR AREA: Turn south off the Arnhem Hwy (7 km east of the South Alligator River) to reach Mamukala wetlands. Mamukala is open all year but is at its most dramatic in September and October when thousands of magpie geese and other birds gather to feed as the waters dry up. There is an excellent observation platform and a 3 km walk (1–2 hours, easy) along the wetlands. Another option is Gu-ngarre walk (3.6 km circuit, 2 hours, easy), which leads through savannah woodlands and monsoon forest, then along the edges of a waterhole. Access is near the Aurora Kakadu Resort.

JABIRU AREA: Bowali Visitor Centre, on the Kakadu Hwy just west of Jabiru, is the park headquarters and a wonderful starting point for learning about Kakadu and Aboriginal culture. There are audiovisual displays and a ranger is on hand to answer questions. Bowali walking track (4 km return, 1.5 hours, easy) starts opposite the Crocodile Hotel and winds its way through open savannah woodland to the visitor centre (the track is also a bike trail).

EAST ALLIGATOR AREA: Ubirr is one of the best art sites in the park; good views of the rock art are provided by a 1 km circuit walk. Another track (500 m return, 1 hour, medium difficulty), involving a fairly steep climb, leads to a rocky vantage point with a spectacular view – particularly at sunset – over the Nardab floodplain. Bardedjilidji walk (2.5 km, 2 hours) is a short, but fascinating, trail that meanders through the sandstone outliers.

YELLOW WATER AREA: The local Aboriginal name for Yellow Water is Ngurrungurrudjba. It is one of the most accessible and beautiful wetland areas in northern Australia. When the waters recede in the Dry season the wildlife is concentrated in this one area that is part of the South Alligator floodplain. Commercial boat tours travel through the wetlands and guides provide commentaries about the landscape and wildlife. A boardwalk offers another perspective of the wetland during the Dry season. Warradjan Cultural Centre near Yellow Water is a fascinating place with outstanding displays of Aboriginal culture. It really is a must-see for visitors to learn about the culture of Kakadu's Traditional Owners.

WHERE: 235 km east of Darwin to the Bowali Visitor Centre, one entrance of the park. Drive from Darwin via Stuart Hwy then Arnhem Hwy; from Pine Creek via Stuart Hwy then Kakadu Hwy.

PERMITS: A fee applies to visitors entering Kakadu National Park. NT residents and children under 16 years of age are exempt. Camping permits are required for some campsites. Some campsites have a quota for camping, so organise permits well in advance of your visit.

BEST TIME TO VISIT: During the drier months from May to September, the whole park is generally open. During the Wet season, while some of the park is inaccessible due to the water and the weather can be very hot and humid, it is an incredible opportunity to see waterfalls turn into gushing torrents and watch thunderstorms roll in over the park. Cooinda is

Top: Spirit beings on a rock-face at Burrungkuy (Nourlangie), Kakadu National Park

Bottom: Aboriginal fine art and artefacts are on display in the Bowali Visitor Centre

beautiful at this time, with a huge increase in bird and wildlife activity as the wetlands fill up. It is also the perfect time to do scenic flights over the park to see spectacular aerial views of the entire area inundated with water and wildlife.

TIPS FOR VISITORS: **Saltwater crocodiles populate the rivers and coastal areas of Kakadu.** Visitors are warned to stay out of the water, unless there is clear advice to the contrary. The only places likely to be free of these dangerous reptiles are located up in the escarpment country.

Keep children away from the water's edge in crocodile-prone areas.

CONTACT: Parks Australia Kakadu; Bowali Visitor Centre: 08 8938 1120
www.kakadu.com.au
www.environment.gov.au/parks/Kakadu

Bowali Visitor Centre

The visitor centre, near the town of Jabiru, is a great first point of call before entering Kakadu. Staff at the centre can assist you with travel plans in the park. Interpretive displays show different views of Kakadu's significance and detail its many sights and activities in the park.

The Marrawuddi Gallery, within the centre, displays fine art from Aboriginal artists from Kakadu. The design of the building itself is inspired by an Aboriginal rock shelter and is internationally acclaimed. Bowali is the name locals give to the area where the centre is located.

WHEN: 8 am–5 pm daily; closed Christmas Day
CONTACT: Kakadu Hwy, Kakadu National Park, Jabiru; 08 8938 1120
www.parksaustralia.gov.au/kakadu/plan/visitor-centres/

Burrungkuy (Nourlangie) and Ubirr

Burrungkuy and Ubirr are the best-known rock-art sites in Kakadu. Located in environments rich in natural resources and comprising several large rock outcrops with numerous caves and overhangs, these sites were important centres of precontact Aboriginal occupation.

Traditionally, Aboriginal people camped in the rock shelters at Ubirr, where the smooth surfaces were ideal for painting. Over 120 rock-art sites here display a range of styles, including large naturalistic portrayals of extinct animals, simple stick figures with large headdresses, X-ray paintings of fauna such as turtles and fish, and animated and ornamented figures in motion. One painting depicting a Tasmanian thylacine is considered to be around 3000 years old.

Other more recently executed post-contact art portrays the trading period with Macassan fishermen and the arrival of Europeans. One of the most amazing paintings is that of a sailing ship, depicted in white ochre, which chronicles the early contact with Europeans. Such ships were seen in the area between 1880 and 1950, when they brought supplies to buffalo-hunting camps on the floodplains of the Alligator River, and returned to Darwin with hides. Many Aboriginal people worked in these camps.

At Burrungkuy, shell and animal-bone fragments in one area suggest occupation over the past 6000 years. The most visited site is the Anbangbang gallery, where evidence of occupation dates back 2500 years. The main rock art you can see today is the work of the artist Najombolmi, who decorated the walls in 1964. In an effort to preserve his Indigenous culture he painted spirit beings, family groups and people travelling to a ceremonial gathering. Nanguluwur also has X-ray paintings of barramundi and a short-necked turtle, painted in 1964 by a friend of Najombolmi.

On the northern side of Burrungkuy is a smaller gallery, Nanguluwur, which displays most of the rock-art styles found in Kakadu.

There are depictions of Algaihgo, the fire woman, one of the First People who created the world. She planted the yellow banksias in the woodlands and used their smouldering flowers to carry fire.

High up on the rock face are hand stencils, the subject of rock art in this area since Aboriginal people first came here around 50 000 years ago. On some hands, the three middle fingers are held together and separated from the outer fingers, a style of hand stencil that is often found alongside 'dynamic art' estimated at over 20 000 years old. High on the ceiling of the shelter are small depictions of people, painted in the dynamic style. These figures, adorned with headdresses, carry boomerangs used for hunting about 20 000 years ago when the climate was drier and open grasslands were prevalent. Boomerangs are of little use in the woodland forests of today.

Burrungkuy is accessible by an easy 1.5-km walking track that includes two lookouts, and Ubirr by an easy 1 km circuit track (allow at least 45 minutes). From Ubirr, an additional 250 m, moderately steep climb gives an unforgettable panoramic view across the vast Nadab floodplains of the East Alligator River. Time your walk to the top of Ubirr rock to catch an incredible sunset over the floodplains. Also, later in the Wet season, when the rain is not as heavy, the floodplain is still an explosion of plant and animal life. The view across the floodplains is particularly striking at this time. The 12 km Barrk sandstone walk over Burrungkuy is challenging, and should not be attempted solo. A range of guided tours are available, including the Wurrgeng cultural walk.

WHERE: Ubirr is 39 km from Jabiru via the Arnhem Hwy.

ACCOMMODATION: Muirella Park (Djarradjin) is a managed camping area with showers and toilets. Fees apply and are collected on site. Check seasonal access. Sandy Billabong is a simple bush camping area with basic toilet facilities. Fees apply and are collected on site.

IMPORTANT: Drinking water is not available at either site, so you must bring your own.

BEST TIME TO VISIT: Ubirr is open year round, but May to September are the best times to go during the drier months. In the Wet season, from December to March, opening hours are limited and access may be restricted due to flooding. From June to September local rangers give talks at Ubirr and Burrungkuy about rock art and culture. Visit www.kakadu.com.au for more information.

OPEN: Ubirr is open from 8.30 am to sunset from April to November, and from 2 pm to sunset from December to March. However, the road to Ubirr may be closed due to flooding at this time so check access before visiting.

www.parksaustralia.gov.au/kakadu/do/rock-art/burrungkuy

www.parksaustralia.gov.au/kakadu/do/rock-art/ubirr

Karlu Karlu (Devils Marbles) Conservation Reserve

Karlu Karlu is one of the most iconic outback destinations in the Northern Territory, with massive red and orange boulders precariously piled atop each other in a broad, desert landscape. The area is culturally and spiritually significant for four Aboriginal groups: the Alyawarre, Kayteye, Warumunga and Warlpiri people. Karlu Karlu is simply the Alyawarre name for the area, with no further meaning than that.

ABORIGINAL CULTURAL HERITAGE: Traditionally, certain parts of Karlu Karlu were off limits to the local Aboriginal people. Many parts were considered so dangerous that only the Elders could visit them for important ceremonies. The only areas open to all Aboriginal people to gather bush foods and medicines and to hunt were the central areas.

The Dreaming of Karlu Karlu tells the story of Arrange, a devil man. As the Alyawarre people tell his story, he travelled through the land twirling his hair into string to make a hair belt – a traditional ornamentation worn only by initiated Aboriginal men. The clusters of hair he dropped became the large red boulders seen today.

The entire area is a sacred site for both men and women. Local Aboriginal women often visit the reserve to gather wild figs. Small waterholes found in the northwest creek are also very valuable to Aboriginal people for collecting water.

Since 2008, the reserve has been jointly managed by the Traditional Owners and Northern Territory Parks and Wildlife. Today it is protected under Northern Territory law as a Registered Sacred Site.

NATURAL FEATURES: The granite blocks from which the marbles were shaped were originally large slabs. Over millions of years, flaking and erosion gradually rounded the corners so many of the boulders are now spherical or egg-shaped. Ranging in size from 50 cm up to 6 m in diameter, the boulders continue to flake and erode, creating a landscape that is ever changing.

Animals, birds and plants of the arid zone are found in the area, and the shadows and nooks of the boulders provide a cool refuge for them in summer months. Attached to the underside of overhanging rock are clusters of bottle-shaped mud nests, home to fairy martins; small dragons and lizards live in the crevices.

THINGS TO DO: The Devils Marbles has a network of self-guided walks. As you wander around you can find new viewpoints to admire.

WHERE: 390 km north of Alice Springs; 100 km south of Tennant Creek via the Stuart Hwy.

CAMPING: A simple bush camping area with fireplaces and pit toilets is located at the southern end of the reserve. No water or firewood is provided, so bring your own.

BEST TIME TO VISIT: At sunset and sunrise, the rocks and boulders are bathed in magnificent orange light. A short self-guided walk (15 minutes return, easy) leaves from the carpark, with signs giving geological information. A network of tracks meanders through the rock formations and you can climb some of the more accessible boulders for an excellent view of the surrounding desert.

CONTACT: PWCNT Alice Springs: 08 8951 8250;
PWCNT Tennant Creek: 08 8962 4599
www.nt.gov.au/leisure/parks-reserves/find-a-park-to-visit/karlu-karlu-devils-marbles-conservation-reserve

Gravity defying stones at Karlu Karlu (Devils Marbles) Conservation Reserve

Litchfield National Park

Litchfield National Park is a true gem. Its 146 000 hectares of diverse landscapes include most types of Top End habitats. Spring-fed waterfalls flow from atop the plateau, creating beautiful, crocodile-free swimming holes, and outliers of imposing, weathered rock rise from grassy plains dotted with massive termite mounds.

ABORIGINAL CULTURAL HERITAGE: Aboriginal people have lived in the region for thousands of years. In the park are the traditional lands of the Koongurrukun, Marranunggu, Werat and Waray clans.

NATURAL FEATURES: The park is dominated by the Tabletop Range, from which spring-fed waterfalls plunge over its sheer escarpments and craggy rock faces. The constant flow of water from springs and Wet-season floods has gouged out ravines and large rock holes at the base of the range. Creeks spill into the Finniss and Reynolds rivers, which meander westwards across the floodplains to the coast.

Two eucalypt species dominate the tropical woodland, the Darwin woollybutt and stringybark. Banksias, grevilleas, acacias and other flowering species attract birds and insects. Carpentaria palms and aquatic pandanus are common around monsoonal rainforests and along the creeks. Some of the Carpentaria forests are extremely tall, with each tree competing for sunlight. Cypress pines grow on the upper slopes around Florence Falls.

In and around the rock pools, water monitor lizards are common. The golden silk orb-weaving spider is also common around waterways, where you will notice their large shimmery, golden webs. Bats inhabit the caverns of the sandstone escarpment. At Tolmer Falls live several colonies of the rare orange leaf-nosed bat and of the ghost bat. The moist tropical vegetation is also home to a range of python species, which are not venomous.

In the woodland environment there are agile wallabies, antilopine wallaroos, common brushtail possums, quolls, sugar gliders and dingoes. The prolific birdlife includes honeyeaters, rainbow bee-eaters, rainbow lorikeets, olive-backed and yellow orioles, dollarbirds, common koels, red-tailed black cockatoos and figbirds. The river floodplains are also important breeding sites for birds such as magpie geese and are home to saltwater crocodiles.

Things to do

WALKING: Clearly marked trails leave from carparks in most popular areas. At Wangi Falls, a beautiful walk (1.6 km return, 1 hour, medium difficulty) leads around the pool via the top of the falls and includes a boardwalk with wheelchair access. At Tolmer Falls, a 20-minute walk (1.6 km return, 45 minutes, easy) leads from the carpark to an observation platform overlooking a massive rock pool with magnificent Tolmer Falls spilling into the void. Tjaynera Falls (Sandy Creek) and a delightfully cool rock pool are at the end of a rocky track (3.4 km return, 1.5 hours, medium difficulty). Leading from the carpark, the track follows the creek past ancient cycads. An easy stroll around magnetic termite mounds in the north-east of the park is enhanced by a boardwalk with information panels, while one of the best walks in Litchfield is among the sandstone pillars of the Lost City. The Tabletop Track (39 km, 3–5 days, difficult) is a circuit that links many of the park attractions and can be accessed at Florence Falls, Tjaetaba Falls (Greenant Creek), Wangi Falls and Walker Creek. Overnight campers must stay at designated campgrounds; there are three on the track.

SWIMMING: Florence and Wangi are impressive waterfalls that plunge into rock pools. They are ideal for swimming and safe from crocodiles during the Dry season. At Buley Rockhole, water cascades over rocks into a series of small plunge pools, offering visitors a range of swimming spots. Another good swimming spot, at the end of a 20-minute walk, is above Tjaetaba Falls. Surprise Creek Falls and Tjaynera Falls are delightful and rarely visited sites just off 4WD tracks. Cascade Falls is a hidden gem. Not as crowded as its famous neighbours, it is reached by an access road off Litchfield Park Rd. The 30-minute walk (medium difficulty, sturdy shoes required) follows Cascade Creek and leads to a series of pools and waterfalls. The falls are almost always closed in the Wet season as the entire track and carpark gets inundated. The Finniss and Reynolds rivers are off-limits to swimmers because they are saltwater crocodile habitats.

IMPORTANT: Visitors must observe crocodile warning signs and be croc-wise at all times.

Top: Visitors cooling off at Florence Falls, Litchfield National Park
Bottom: Katherine Gorge glows in the sunlight in Nitmiluk National Park

WHERE: 100 km south of Darwin. Drive from Darwin via the Stuart Hwy then through Batchelor. The roads to Litchfield are clearly signposted.
CAMPING AND ACCOMMODATION: Campsites are located throughout the park and generally have both 2WD and 4WD access. There is caravan access at Wangi Falls but no power. Litchfield Tourist Park is the closest commercial accommodation to the national park, with a range of options to suit various budgets. www.litchfieldtouristpark.com.au
BEST TIME TO VISIT: In the Dry season, from May to September, the weather is generally sunny and clear, and the temperature is warm but not too hot. This is the most popular time to visit Litchfield. However, do not overlook a visit in October and November. As the rains begin for the Wet season, the falls become magnificent torrents of water and the rainforests and woodlands become lush and green. Tourists are also fewer. Please take precautions in wetter weather and check the local forecasts – if the rains have been heavy, roads and many waterholes may be closed.
CONTACT: Litchfield Tourist Park: 08 8976 0070. www.nt.gov.au/leisure/parks-reserves/find-a-park-to-visit/litchfield-national-park

Nitmiluk National Park

In Nitmiluk National Park is the spectacular country of the Jawoyn people, who are made up of seventeen clans. Impressive stone country, towering escarpments with hidden caverns and caves, gushing waterfalls, broad valleys and a myriad of wildlife are an idyllic backdrop to the many Aboriginal art sites and the rich cultural heritage of the land. The powerful Katherine River, rising in Arnhem Land, has cut through the ancient sandstone to create a series of spectacular gorges.

An outstanding feature of the park is Leliyn (Edith Falls). The Edith River comes off the Nitmiluk escarpment to create the falls. Located 40 km north of Katherine, down a 20 km bitumen road from the Stuart Hwy, the falls descend into the large Leliyn plunge pool. The nearby campground has a small kiosk, a BBQ area, toilets, showers, a laundry and disabled access.

ABORIGINAL CULTURAL HERITAGE: *Nitmiluk*, pronounced 'nit-me-look', is the Jawoyn name for the Katherine Gorge. It literally means 'cicada place'. The name was given to the area by Nabilil, a dragon-like creation-time figure who heard the 'nit, nit nit' song of the cicadas as he travelled through the land. Many other places in the area were also named because of the local wildlife. Nabilil came from the west carrying water in a dilly bag and fire sticks.

Bula, the most important figure in the Jawoyn Dreaming story, created this land. He arrived from the north and his actions transformed the landscape. The area where he eventually went underground is today called 'Sickness Country'. The Jawoyn believe that if this country is disturbed fire and earthquakes will wreak havoc on the world. The Rainbow Serpent, called *Bolung* by the Jawoyn, still inhabits the second gorge, making it a sacred area and Jawoyn people are very careful not to disturb her.

In the traditions, ceremonies, relationships and stories of the Jawoyn people, the Dreaming characters play significant roles. While not all the Dreaming places are dangerous or sacred, all must be approached with care as they are all significant for the Traditional Owners.

Katherine Gorge was handed back to the Jawoyn people in 1989, and they established Nitmiluk National Park in joint management with the Parks and Wildlife Commission of the Northern Territory.

NATURAL FEATURES: The park lies at the junction of three geological formations – the Pine Creek Geosyncline and the McArthur and Daley basins. Katherine Gorge is a series of thirteen gorges that cut through an ancient sandstone plateau formed some 1400 million years ago. Monsoonal waters have eroded the sandstone over the last 20 million years, creating the massive gorge and countless ravines.

More than 450 plant species have been recorded in the area with some, such as the wattle *Acacia helicophylla*, endemic to the park. The narrow ravines shelter small pockets of monsoonal rainforest plants, while the open plains and valleys have common eucalypt species such as Darwin woollybutt, fan-leafed bloodwood, river red gum and the beautiful salmon gum. Speargrass and native sorghum are widespread and spinifex clumps grow in the high rocky terrain.

The waterways of Nitmiluk are a habitat for fish and other marine creatures, the most common being barramundi and freshwater bream. Archerfish can be spotted near the riverbanks, along with the northern snake-necked turtle. Freshwater crocodiles are common, with the occasional 'salty' finding its way into the gorge during a big Wet season. Gould's sand goanna, the frilled-neck lizard and a variety of frogs are common, while the cane toad is a relatively recent invader. Agile wallabies, antilopine wallaroos and dingoes roam the tropical woodland, while elusive rock wallabies haunt the high rocky outcrops. Most Top End bird species are here, with the rare and colourful Gouldian finch nesting in salmon gums in the Yenberrie Hills, near Leliyn.

Things to do

BUSHWALKING: There is an excellent network of walking trails in the Nitmiluk National Park. Many walks around the Nitmiluk Gorge itself start from the visitor centre and begin with a climb onto the rocky escarpment. Day walks range from 3½ hours to 9 hours and includes the Lily Ponds, Butterfly Gorge, Windolf, Baruwel and Smitt Rock walks. Longer 2–3 day hikes include the Eighth Gorge, Waleka and Jawoyn Valley walks. The Jatbula Trail (62 km, 5 days, difficult) leads from the northern side of the Katherine River to Northern Rockhole, Biddlecombe Cascades, Crystal Falls, the Amphitheatre, 17 Mile Falls and Leliyn. It is considered to be one of the best walks in northern Australia.

The Leliyn Trail (2.6 km return, 2 hours, medium difficulty) is a well-marked loop track that climbs to the top of the escarpment then down to the Edith River, via two beautiful pools. Sweetwater walk (8.6 km return) follows the Edith River to Sweetwater Pool, a good spot for camping and swimming. The track is the last section of the Jatbula Trail. Campers must check the availability of the Sweetwater campground as it is preferentially reserved for Jatbula Trail hikers.

For more information on walking see the southern walks guide: www.nt.gov.au/__data/assets/pdf_file/0013/200614/nitmiluk-national-park-southern-walks-information-sheet.pdf

CANOEING: Canoe hire (per hour or for several days) is available from Nitmiluk Tours. A scenic boat ride takes canoeists through the first gorge to the second gorge, where canoeing can commence. Canoeing through the second gorge and beyond is self-guided and canoeists must carry their own canoe between gorges. Generally, in the time permitted in a day trip, canoeists go as far as the third gorge. For trips further up the gorge, camping is recommended. Canoeists may only camp at the designated camping spots. Overnight trips to the higher gorges are a spectacular and rewarding experience away from the crowds. Late in the Dry season, the river is languid and the water level low so portage becomes strenuous. It is better to plan your trip for earlier in the season. Canoeing is banned during the Wet season. For more information see the Nitmiluk Canoe Guide: www.nt.gov.au/__data/assets/pdf_file/0007/270772/nitmiluk-national-park-canoeing-guide.pdf

SCENIC TOURING: Nitmiluk Tours run cruises up the gorge, ranging from 2-hour trips to half- and full-day safaris. In the Wet season, a jet boat travels through the rapids to the third gorge. Helicopter rides leave from a helipad within the park and provide an excellent overview of the area. Nitmiluk Tours also offer accommodation options, from camping to chalets to a luxury lodge. See: www.nitmiluktours.com.au

SWIMMING: There are delightful swimming holes at Southern Rockhole, Northern Rockhole, 17 Mile Falls, Biddlecombe Cascades and Crystal Falls. Check with the rangers before swimming in Leliyn and Katherine Gorge because saltwater crocodiles can be present after the Wet season. Always watch for closures.

WHERE: 345 km south-east of Darwin; 30 km north-east of Katherine. Drive from Darwin via Stuart Hwy to Katherine then take Gorge Rd.

CAMPING AND ACCOMMODATION: Campsites with facilities are located at Nitmiluk Centre and non-powered sites are available at Leliyn (Edith Falls). Bush campsites are located along the longer walking trails and the Katherine River. Campers must register and fees do apply – contact the visitor centre. Nitmiluk Tours also offer accommodation options, from camping to chalets to a luxury lodge. Numerous accommodation options are also available in and around Katherine.

PERMITS: Permits are required for camping, walking and boating. Contact the Nitmiluk Visitor Centre.

BEST TIME TO VISIT: In the Dry season, from May to September, when access roads and all gorges and walking tracks are open.

INTERESTING FACT: Katherine Gorge was the location for Charles Chauvel's 1950s Australian film classic *Jedda*.

CONTACT: Nitmiluk Visitor Centre: 08 8972 1253; PWCNT Nitmiluk: 08 8972 1886; PWCNT Leliyn (Edith Falls): 08 8975 4852; PWCNT Katherine: 08 8951 8250
www.nt.gov.au/leisure/parks-reserves/find-a-park-to-visit/nitmiluk-national-park

Tjoritja (Western MacDonnell Ranges)

The MacDonnell Ranges are an ancient landscape of parallel ridges sculpted by the elements over millions of years. They rise dramatically from the flat terrain of Central Australia. In one of the oldest and driest regions of the world, hidden gorges and waterholes in West MacDonnell National Park provide a refuge for plants and wildlife, while the range tops are covered in spinifex and hardy drought-tolerant shrubs.

ABORIGINAL CULTURAL HERITAGE: The Arrernte people have lived in this area for over 30 000 years and Tjoritja plays a major role in their mythology. The desert people lived well here, walking throughout the country to gather food from underground larders, picking fruit and seeds, and hunting animals and birds. Over generations they accumulated knowledge about plants and animals and where to find water. Conflict arose when Europeans arrived and vied for the best watering areas. Bloody battles ensued and during the dispossession that followed, many Aboriginal people were sheltered by missionaries and influenced by Christianity. Today, there are important Dreaming trails and sacred sites in the MacDonnell Ranges still visited for ceremonial purposes.

NATURAL FEATURES: Some 850 million years ago, Central Australia was covered by an inland sea; around 600 million years ago, severe earthquakes caused massive uplifting which formed the chain of mountains now known as the MacDonnell Ranges. Steady erosion by wind and water has carved out spectacular gorges and canyons, some of which retain pools of water throughout the year. Narrow, steep-sided chasms such as Redbank, Glen Helen, Ormiston and Serpentine gorges intersect the 'West Macs', as they are known locally. At 1380 m, Mt Sonder is a landmark of the park and the fourth highest peak in the Northern Territory. The 1531-m Mt Zeil in the extreme north-west of the park is the highest peak in the ranges.

Eucalypt and acacia trees dominate the lower terrain of the park while mallee, mulga and spinifex grasses cling to the dry rugged hills. The MacDonnell Ranges are a refuge for rare and threatened plants and up to 40 species can be traced back to times when Central Australia was wetter and covered in lush rainforest. These ancient species include the MacDonnell Ranges cycad (*Macrozamia macdonnellii*), maidenhair fern, skeleton fork fern and mountain hakea. Some common trees include the desert she-oak, river red gum, corkwood and coolibah. Here, too, is the beautiful smooth white-barked ghost gum (*Corymbia aparrerinja*), which often features in Aboriginal mythology and was made famous in the paintings of Albert Namatjira. After heavy rains the desert comes alive with wildflowers including Sturt's desert pea, the desert rose, native hops and daisies. With Europeans came a variety of feral animals, including cats, foxes, rabbits, horses, donkeys and camels, which either preyed on small mammals in Central Australia or severely degraded their habitats. Twelve mammal species have disappeared from the region since European contact and others, such as the bilby, rufous hare wallaby, mulgara and black-footed rock wallaby are endangered. The latter has dramatically declined since the 1930s, and has vanished completely from Uluṟu–Kata Tjuṯa National Park. Red kangaroos, other rock wallaby species, goannas and a variety of other reptiles are still common in the West MacDonnells.

The park has more than 160 bird species. Emus, spinifex pigeons, painted finches, western bowerbirds and dusky grasswrens are common, while at places such as Ellery Creek Big Hole, river red gums are

Top: Glen Helen Gorge juts sharply out of the water, Tjoritja (Western MacDonnell Ranges)

Bottom: Hiking through Ormiston Gorge, Tjoritja

home to western ringnecks and pied butcherbirds. Zebra finches, honeyeaters and pigeons drink from the rock pools alongside water birds such as grebes, darters and white-faced herons.

CAMPING AND ACCOMMODATION: Campsites with full facilities, 4WD-only sites and basic walk-in sites are scattered throughout the park. Glen Helen Resort, 08 8956 7489, is the commercial operation closest to the park and offers caravan and motel accommodation. There is a wide range of accommodation available in Alice Springs.

Things to do

WALKING, CYCLING AND 2WD TOURING: These are all good ways to become acquainted with the park. Also, an aerial view from a fixed-wing aircraft or helicopter is stunning.

SWIMMING: It is possible to swim at many of the waterholes but the water can be extremely cold.

BUSHWALKING: Walks are numerous and the descriptions given in 'Places to visit' are a brief guide only to what is available in various sections of the park.

CYCLING: A sealed bicycle path leads off Larapinta Dr, opposite John Flynn's grave, 7 km from Alice Springs. The path, stretching some 17 km to Simpsons Gap, is even and well-formed, suitable for the whole family. It winds through desert habitats that contain river red gums, witchetty bush and mulga.

SCENIC TOURING: Drive west from Alice Springs along Larapinta Dr, past Simpsons Gap and Standley Chasm, and turn right onto Namatjira Dr. Named after the renowned Aboriginal artist, Albert Namatjira, the road winds through spectacular scenery with rolling escarpments and layered sandstone walls, reminiscent of many of the painter's works.

Places to visit

SIMPSONS GAP: Sacred to the Central Arrernte Aboriginal people, the Gap is known as *Rrengetyirpe*. The Dreaming stories of the area involve the goanna, eagle and rock wallaby. The Gap, located 18 km from Alice Springs, is open daily, 5 am–8 pm. There are several well-marked trails including Ghost Gum walk (15 minutes return, easy), a short trail that starts at the visitor centre and takes in the vegetation of the area. Cassia Hill walk (1.5 km, 1 hour return, easy) leads through clumps of witchetty bush and mulga, and rewards visitors with views over Simpsons Gap and the surrounding country. Woodland Trail (17 km return) passes through mulga woodlands and leads to Bond Gap, a narrow chasm with an ice-cold pool. This part of the national park can be busy during the peak season, but the gap has a permanent waterhole and there is the opportunity to see the black-footed rock wallabies that live in the boulder-strewn gorge. There is a small campsite but it is only for use by those walking the Larapinta Trail.

ELLERY CREEK BIG HOLE: Called *Udepata* in Arrernte, this area is sacred to the Western and Eastern Arrernte people. The Honey Ant Dreaming is the main Dreaming story of the waterhole, although there is also a Fish Dreaming. There are easy walks around this large waterhole, which is located 92 km from Alice Springs. It is a beautiful place to swim, picnic and to view the birdlife. If you want to swim across to the small sandy 'beach', take an inflatable li-lo for safety, and so that you can float back on the still, deep water, marvelling at the blueness of the sky. The permanent water here made it an important meeting place for the Arrernte people.

SERPENTINE GORGE: Called *Ulpma* by the Western Arrernte people, Serpentine Gorge is considered a sacred site. The Dreaming story of the gorge is associated with the Eaglehawk ancestor, but the full story can only be told be traditionally initiated Aboriginal men. There are special Arrernte ceremonial places on the western cliffs and in the gorge itself. A short, easy walking track from the carpark takes about 25 minutes to reach this sheltered oasis. The narrow gorge extends for about another 2 km and there is an easy, well-marked trail that leads to a lookout. The water attracts birdlife, including tiny fairy martins, and insects such as dragonflies skim across its surface. The Centralian flannel flower and the MacDonnell Ranges cycad are rare and endemic, and both grow in the gorge.

OCHRE PITS: For thousands of years Aboriginal people gathered red and white ochre from the banks of a sandy creek at this site, 110 km west of Alice Springs. The ochre was used for medicinal and cultural purposes and for trading with other clans. Red ochre mixed with grease can be applied as an ointment and can relieve congestion when mixed with eucalyptus leaves. White ochre can be mixed with water and blown from the mouth to abate the heat of the sun and it was also used as a charm. Ochre can also be used on wooden weapons to increase the success of hunting and to protect them from termites.

ORMINSTON GORGE AND POUND: This gorge is located 135 km west of Alice Springs and has a near-permanent 15 m-deep waterhole framed by sheer 300 m-high cliffs. To the Western Arrernte people it is a sacred site known as *Kwartatuma*. The Dreaming story of the area involves the hunting of a group of emus that journeyed to the waterhole from the east. The Pound is a huge rock-walled amphitheatre almost 10 km across. There are a number of walks including Waterhole walk (500 m, 10 minutes one way), a short stroll from the carpark around the waterhole; Ghost Gum Lookout walk (20 minutes one way); and Ormiston Pound walk (7 km circuit, 3–4 hours), which winds around the slopes of the gorge, descending to the floor of the Pound and returning along the gorge past the waterhole. The long-tailed dunnart and central rock-rat were rediscovered here in 1996.
REDBANK GORGE: Located 165 km west of Alice Springs, Redbank Gorge is also a sacred site for the Western Arrernte people. Known as *Yarretyeke* in Arrernte, the Dreaming story of the area is connected to the euro, a small kangaroo species. However, the full story is restricted to traditionally initiated Aboriginal men only. The Gorge walk (2 km, 1.5 hours return) is a short hike up a stony creek bed from the carpark to the gorge, which is little more than a small slit between two towering quartzite walls. During dry periods, a path of fine sand marks the bottom of the gorge and it is easy to walk through, but at other times a deep pool of icy water greets visitors. It is advisable to swim in wet suits or to take an air mattress to navigate the waters. Redbank Gorge marks the beginning of a marked trail to Mt Sonder (16 km return, 6–7 hours), which lies to the east.
LARAPINTA TRAIL: This is an award-winning walking trail (223 km, several weeks) considered one of the best walking tracks in the world. It runs along the backbone of the West MacDonnells, from the old telegraph station just north of Alice Springs to Mt Sonder in the north-west of the park, and is divided into 12 sections. People with basic bushwalking experience can easily traverse section one from Alice Springs to Simpsons Gap, but some other sections are more difficult. For further details contact PWCNT: 08 8951 8250, or visit: www.larapintatrail.com.au

WHERE: The MacDonnells stretch 170 km west from Alice Springs. Drive from Alice Springs via Larapinta and Namatjira drives; from Kings Canyon and Yulara via Mereenie Loop Rd.
PERMITS: A permit is required for Mereenie Loop Rd, which passes through Aboriginal land. It is available from Alice Springs Visitor Centre: 08 8952 5800 or Kings Canyon Resort: 08 8956 7442. Permits are required at some campsites.
BEST TIME TO VISIT: May to September.
CONTACT: Simpsons Gap ranger station: 08 8955 0310; Ormiston Gorge ranger station: 08 8956 7799; PWCNT Alice Springs: 08 8951 8250: Glen Helen Resort: 08 8956 7489. www.nt.gov.au/leisure/parks-reserves/find-a-park-to-visit/tjoritja-west-macdonnell-national-park

Uluṟu–Kata Tjuṯa National Park

Located in the red heart of the Central Desert, the ancient forms of Uluṟu and Kata Tjuṯa lie geographically, spiritually and symbolically at the centre of the Australian continent. Rising majestically above the red-sand plains, they dominate the landscape and are shrouded in myth and mystery. Their colours and moods are ever-changing with the interplay of light from the sun, cloud and rain.

Protected within Uluṟu–Kata Tjuṯa National Park, Uluṟu (Ayers Rock) and Kata Tjuṯa (The Olgas) rise like giant red icebergs from the flat 'sea' of the surrounding desert. At around 350 m high, Uluṟu is the world's largest monolith, higher than the Eiffel Tower, with a circumference measuring 9.4 km and an estimated depth of 6 km below the Earth's surface.

For the local people Uluṟu and Kata Tjuṯa are far more than just rock formations. They make up a living cultural landscape that is sacred to the Yankunytjatjara and Pitjantjatjara Aṉangu people.

On 26 October 1985, Uluṟu and Kata Tjuṯa were handed back to the Aṉangu people, the Traditional Owners of the land, in what

Top: The familiar sight of Uluṟu changes close up

Bottom: The ancient forms of Kata Tjuṯa (The Olgas)

remains one of the most significant moments in Australia's Aboriginal land rights movement. It had taken over 35 years of campaigning for the A<u>n</u>angu to be recognised as the park's Traditional Owners and given the deeds to their land. From that day, the A<u>n</u>angu agreed to lease the park to the federal government for 99 years. This allows public access and also provides funds for the local community. The national park is jointly managed by the A<u>n</u>angu people and Parks Australia.

In 1987, the area won World Heritage listing for its natural wonders. In 1993 Ulu<u>r</u>u–Kata Tju<u>t</u>a National Park became the official park name and the next year it won another World Heritage listing for its cultural value. The park is ranked as one of the most significant arid-land ecosystems and is classified by UNESCO as a Biosphere Reserve.

ABORIGINAL CULTURAL HERITAGE: Ulu<u>r</u>u is a site of ceremonial significance for many Aboriginal groups of Central Australia, including the Pitjantjatjara and Yankuntjatjara A<u>n</u>angu people, who have lived in the region for at least 10 000 years. There are more than 40 sacred Aboriginal sites in the area where ancestral spirits still reside, making the land deeply important to the cultural identity of the A<u>n</u>angu. The Pitjantjatjara and Yankuntjatjara people still abide by ancient laws and traditions, referred to as *Tjukurpa*, which provide the foundation to their unique culture.

Before the arrival of Europeans, the Indigenous people moved around this land, which varied from mulga flats and sand dunes to rocky hills and pockets of vegetation around the base of rocks such as Ulu<u>r</u>u. Each of these environments was used at different times of the year, depending on the food and water available. Water was present in claypans, rock holes, soaks and springs. Around the base of Ulu<u>r</u>u are rock shelters and caves, decorated with hundreds of rock paintings – some executed as late as the 1940s – but the ravages of weather and over-visitation by tourists in the past have resulted in severe deterioration. The art sites at Kata Tju<u>t</u>a, where there are more engravings than paintings, are better preserved. Today, Aboriginal people of Central Australia call themselves A<u>n</u>angu, and some of the most important cultural areas in the park are out of bounds to non-Indigenous people.

NATURAL FEATURES: Ulu<u>r</u>u and Kata Tju<u>t</u>a are remnants of a huge bed of sedimentary rock, worn down by nature over some 40 million years after an inland sea retreated. It is believed Kata Tju<u>t</u>a may have been a single rock bigger than Ulu<u>r</u>u before it was weathered back to 36 separate but dramatic rock domes, one of which is almost 200 m higher than Ulu<u>r</u>u.

Between Ulu<u>r</u>u and Kata Tju<u>t</u>a lies an ancient valley comprising sand layers that hold water, much of which seeps out into Lake Amadeus, about 40 km north of the national park. Some of this water is estimated to be 7000 years old. The surrounding dune country is even older, with dunes unchanged for 30,000 years, apart from the loose sand on the dune crests.

Ulu<u>r</u>u and Kata Tju<u>t</u>a are among the most photographed and filmed destinations on Earth; the red rock changes colour quickly during the day, and particularly around sunset. Both areas are spectacular during storms and after heavy rain.

The arid landscape around the park comes alive after soaking rains, and vivid wildflowers of white, pink, yellow and blue contrast against the red earth and azure sky. Daisies, desert fringe-myrtle, emu bush and parrot peas are common. Spinifex and other grasses form a thick layer on the desert floor, while mulga is the dominant tree species, tangled and black during dry times, lush and green after a flood. After rains, the green-grey bush tomato flowers and produces small purplish fruit highly prized by the Aboriginal people. The seeds of desert oak, umbrella bush and bloodwood provide food for desert animals, while honey grevillea flowers provide sweetness and energy for a range of birds and insects.

Once 46 species of mammals were found in the park, but today this number has been reduced by more than half. Recently, the mala was reintroduced and moves are being made to reintroduce other locally extinct animals. The insect-eating mulgara, which lives in burrows on the dry sand plain area of the park, is the only mammal currently listed as vulnerable. It shares its habitat with numerous dunnart species and the unadorned desert-skink; watch for this reptile around clumps of spinifex, where it likes to forage. Here, too, is the spinifex hopping mouse, although it prefers to shelter in its burrow during the day, emerging at dusk to zigzag between grassy clumps on the desert floor. Seven species of bat live in the caves and rock crevices of the park. More visible mammals are common wallaroos (euros), red kangaroos, and herds of feral camels, all seen grazing on the plains. Around the rocks you might glimpse dingoes and emus, while rock wallabies hop around the escarpments.

Reptiles are abundant, with some 73 species recorded. Along with numerous skinks, there are sand monitors, the awesome 2 m-long perentie, geckos, and a range of snake species, such as the venomous king brown and the desert death adder. In the shrublands and grassy tussocks watch out for the fierce-looking, but harmless and somewhat delicate, thorny devil.

There are 178 bird species recorded in the park, including some species that are rare in the area such as the elusive striated grasswren, a spinifex dweller. Some of the special birds to be seen at Uluṟu include the oriental plover, princess parrot, grey honeyeater and western bowerbird, while the chiming wedgebill and grey falcon may be seen at Kata Tjuṯa. Other desert birds, such as cockatiels, budgerigars, little button-quails, zebra finches, crows and honeyeaters, are also common. Wedge-tailed eagles and other raptors including black-shouldered kites glide effortlessly on the thermals looking for prey.

Things to do

THE CULTURAL CENTRE: Visit the centre to learn about Aṉangu history and culture, and the arid-zone landscape. This will give you a better appreciation of the park. Also you can visit the Walkatjara Art Centre, which is owned and directed by the Aṉangu people from the Mutitjulu community. It showcases their vibrant paintings, which depict traditional stories from the area.

SCENIC VIEWS: There are parking areas at Uluṟu and Kata Tjuṯa where visitors will have good views of the landscape at sunrise and sunset. Arrive early, especially to watch and photograph the changing colours of Uluṟu, as crowds can be heavy during the peak tourist season. Off the Kata Tjuṯa Road there is a 30-minute return walk to the dune viewing area, which provides seating, shade and panoramic views of Kata Tjuṯa and the sand dunes (tour groups only after 4 pm).

WALKING: There are a number of walks that lead to areas around the base of Uluṟu. Kuniya walk (1 km, 45 minutes return, easy), on the southern side of the rock, is a short stroll that leads past rock-art sites to a picturesque waterhole, home of Wanampi, an ancestral water snake, and for centuries an important camping place for Aboriginal people. Before taking the walk, pick up a self-guiding brochure at the Cultural Centre, which explains the Aboriginal mythology of the area. Mala walk (2 km, 1.5 hours return), on the north-western side of the rock, is an easy trail that passes several caves used by the Aṉangu until recently, then ends at Kantju Gorge. Signs along this walk give explanations of Aboriginal creation times. A free ranger-guided tour of Mala walk is conducted daily from the base of Uluṟu during the Dry season – departure times vary depending on the seasons. A self-guiding brochure is also available for this walk at the culture centre. Both of these walks are wheelchair accessible.

Two longer walks allow visitors to appreciate the immensity of Uluṟu and Kata Tjuṯa. The Base of Uluṟu walk (10.6 km circuit, 3–4 hours) leads around the base of the rock. The walk takes in the Mala and Kuniya trails and you are asked to walk in a clockwise direction. Valley of the Winds walk (7.4 km circuit, 3 hours, medium difficulty) in Kata Tjuṯa is spectacular. The track is steep and rocky in places as it leads through deep canyons and broad valleys, and there are two lookouts along the way.

Several shorter walks include Walpa Gorge walk (2.6 km, 1 hour return), a gentle, rising track in Kata Tjuṯa that leads to the end of a gorge where vine-like spearwood (*Pandorea pandorana*) flourishes amid the rocks. When in flower, this shrub is covered in large, creamy white bells. The long stems, tough and flexible, were used by Indigenous people to make spears.

SACRED SITES: Maps provided by the Cultural Centre clearly mark the sacred sites of the park. Out of respect to the Aṉangu people and their culture, some sites may not be visited, filmed or photographed.

Please respect the wishes of the Traditional Owners. **Uluṟu itself is a scared site. The Aṉangu people ask all visitors to respect their cultural and spiritual beliefs and refrain from climbing the rock.** From 26 October 2019, coinciding with the 34th year of the return of Uluṟu to its Traditional Owners, climbing the rock will be banned.

WARNING: High temperatures at Uluṟu can cause heat stroke and exhaustion. Walkers are advised to wear a hat, strong shoes, use sunscreen and drink plenty of water. Avoid wearing lycra and other fabrics that do not breathe because the red rocks create more heat in already high temperatures and wearing clothes made of these materials can lead to heat stroke.

Stay on marked trails and walk in the cooler hours of the day – preferably early morning.

WHERE: The park is 440 km south-west of Alice Springs. The 450 km drive to Uluṟu–Kata Tjuṯa from Alice Springs takes roughly 5 hours via the Stuart and Lasseter hwys. The highways are sealed roads, so a 4WD is not required. Jetstar, Virgin Airlines and Qantas fly to Uluṟu.

CAMPING AND ACCOMMODATION: There are no camping or other accommodation options within the national park itself. Yulara, 20 km from Uluṟu, is the closest base to explore the park. There are hotels to suit all budgets, as well as camping and caravan facilities.

PERMITS: A park-use fee is charged per person. This is valid for three days; annual tickets are also available. All tickets are payable at the park entry station.

BEST TIME TO VISIT: May to October, when the average daytime temperatures range from 23–31°C, and night temperatures range from 7–13°C.

DO NOT MISS: The play of light on Uluṟu at dawn or dusk. It is spectacular.

CONTACT: Culture Centre: 08 8956 1128; Ayers Rock campground: 08 8957 7001: Ayers Rock Resort: 1300 134 044

www.travelnt.com; www.environment.gov.au/parks/uluru

TOURS AND STAYS

Ayal Aboriginal Tours Kakadu

Local Aboriginal guide, Victor Cooper, is a Traditional Owner and former park ranger who knows the area well and enjoys sharing his knowledge and stories with visitors during his small-group tours. They include the Kakadu Aboriginal Rock Art Tour, which visits Ubirr, one of Kakadu's major rock-art sites; and Buffalo Camp History and Wildlife Tour, in which visitors travel in an air-conditioned 4WD along the Arnhem Hwy towards the Alligator River floodplains. Ayal Aboriginal Tours also offer private tours that provide an exclusive Kakadu National Park experience for up to 4 people in a 4WD vehicle or up to 12 in a bus.

CONTACT: 08 8979 0483; 0429 470 384

www.ayalkakadu.com.au

Bremer Island Banubanu Beach Retreat

Banubanu Beach Retreat is an eco-resort in East Arnhem Land, built in partnership with the Yolŋu people on whose land the retreat is located. The resort offers a peaceful island getaway as it allows a maximum of only 20 guests at any one time. There are 3 accommodation options to suit all tastes: the Deluxe Beachfront eco tents, the eco-friendly Beach House cabin, and the Hideaway cabin with all the comforts of home. Day visits to the retreat are also available, where guests will receive a welcome drink, use of the facilities and a 2-course lunch. Banubanu Beach Retreat offers a range of tours and experiences, such as fishing charters, guided mud-crabbing tours, bird watching, bushwalks and swimming.

WHERE: Bremer Island is located just off the coast of Nhulunbuy in East Arnhem Land, and is accessible by light aircraft or boat from Nhulunbuy.

COST: Day visits cost $74 per person when transport to Bremer Island is arranged separately; $230 per person including boat transfers to Bremer Island;

Top: Enjoy crystal clear waters at Bremer Island Banubanu Beach Retreat

Bottom: Davidson's Arnhem Land Safaris gives exclusive access to the registered Aboriginal Sacred Site of Mt Borradaile

Top left: Cruising along Yellow Water Billabong in Kakadu National Park

Top right: Enjoy the view at Nadab Lookout, Ubirr Rock, with Kakadu Cultural Tours

Bottom: Didgeridoo workshop at the Kakadu Culture Camp

$375 per person including light aircraft transfers to Bremer Island. For cost of accommodation at the retreat and packages see the website.
CONTACT: 08 8987 8085
www.banubanu.com

Davidson's Arnhem Land Safaris

Set at Mt Borradaile, the idyllic 700 sq km area that is home to Davidson's Arnhem Land Safaris is a registered Aboriginal sacred site, with caves that have seen 50 000 years of Indigenous occupation. While the area is managed by the Traditional Owners, the Amurdak people, Davidson's was given the great privilege of an honorary custodian status when, in 1986, the Traditional Owners asked Max Davidson if he would start a tourism venture at Mt Borradaile. Davidson's Safaris now provides the Amurdak people with a valuable source of income, and their style of eco tourism is helping to preserve the many significant and sacred sights in the area.

Davidson's Safaris offer something for every taste, such as a billabong cruise, visiting ancient rock art and catacombs, fishing, or exploring for rare species of animals. There is a modern eco lodge on site, with a range of cabin facilities and a first-class dining experience. Guests often take a few of the tours on offer and really explore this restricted area of Arnhem Land.

TIPS FOR VISITORS: Alcohol must not to be brought into Arnhem Land and strict penalties apply to those who do bring it in. There is a fully licensed bar at Davidson's Eco Lodge.
WHERE: Mt Borradaile, Arnhem Land
PERMITS: Access to Mt Borradaile is restricted and permits are required to enter the lands. When you book with Davidson's, permits will be organised for you and the price included in your accommodation fees.
CONTACT: 08 8979 0413
www.arnhemland-safaris.com

Djabulukgu Association cultural 4WD and boat tours

Visitors experience Indigenous culture and see the stunning scenery of Northern Kakadu during the Arnhemlander 4WD Tour and the Magela Cultural and Heritage Tour. They can also cruise the East Alligator River in the Guluyambi Boat Tour for breathtaking views of the surrounding area.

CONTACT: 1800 525 238
www.djabulukgu.com.au/index.php/enterprise/kakadu-cultural-tours

Kakadu Animal Tracks Safari

This award-winning, 1-day tour offers insights into Aboriginal culture and bush-food gathering and cooking. In the daylight hours, visitors will see stunning wildlife from the Kakadu area and in the evening enjoy a bush-food campfire cook up.

CONTACT: 0409 350 842
www.kakadutoursandtravel.com.au

Kakadu Cultural Tours

Kakadu Cultural Tours are fully owned and operated by the Djabulukgu Association, which represents the Traditional Owners of Northern Kakadu and parts of Western Arnhem Land. This enables their tour groups to have access to exclusive country and sites. Kakadu Cultural Tours specialises in Aboriginal cultural and nature-based cruises, tours and wilderness lodge accommodation. Small tour groups are escorted by predominantly Aboriginal guides and this ensures a unique cultural experience. Kakadu Cultural Tours offer these packages:

GULUYAMBI CULTURAL CRUISE: Enjoy a boat tour along the East Alligator River. Scenically spectacular, this river is a fine example of Kakadu's pristine wilderness.

A local Aboriginal guide provides guests with an insight into the river system and its abundant food chain, as well as their own culture and ancestral history, traditional uses for plants and animals and bush survival skills. The tour includes a display of traditional hunting and gathering implements. With a limit of only 25 guests, the cruise is an intimate and personalised cultural experience.

WHERE: The tour departs from the upstream boat ramp on the East Alligator River. Follow the Arnhem Hwy 5 km west of Jabiru and turn north onto the Oenpelli Rd. After approximately 36 km, turn right and follow the signs for Guluyambi Cultural Cruise and Upstream Boat Ramp (East Alligator River). The road is sealed all the way. Allow 45 minutes to drive from Jabiru. Allow 4 hours to drive from Darwin.

WHEN: Tour departs 9 am, 11 am, 1 pm and 3 pm daily, May to November. Duration: 1 hour and 45 minutes.

COST: Adult: $79; child 4–14 years: $52

ARNHEMLANDER CULTURAL AND HERITAGE TOUR: This 4WD day tour of Arnhem Land and Northern Kakadu is an outstanding way to experience the world-famous landscapes of sandstone outcrops, rock-art sites, forests, floodplains and billabongs. The tour crosses the East Alligator into Arnhem Land and takes guests to the Injalak Arts and Crafts Centre in Oenpelli, where you can see traditional painting and pandanus basket-weaving techniques, as well as the Mikkinj Valley, with its stunning scenery of billabongs, wildlife and towering escarpment.

WHEN: Tour departs 7.45 am daily, May to November. Duration: 8 hours.

WHERE: The tour departs from Jabiru, with pickups from all accommodation in Jabiru.

COST: Adult: $273; child 4–14 yrs: $218. Cost includes Arnhem Land permits, refreshments and lunch.

HAWK DREAMING WILDERNESS LODGE: Experience a beautiful and remote area of Kakadu that is restricted to guests and local Indigenous residents only. The lodge is located at Cannon Hill, a very special and well-renowned part of Kakadu. The whole area is a registered sacred site and is important to the local Aboriginal people, many of whom live near the lodge. Sandstone outliers surrounding Cannon Hill are sites of significant rock art, which date back thousands of years. As well as the cultural significance, Cannon Hill is an area where you can see a wide diversity of vegetation in Kakadu, with abundant wildlife and untouched bushland making it a breathtaking place to visit.

Guests stay in comfortable tented cabins, with ensuite facilities and decks. These are spread out nicely through the shady grounds. Knowledgeable and experienced camp hosts and guides take guests on evening tours to explore rock-art sites and to watch the sunset from the escarpment. The cost includes breakfasts and three-course home-style dinners. There are 2- and 3-day tour options available, which include the Guluyambi Cultural Cruise and the Arnhemlander Cultural and Heritage Tour. See the Kakadu Cultural Tours website for more details.

WHEN: Between 15 May and 30 September annually.

COST: Twin share adult: $294 per per night; child: $234 per night; solo traveller: $420 per night. The cost includes meals, accommodation and a rock-art sunset tour. Accommodation and tour packages include transport to and from the Border Store.

CONTACT: 1800 525 238
www.kakaduculturaltours.com.au

Kakadu Tourism Adventure Tours

Visitors are taken in 4WD vehicles to the less accessible parts of Kakadu, going off-road to visit waterfalls, swimming holes and escarpments. The Adventure Tours offer 4WD all-day tours that operate throughout the Dry and shoulder periods. Itineraries change according to access and time of the year. The tour has a fleet of 4WDs; meals and refreshments are provided throughout the day.

CONTACT: 08 8979 1500
www.kakadutourism.com/tours-activities/spirit-of-kakadu-adventure-tours

Karrke Aboriginal Cultural Experiences

Owned and operated by Christine Breaden and Peter Abbott, Karrke Tours was established to preserve the cultural knowledge, language and heritage of the Luritja and Pertame Southern Arrernte people. *Karrke* is the name of the western bowerbird in Arrernte. The walking tour runs for one hour and gives an insight into numerous cultural practices of the local people from the community of Wanmarra. The tour includes education about bush medicine, bush tucker, important flora and fauna, language, and traditional painting. It is an ideal tour to do after exploring the nearby Kings Canyon.

WHERE: Karrke is located next to Kings Creek Station on the Luritja Hwy; turn-off on a dirt road, then drive 2 km to the Wanmarra Community.
WHEN: 9 am, 10.30 am, 2 pm and 4 pm Wednesday to Sunday.
COST: Adult: $60; child 6–11 years: $10; young adult 12 years and over: $40. Cash only.
CONTACT: 08 8956 7620
www.karrke.com.au

Lirrwi Tourism

Share the unique culture of the Yolŋu people of North-East Arnhem Land with Lirrwi Tourism's homeland experiences. Homelands are the ancestral lands and seas of various Yolŋu clans. They are built around a family group and are sacred places, rich in culture, and restricted, remote and incredibly beautiful. A visit to these homelands is a unique experience. Family lives are not regimented as they often are in the western world. Each day is in sync with the environment, wildlife and climate. Expect the unexpected every day, and immerse yourself in Yolŋu culture.

Day tours

BAWAKA HOMELAND HIGHLIGHTS: Visitors go to a small family community to become involved in their daily activities. The day trip of approximately 8 hours includes a welcome to country or smoking ceremony on arrival and the opportunity to learn about traditional lore, language and the unique kinship system of the Yolŋu people. Guests will also participate in a range of activities, which may include traditional pandanus weaving or spearfishing, collecting bush foods and medicines, cooking or dance. Each day is different.
COST: $440 per person, subject to a minimum of 8 participants. Includes pick up and drop off at your accommodation, lunch, cultural experiences and a Yolŋu driver and guide.
GULULU DAY TOUR: A Yolŋu-guided tour of approximately 8 hours of some of the culturally significant and spectacular coastal locations of North-East Arnhem Land.

Visiting the Bawaka Homeland in Arnhem Land with Lirrwi Tourism

PERMITS: Each person must purchase a Dhimurru visitor permit.
COST: $330 per person, including lunch and all transport; subject to a minimum of 8 participants.
MULTI-DAY TOURS: A multi-day tour ensures a thorough immersion in Yolŋu life. There is a range of options available. Multi-day trips include the 4-night, 5-day homeland adventure, educational tours for school groups, and women's tours. Specialty tours can also be organised on request to suit your interests and timeframe, including art tours and *yidaki* master classes. Contact Lirrwi Tourism for more details.
CONTACT: 08 8987 2828
www.lirrwitourism.com.au

Lord's Kakadu and Arnhem Land Safaris

Lord's Safaris is a family-owned company with more than 25 years of experience in the tourism industry. Located in Kakadu, Lord's exclusively offers tailor-made private tours for small groups of up to 7 guests. Tours are run throughout the Northern Territory, with the option of visiting some of the Territory's most impressive sites, such as Kakadu, Arnhem Land, Koolpin Gorge and Bamurru Plains. Lord's also have their own campground in Kakadu, offering permanent tents with floors, beds, doors and solar-powered lights and fans, for up to 12 guests. Whatever you decide to see, Lord's Safaris offers personal, customisable tours, coupled with a lifetime of knowledge of the culture, nature and landscapes you will visit, to create a truly memorable and unique experience.

TIPS FOR VISITORS: All tours are custom-made, but the website offers sample tours that can be used as examples if you need ideas when planning your own adventure with Lord's Safaris.
WHERE: Kakadu
CONTACT: 0438 808 548
www.lords-safaris.com

Pudakul Aboriginal Cultural Tours

The Limilngan-Wuna people are the Traditional Owners of the land at the forefront to Kakadu National Park. Pudakul Tours operate on the area of the Adelaide River Floodplains and the Mary River, and give visitors an opportunity to learn about the cultural practices and spiritual beliefs of these Aboriginal people. *Pudakul* is the name of the macaranga tree, or freshwater hibiscus. Traditionally, the Limilngan-Wuna people use the plant to make spears.

LIMILNGAN-WUNA CULTURAL TOUR: This tour offers an educational experience set around the Adelaide River floodplains. It provides a connection to culture, with the opportunity to learn the techniques used in basket weaving and dilly-bag making. Visitors can have a go at spear throwing, play a didgeridoo and clap sticks, or go on a bush-tucker walk and learn about local bush medicine. The 2-hour tour is an enjoyable introduction to the area, and ideal to do on the way to Kakadu or Litchfield national parks.
WHERE: 45-minute drive from Darwin along the Arnhem Hwy. Transfers can be arranged from Darwin at additional cost; minimum numbers apply.
WHEN: 10.30 am–12.30 pm daily, 1 May to 30 November.
COST: Adult: $99; child 16 years and under: $55; family (2 adults/2 children): $250. Price includes a damper and billy-tea morning tea.
WETLAND DISCOVERY TOUR: Learn about the magnificent and unique wetland region through the cultural lens of the Limilngan-Wuna people. The guided tour begins with a scenic boat cruise along the picturesque Corroborree Billabong. The billabong is part of the Mary River Wetlands and is home to a spectacular range of bird life, crocodiles and other wildlife. The tour then travels 30 minutes to the Pudakul Aboriginal Cultural Tours centre for a 90-minute experience learning about the local history and culture.
COST: Adult: $165; child: $145. The Wetland Tour includes a Darwin CBD, and local surroundings including Palmerston, pick-up at approximately 6.30 am. Guests will then be returned to their accommodation at approximately 2 pm.
CONTACT: 08 8984 9282
www.pudakul.com.au

Top left: Learning about bush medicine on Pudakul Aboriginal Cultural Tours' Bush Tucker walk

Top right: Enjoy stunning sunset views when cruising the wetlands with Lord's Kakadu and Arnhem Land Safaris

Bottom left: Guests on Nitmiluk Tours can sample Indigenous-inspired canapes

Rainbow Valley Cultural Tours

In Southern Arrernte language, Rainbow Valley Reserve is referred to as *Wurre.* This tour, run by Traditional Owner Ricky Orr and his family, is an introduction to the culture and bold country of the Pertame and Luritja people. Ricky's tours allow visitors to access places in the Rainbow Valley Reserve that are not open to the public, including an ancient rock-art site and other archaeological sites. The tours also inform visitors about the cultural significance of the Rainbow Valley landscape, including information on Dreamtime stories and bush foods and medicines. The tours end with a viewing of spectacular sunsets over the sandstone ridges and bluffs – a perfect opportunity to take photographs.

WHERE: Rainbow Valley is located 97 km south of Alice Springs. The turn-off to the reserve is 75 km south of Alice Springs along the Stuart Hwy. From here, it is a 22 km-stretch east along an unsealed road that has some sandy patches. Access is recommended for 4WD only.
WHEN: Starts 2 pm Monday, Wednesday and Fridays. The tour finishes after sunset.
COST: Adult: $100; child: $60.
CONTACT: 08 8956 0661 or 0427 075 963 www.rainbowvalleyculturaltours.com

RT Tours Australia

Bob Taylor, owner and operator of RT Tours, hosts visitors in his traditional Arrernte lands and shares with them his passion for his ancient culture, the untouched country and good food. His small group tours are personal and fun, and give visitors an insight into the adaptation of Aboriginal Australia in the modern world. A variety of tours are available including half-day or evening tours, fantastic art tours, or overnight stays so you can tour at your own pace. The longer stays are tailored to include both hotel accommodation and camping, as well as restaurant meals and open-fire cooking. Bob is a chef by trade so visitors can expect some delicious fare. His tours are the perfect way to learn about and experience Australia's desert. There are various tours that visit Mbantua (Alice Springs), the East and West MacDonnell Ranges, Uluṟu; Kata Tjuṯa or Watarrka (Kings Canyon).

Top: RT Tours runs small-group tours with a personal touch

Bottom: Rainbow Valley Tours' owner–operator Ricky Orr teaches visitors about his traditional lands of the Rainbow Valley Reserve

COST: Bush lunch tour: $150 per person; campfire dinner tour: $160 per person. The cost of longer and more personalised tours depend on tour length and itinerary. Contact Bob for more information.
CONTACT: 08 8952 0327; 0438 532 118
www.rttoursaustralia.com.au

SEIT Outback Australia

SEIT Outback Australia takes its name from an acronym of some key words that describe the kinds of experiences they offer: Spiritual, Emotional, Intellectual and Task-oriented (hands-on). SEIT promises to engage guests in these 4 ways through their large range of tours showcasing the Uluṟu–Kata Tjuṯa region. Experience Australia's most famous landmark, Uluṟu, in the way of your choosing: a 2-hour sunset tour; 6-hour guided trek around its base, exploring waterholes and Aboriginal rock-art sites as you go; or a Fork and View or Billy Tea experience, during which you will be served quality meals on board a converted double-decker touring bus while enjoying views of Uluṟu.

SEIT also offers the option of private touring for those who would like to customise their experience. These tours can include airport transfers and visits to the West MacDonnell Ranges, Rainbow Valley, Alice Springs, Kings Canyon and the Uluṟu Fork and View experience.

TIPS FOR VISITORS: SEIT tours are run in English, but they offer free iPods featuring audio guides in French, Italian, Spanish, German, Mandarin, Portuguese and Russian. The audio guides will be provided at the beginning of the tour.
WHERE: Yulara
CONTACT: 08 8956 3156
www.seitoutbackaustralia.com.au

SEIT Outback Australia tour guide with a litle thorny devil lizard

Venture North Safaris

Family-owned Venture North Safaris is a multi-award winning tour company that specialises in small-group tours exploring the rich cultures and environments of the Northern Territory. Venture North offers a range of multi-day, 4WD tours around remotes areas of Arnhem Land, Kakadu, Garig Gunak Barlu, Litchfield and Nitmiluk national parks and the Kimberley. For those who love fishing, there are also multi-day fly in/fly out fishing charters available, where guests are flown from Darwin to the Cobourg coastal camp (flights take 1 hour), and provided with an exclusive fishing experience, all equipment, meals and accommodation and shown the best places to fish in one of Australia's true wilderness areas by experienced guides.

TIPS FOR VISITORS: Venture North offers the chance to create completely customised private charters as

Top: Expansive views on the Corroboree Billabong Cruise with Venture North Safaris

Bottom: Venture North Safaris' Rock Art Tour in Gunbalanya, Arnhem Land

well. All details and booking forms can be found on the website.

WHERE: Venture North tours operate out of Darwin.
CONTACT: 08 8927 5500
www.venturenorth.com.au

Voyages Indigenous Tourism Australia – Ayers Rock Resort

Ayers Rock Resort is an oasis of hotels (including the Longitude 131 Lodge), tour providers and cultural and natural experiences located right in the heart of Australia, just 20 km from Uluru. The resort is owned by the Indigenous Land Corporation (ILC), and has implemented an Indigenous Training and Employment Strategy, aiming to employ Indigenous trainees at the resort each year and reach 50 per cent Indigenous employment by 2018. Furthermore, all profits from business activities go towards supporting the ILC's Indigenous programs across Australia.

Ayers Rock Resort and the hotels situated there offer a wide range of accommodation and tourism opportinities to suit any needs from family holidays to culinary, adventure and luxury experiences. The resort also hosts functions, has a variety of dining and restaurant options, and provides a wonderful place from which to explore the Uluru–Kata Tjuta region. Details on all accommodation and tour packages are available on the website, including hotel-specific phone numbers and contact details.

WHERE: Ayers Rock Resort is located approximately 20 km from Uluru along the Uluru Rd/Lasseter Hwy.
WHEN: 8 am–6:30 pm Monday to Friday; 9 am–5 pm Saturday and Sunday (office).
CONTACT: 02 8296 8010
www.ayersrockresort.com.au

Yellow Water Cruise

Past winner of the Qantas Australian Tourism Award for Major Tour and/or Transport Operators, this tour company has exclusive use of the spectacular Yellow Water Billabong. It operates year round and provides up to six cruises a day of 90 or 120-minute duration. The sunrise and sunset cruise are very popular, and many people take more than one cruise during their stay to see the changes in the wildlife at different times of the day.

CONTACT: 08 8979 1500
www.kakadutourism.com/tours-activities/yellow-water-cruises

Ayers Rock Resort is an oasis in the desert, 20 km from Uluru

ART GALLERIES, CULTURAL CENTRES AND MUSEUMS

The art centres included here are all Aboriginal-owned and operated. They preserve and support culture, offer new opportunities, develop artistic skills and provide meaningful employment and a source of income for the artists and their families. The art at these centres is sold ethically.

Visitors to the art centres are asked to show their respect to the Traditional Owners by wearing modest clothing, requesting permission before taking photographs, especially of people and artworks, and taking into consideration the importance of the sacred images and stories in all the artworks.

As many of the art centres are on Aboriginal land, visitors should always contact the centre in advance to make an appointment, and to check if permits are required. If so, they must be organised before travel. In many areas in Central Australia, visitors need permits to drive on the roads even if they are not stopping. This is because the land is Aboriginal-owned and it is important to regulate the number of people on the roads and going through these areas.

Driving to the art centres that are in remote communities can be challenging. Before leaving major towns, visitors are advised to get up-to-the-minute reports on road conditions, and pick up current maps and safe-driving tips from tourist information offices. Ensure that you are well-prepared with sufficient fuel, water and emergency supplies. It is also advisable to let someone know where you are driving to before you set off.

Anindilyakwa Art and Cultural Centre

Anindilyakwa Art promotes the Aboriginal artists of Groote Eylandt and helps them to sell their works. The centre displays work in a range of mediums, including ochre and acrylic paintings on canvas, bark and shell; wooden objects such as *yidakis* (didgeridoos) and clap sticks; carvings; traditional weaving using pandanus and natural dye methods; and traditional and unique jewellery design.

WHERE: Groote Eylandt, 50 km from the eastern coast of Arnhem Land. The airport is located at the north of Groote Eylandt, near the Angurugu community. Groote Eylandt is a 90-minute flight from Darwin.
WHEN: Monday: 8.30 am–4.30 pm; Friday: 8.30 am–4.30 pm.
COST: Entry is free.
CONTACT: 08 8987 6266
www.ankaaa.org.au/art-centre/anindilyakwa-arts-centre-arnhem-land

Arlpwe Art and Culture Centre

Arlpwe Art and Culture Centre is comprised of an Aboriginal art gallery, two art centres and a pottery studio. It services the local Aboriginal artists of the small Central Australian community of Ali Curung. The Katetye people are the traditional custodians of the area, with Allawara, Warlpiri and Warramungu language groups also forming the local community. Central Desert-style paintings, including distinct dot painting landscapes and ceremonial body designs, feature prominently in the works on display here. The pottery studio was introduced as a new medium to the community. It has stimulated a unique creative development in the artists who can express their culture in new ways. The pottery training school also involves classes for children at the primary school, engaging the next generation in the process of artistic communication. Artists here are proud of their work, and their authentic Aboriginal paintings, artefacts and artworks help keep the Indigenous culture alive for all future generations.

WHERE: Ali Curung, 350 km north of Alice Springs. From Alice Springs follow the Stuart Hwy and turn right at the signpost. A sealed 22 km road east leads to the community. The drive takes about 4–5 hours.
WHEN: 9 am–5 pm, Monday to Friday.
CONTACT: 08 8964 1640
www.australianaboriginalartgallery.com.au

The Artists of Ampilatwatja

The Ampilatwatja (pronounced um-bludder-witch) community is the cultural heart of the Alyawarr nation. For the Alyawarr people, art is an important way to express connection to country. The works produced at this community are distinct from any other Aboriginal art, even that from nearby communities in Central Australia. The depiction of the land is generally done with bold, bright colours and fine dots. The artists mostly paint *Arreth*, which means 'strong bush medicine'. Every plant and animal plays an irreplaceable role in the ecological system of the land that has sustained the Alyawarr people for generations. Artists pay homage to their country, demonstrating their deep connection to it. The stories in their art of the landscape transcend surface meaning. Through the delicate layered dots of the paintings, artists only reveal the 'outside' stories to the general public. However, through the lens of their own deep cultural foundations, the artists and their people interpret the 'inside' stories of information that is held sacred. It allows us all an insight into the rich lives of the Alyawarr people, without encroaching on any religious laws of their culture.

WHERE: PMB 78 Amplilatwatja, via Alice Springs.
WHEN: Please contact the art centre to arrange a visit.
PERMITS: One-day visits do not require entry permits and all visitors are welcome.
CONTACT: 0437 426 549
www.ampilatwatja.com

Buku-Larrnggay Mulka Art Centre

Buku-Larrnggay means 'the feeling on your face as it is struck by the first rays of the sun', that is, when facing east. *Mulka* means 'a sacred but public ceremony'.

This large Yolŋu community-controlled art centre in the small community of Yirrkala in North-East Arnhem Land supports many award-winning Yolŋu artists. It is home to some of Australia's most significant artworks. In 1976, the Yolŋu artists established Buku-Larrnggay Arts in the old mission health

A young Indigenous artist creating a limited-edition print at Buku-Larrnggay Mulka Art Centre

centre. Today Buku supports traditional and contemporary art across the wide range of media that the Yolŋu artists work in. This centre is comprised of a print workshop, numerous gallery spaces, a museum, and The Mulka Project, a digital production and archiving studio housing tens of thousands of historical films and digital images.

Art from this region has a rich history. There is strong evidence to suggest that art from the Yolŋu people of Yirrkala was the catalyst for a growing interest in Aboriginal art in the 1970s, particularly the profound realisation that traditional Aboriginal art is unique on a global scale. Additionally, it was artists in Yirrkala who first recognised the potential of Aboriginal visual art as a political tool. In 1963, the now famous Yirrkala Church Panels were hung in the Methodist church at Yirrkala to recognise the local clans and their lands. These title deeds can still be seen today at the art centre's museum. Later in that same year the Yirrkala Bark Petition was presented in Australian Parliament in a bid from Yirrkala Elders to hold the rights to their own traditional lands.

Buku-Larrnggay Mulka Centre services the Yirrkala community and also approximately 25 homeland centres in a 200 km radius. Yirrkala is the traditional home of the *yidaki* and some of the world's finest examples of the instrument come from this art centre. Other art and cultural works on display, and for purchase, include *larrakitj*, which is a traditional memorial pole used in funerary ceremonies; *gunga djäma,* woven pieces such as baskets, mats and dilly bags; *dharpa*, wood sculptures; and *nuwayak*, sacred clan title deeds painted onto the bark of the stringy-bark tree.

Artists from this region are well known for their traditional carving and barks. Their works are consistently selected in competitions and awarded major prizes across the country, including in the prestigious Telstra National Aboriginal and Torres Strait Islander Art Award in a range of categories. Their art is also exhibited in major galleries around the globe, including the Musée du Quai Branly in Paris. Yirrkala is home to the famous artists of the Yunupingu, Marika and Maymuru families, among others. There is also a group of younger, emerging artists. Art from Buku-Larrngay Mulka retails from $200 for a smaller work, to thousands of dollars for larger, very detailed pieces. It is fine art and the prices reflect the skill in these traditional pieces.

WHERE: 138 Tuffin Rd, Yirrkala. Qantas and Airnorth fly to Nhulunbuy. The road is impassable in the Wet season (from December to May). Car hire recommendations include Manny's Car Rentals: 08 89872300, Gove Rentals: 08 8987 1700 and Nhulunbuy Ute Hire: 08 89872872.
WHEN: 8 am–4.30 pm Monday to Friday; 9 am–12 pm Saturday.
CAMPING AND ACCOMMODATION: There are two hotels in the vicinity, the Walkabout Lodge and the Gove Peninsula Motel. Camping is available only in certain designated areas, and permits are required through Dhimurru Land Management: 08 8987 3992.
PERMITS: While the community is on Aboriginal land, no permit is required to visit the art centre when coming from the nearby town of Nhulunbuy or the Gove airport. Permission from the Northern Land Council (08 8920 5100) is required to drive here from Darwin or Katherine (approximately 10 hours). Yirrkala is a dry area where alcohol is forbidden without a permit.
COST: Entry to the centre is free. A gold coin donation is required to visit the museum.
CONTACT: 08 8987 1701
www.yirrkala.com

Bula'Bula Arts

Bula'Bula Arts is the cultural heart of Ramingining, the small community located in the heart of the heritage-listed Arafura

Wetlands, in North-East Arnhem Land. While an art centre has existed in the community since the 1970s, Bula Bula Arts Aboriginal Corporation was formally established in the 1990s. The centre is not for profit, and its main objective is the preservation and cultivation of Yolŋu culture. *Bula'bula* is the voice of the kangaroo, and refers to the song cycle of the area's main creative being, Garrtjambal, the red kangaroo.

Bula'Bula Arts supports approximately 150 artist members from Ramingining and its surrounding homelands, with a core group of around 30 artists. The community sits on the traditional lands of the Djadawitjibi people of the Djinang group, but is now home to more than 16 clans speaking 14 different languages. The work of these artists is captivating, with deep spiritual and ritual connections to the sophisticated social structures of Yolŋu culture. The centre is world renowned for the hollow-log memorial installed at the National Gallery of Australia, which was created there. Many of the leading artists have featured in movies such as *Ten Canoes* and *Charlie's Country*.

Bula'bula Arts represents a strong group of weavers and painters with both traditional and contemporary styles. Works includes bark and canvas paintings, hollow logs, prints, and traditional fibre work, such as woven dilly bags, bush string bags, mats and baskets. Visits can include participatory art experiences such as weaving or bark painting and visits to artist's homelands. Contact Bula'bula for more information.

WHERE: Ramingining is located in the Arafura Wetlands. It is 580 km east of Darwin, 435 km west of Nhulunbuy, and 30 km inland from the Arafura Sea. Fly Tiwi flies between Darwin and Ramingining on Monday, Wednesday and Friday. The road to Ramingining is only accessible during the Dry season, and only by 4WD.

Top: Traditional painting by Roy Burnyila of Bula'Bula Arts

Bottom: Skillful and stunning fibre work by Robyn Djunginy Malibirr of Bula'Bula Arts

ACCOMMODATION: Ramingining offers newly renovated accommodation for visitors.
PERMITS: Ramingining is Yolŋu land and permits must be obtained before travelling to the community. They may be obtained from the Northern Land Council.
www.nlc.org.au/articles/cat/permits/
CONTACT: 08 8979 7911
www.bulabula-arts.com

Darwin Aboriginal Art Fair

The Darwin Aboriginal Art Fair (DAAF) showcases the diverse work of more than 2000 Aboriginal and Torres Strait Islander artists, from more than 60 Aboriginal and Torres Strait Islander art centres around Australia. The event promotes the production of authentic Aboriginal art and its sale within an ethical and sustainable business environment. Attracting more than 10 000 visitors to the fair and ancillary events, the sales volume of DAAF is much greater than that of any other Australian art fair. Both emerging and established artists display their work, which include paintings on canvas, bark and paper; sculpture; fibre art; textiles; cultural artefacts and regalia. DAAF boasts a program filled with artist workshops and demonstrations, public talks, traditional dance performances, children's activities, film, fashion and more. Visitors can expect to experience the vibrancy of the dynamic contemporary Indigenous art scene and engage with the artists themselves.

DAAF is part of the Darwin Festival. It runs in the same week as the National Aboriginal and Torres Strait Island Art Awards and the Garma Festival, and has formed a close partnership with the National Indigenous Music Awards. Together the four events mark the most prestigious national celebration of Aboriginal and Torres Strait Islander arts in the world.

WHERE: The Darwin Convention Centre, 10 Stokes Hill Rd, Darwin.
WHEN: Annually in August.
COST: Entry to the art fair is free.
CONTACT: 08 8981 0576
www.darwinaboriginalartfair.com.au

DAAF Film Gala

The film gala is an intimate event that presents two Aboriginal feature films at Darwin's beautiful open-air cinema. One night is generally a featured film and the other a fundraiser. The movie screenings are accompanied by panel discussions, master classes, and performances relevant to the film. They are preceded by a collection of short films from Aboriginal and Torres Strait Islander art centres. In 2017, the iconic story of the Namatjira family, *Namatjira Project,* was the feautured film and was complemented by a master-class watercolour workshop with members of the Namatjira family, a music performance and a panel discussion.

WHERE: The Deckchair Cinema, Jervois Rd off Kitchener Dr, Darwin Waterfront.
COST: Ticket price varies for each film. See the DAAF program for more details.
www.deckchaircinema.com/films/daaf-indigenous-film-gala-namatjira-project-darwin-festival

From Country to Couture: The DAAF Fashion Show

The DAAF Fashion Show was added to the program of events in 2016, and in 2017 was sold out to more than 400 guests. The show represents the growth and interest in contemporary Aboriginal and Torres Strait Islander textile art through a combination of fine art with high-end fashion. Together, the two create an electric energy through which traditional cultural stories are conveyed. Garments are made in various prints and fabrics, and showcase the textile and fashion work from Aboriginal art centres Australia wide. The spectacular and increasingly popular fashion show is not to be missed.

Location and ticket prices may vary each year. See the DAAF program for more information.
www.darwinfestival.org.au/events/country-couture-daaff-fashion-show

Desert Mob

One of Australia's major Aboriginal art events, Desert Mob represents artists from more than 30 remote desert communities in Central Australia. The annual event has been running for more than 25 years and provides a snapshot of life in the art centres of the remote Northern Territory, South Australia and Western Australia. This unique gathering includes an arts symposium, exhibition and marketplace. It is the most immediate interface between remote desert community artists and the wider world, and is an exhilarating testament to the dynamism of Aboriginal art. The exhibition displays paintings, sculpture, weaving, woodcarvings, ceramics, prints, photography and work on paper. It includes hundreds of new works each year.

WHERE: Desert mob is held in Alice Springs, in three galleries in the Araluen Art Centre precinct.
WHEN: Desert Mob spans 3 days over a weekend in September. The gallery is opened on the Thursday night, the symposium is held on the Friday, and the marketplace is held on the Saturday from 10 am. The exhibition itself is displayed for 6 weeks across September and October.
COST: Entry is free. While the symposium is also free, a $30 ticket allows access to a morning tea and lunch with presenting artists, art workers and special guests.
www.desart.com.au/desert-mob

Elcho Island Art and Craft

This community-operated art centre opened in 1992 and now services more than 200 Yolŋu artists in Elcho Island's main community

Art on display as part of the Desert Mob Art Fair in Alice Springs

of Galiwin'ku. The art centre is renowned for its high quality weavings, paintings and carvings made by artists who are nationally and internationally profiled. The artists use traditional bush materials, such as natural pigments, in both traditional and contemporary applications of art.

Elcho is home to Gali Yalkarriwuy, the famous *Banumbirr*, or 'morning star pole', artist. The poles celebrate the importance of the Banumbirr creation story and tell many stories about the land and environment passed on through generations. The poles are made from the wood of a specific tree found on the island. They are decorated with carvings and various coloured ochres, and adorned with woven strings and feather bunches. Some are made for special ceremonies such as initiations and memorials. Other works produced include dupan hollow log coffins, bark paintings, *yidakis*, woven pandanus baskets, carvings and shell jewellery. The fibre art from Elcho Island is some of the most spectacular in Australia, with grasses and fibres dyed and woven together to form baskets, dilly bags, mats, fishing nets and jewellery.

Elcho Island Art and Craft assists artists in their work as well as the collection, promotion and distribution of high quality Yolŋu art to a range of Australian and international markets.

WHERE: The art centre is located in the Marthakal Arts Hub, in Galiwinku on Elcho Island, 150 km north-west of Nhulunbuy. Airnorth charters direct flights to Elcho Island from Darwin. The flight is about 90 minutes each way.
WHEN: 9 am–5 pm Monday to Thursday; 9 am–4.30 pm Friday; 9 am–2 pm Sunday.
PERMITS: The art centre is on Aboriginal land and permits must be obtained prior to arrival. Contact the centre's staff for assistance in organising them.
CONTACT: 08 8970 5088
www.palya.com.au/elcho-island-arts-and-crafts/

Top: Longitude 131 takes visitors to see Australia's oldest continuously running arts centre, Ernabella Arts

Bottom: Painted ceremonial poles and fibre work on display at Gapuwiyak Culture and Arts Aboriginal Corporation

Elcho Island Arts Gallery

This gallery also represents artists from Elcho Island and it is easily accessible for visitors as it is located in Darwin.

WHERE: 7 Pavonia Place, Nightcliff.
WHEN: 9 am–5 pm Monday to Thursday; 9 am–4:30 pm Friday; 9 am–2 pm Sunday.
CONTACT: 08 8948 6602
www.elchoarts.com/gallery

Ernabella Arts Tour – Longitude 131

Ernabella Arts is part of a closed community located on the Pukatja homelands, and the oldest continuously running Indigenous arts centre in Australia, established in 1948. The Longitude 131 Lodge (located within Ayers Rock Resort) offers exclusive tours to the art studio and gives guests the opportunity to engage with the resident artists there. The variety of artists at Ernabella today is large, as the centre has changed from its humble beginnings as a craft room to a globally acclaimed contemporary art studio. Allowing a maximum of 4 passengers, this private tour is a full-day experience where guests can learn the meaning behind the artworks from the artists themselves, learn about the ancient techniques used by the artists, and create their own ceramic tile.

TIPS FOR VISITORS: This tour includes a total of 7 hours driving time with 2½ hours at the Ernabella studio and includes morning tea and lunch. Ernabella is a conservative community, so please take this into consideration and wear modest clothing.
WHERE: Tours depart from the Longitude 131 Lodge, located in Yulara.
WHEN: Tours only operate during the winter months (June–August).
COST: $1000 per person.
CONTACT: 02 9918 4355
www.longitude131.com.au/experience/ernabella-arts/

Gapuwiyak Culture and Arts Aboriginal Corporation

The arts corporation of Gapuwiyak, in remote East Arnhem Land, is a recent initiative set up to support the cultural practices of the Yolŋu people living in the region and provide them with leadership opportunities, meaningful employment and professional development. Gapuwiyak is located on the traditional lands of the Gupapuyngu clan, however, people from all major Yolŋu clan groups live in the community and the surrounding homelands. Artists are inspired by the deep and powerful connection to their land and their ancestors, which is continually strengthened through cultural practices such as *bunngul* (ceremony), *manikay* (singing), *giritjirri* (dance), *miny'tji* (sacred designs), and *dhäwu* (stories). The art centre houses its own collection and sells locally produced works. It is particularly well known for its vibrant fibre work, which traditionally uses pandanus leaves and Kurrajong bark. There are also fine examples of bark and canvas paintings, *yidakis* and *larrakitj* (painted ceremonial poles). It also has a media centre, which has a growing archive of old and new media relevant to the community.

WHERE: Gapuwiyak is a small Yolŋu town on the shore of Lake Evella in East Arnhem Land. It is approximately 200 km west of Yirrkala and 250 km south east of Ramingining. Fly Tiwi operates a daily 7 am flight from Darwin to Gapuwiyak. There are also charter companies based in Darwin and Nhulunbuy. Driving from Darwin takes around 12 hours and 4WD is recommended.
CONTACT: 08 898 79110
www.gapuwiyak.com.au

Godinymayin Yijard Rivers Arts and Cultural Centre

Godinymayin Yijard Rivers Arts and Cultural Centre (GYRACC) was built as a meeting place for both local Indigenous and non-Indigenous people to gather and share art and culture. The centre offers exhibitions, live music, song and dance performances, workshops and education programs, and is often the setting for cultural celebrations as well. Communities in the Katherine region are remote, and GYRACC cites their main goal as connecting these communities through a sharing of art, cultures and a 'two-way' learning philosophy, respecting both the Indigenous and non-Indigenous perspectives and histories in the region. The centre holds regular events and exhibitions, and all details and an events calendar can be found on the website.

WHERE: Stuart Hwy, Katherine East. Katherine is located 300 km south of Darwin when travelling along the Stuart Hwy and is accessible by 2WD. There are three main roadside stops between Katherine and Darwin where visitors can re-stock and re-fuel. Katherine is also a major stop on both Greyhound bus and Ghan rail trips through central Australia, and is accessible by air with Airnorth.
WHEN: 10 am–5 pm Tuesday to Friday; 10 am–3 pm Saturday.
CONTACT: 08 8972 3751
www.gyracc.org.au

Hermannsburg Potters

Pottery has become a famous feature of the small Arrernte community of Hermannsburg, in the remote foothills of the Western MacDonnell ranges in Central Australia. It was introduced to the community by missionaries in the 1960s. In 1990, an accomplished NT potter, Naomi Sharp, provided a single kiln and her expertise to guide the potters in ceramic craft. Today, artists, mostly women, translate their cultural and artistic heritage into their unique and exciting style of ceramics. Terracotta clay and hand building and coiling methods are used to make the distinctive pots. These are then decorated with animals, plants, people and historical and contemporary scenes, which are molded, carved and painted into the body and the lid of the pots. As well as traditional imagery, the potters often incorporate dragons, zebras and other animals into their pieces. Pottery is now a way of life for these artists and the innovative design of their pots has become internationally renowned. Hermannsburg pots are shown in galleries across the country and worldwide.

WHEN: Visits to the studio are by appointment only. No photographs are permitted of the artists inside their studio. Contact Hermannsburg Potters to make an inquiry.
CONTACT: 08 8956 7414
www.hermannsburgpotters.com.au

Injalak Arts and Crafts

This is one of the NT's most well known Aboriginal art centres. Situated in the remote community of Gunbalanya in West Arnhem Land, it has around 200 active members from the community and the surrounding outstations. Members are Kunwinjku, Mengerrdji and Erre people and all speak the Kunwinjku language. The artists' works are authentic representations of ancient Dreamtime stories and the ancestral history of the Kunwinjku people. The range of pieces includes bark and paper paintings, carvings, artefacts such as clap sticks, *yidakis*, mimi poles and *lorrkons* (hollow logs), fibre baskets and pandanus floor mats, and limited-edition prints. Injalak is also becoming well known for its screen-printed fabrics. The silk, linen and cotton pieces come in a range of colours and designs and are sought after for use in high fashion and casual wear. Injalak Arts wholesales a range of works, from affordable pieces to artwork for fine art markets in Australia and around the world. The centre also runs rock-art tours (see Injalak Rock Art Tour).

Top left: A traditional dance performance at Godinymayin Yijard Rivers Arts and Cultural Centre (GYRACC)

Top right: Women in traditional paint dance at GYRACC

Bottom right: An Aboriginal man performing in *The Shadow King* production in 2014 at GYRACC

WHERE: From Jabiru, cross Cahills Crossing on the East Alligator River and follow the 17 km dirt road to Gunbalanya. This is an easy 50-minute drive with stunning views. The turn-off to the community is clearly marked. 2WD vehicles make the trip, however 4WD is recommended. Road access to Gunbalanya is only possible from May to October. Be sure to check tide times at Cahills Crossing before leaving.
WHEN: 8.30 am–5 pm Monday to Friday; 9 am–2 pm Saturday; closed Sundays and public holidays. Visits outside of these hours may be possible by appointment.
PERMITS: Permits to visit Gunbalanya must be arranged in advance via the Northern Land Council in Darwin or Jabiru.
CONTACT: 08 8979 0190
www.injalak.com

Injalak Rock Art Tours

Injalak Hill boasts a series of outstanding rock-art galleries that range from 100 to 8000 years old. Injalak Arts has been given exclusive permission by the Traditional Owners to facilitate rock-art tours led by trained and experienced local guides who have detailed knowledge of the rock-art sites. The tour runs for 2½–3 hours. Visitors need to wear good walking shoes and a hat, and bring water, insect repellent and sunscreen.

WHERE: Injalak Arts and Crafts (see Injalak Arts and Crafts).
WHEN: Tours leave Injalak Arts at 9 am Monday to Saturday; no tours on Sundays or public holidays. Tours operate in the Dry season only when the Gunbalanya is accessible by road.
PERMITS: Permits to visit Gunbalanya must be arranged in advance via the Northern Land Council in Darwin or Jabiru.
COST: Adult: $110; child under 18: $33; pensioner concession: $77 (must present pension card). Maximum 12 adults per group. To book a group tour or arrange an alternative time for your tour, contact staff at Injalak Arts and they will endeavour to accommodate all guests.
www.injalak.com/rock-art-tours

Ikuntji Artists

Ikuntji has been the cultural hub of the Haasts Bluff community, within the Western MacDonnell Ranges, since about 1996, reinforcing and reinvigorating cultural practices. Artists from Ikuntji draw their inspiration from their *Ngurra*, or country, and their *Tjukurrpa*, or Dreaming stories. Their work reflects the constantly changing vistas, as the mountains change colour throughout the day depending on the passage of the sun and on the season. The artists use bold colours in their paintings, which show an innovative, contemporary take on a rich cultural heritage. The artworks are diverse, from traditional symbolism and iconography to highly abstract paintings. The eight principle artists who work out of this art centre are highly acclaimed and exhibited in Australia and internationally.

WHERE: Haasts Bluff is 230 km west of Alice Springs. The most direct route is from Alice Springs via Larapinta Dr and Glen Helen Resort. The road includes 170 km of sealed bitumen but 60 km is unsealed. 4WD is recommended.
WHEN: 10 am–4 pm Monday to Friday. Day visitors are welcome but it is necessary to make an appointment.
PERMITS: While public spaces in the community do not require a permit, travelling on Aboriginal land may. See the Central Land Council website for more information: www.clc.org.au/frequently-asked-questions/cat/permits
CONTACT: 08 8956 8783
www.ikuntji.com.au

Jilamara Arts and Crafts

Jilamara Arts is located in the community of Milikapiti on Melville Island and displays Tiwi Island art from 60 local artists. They have contributed significantly to Australia's contemporary Indigenous art scene and are highly respected for their astonishingly rich art. The artists are renowned for

Top: Michelle Woody of Jilamara Arts and Crafts collecting ochre for painting

Bottom: Artist Conrad Tipungwuti of Jilamara Arts and Crafts

their use of natural ochres in paintings of various mediums, *tunga* baskets, *tutini* poles and carvings. The Tiwi Islands have been separated from mainland Australia for at least 3000 years, leading to the creation of a regionally distinct artistic tradition.

WHERE: Fly Tiwi operates a daily direct flight to Snake Bay from Darwin, or from Garden Point. See www.flytiwi.com.au/gardenpoint for more information. Air charter services include Territory Air Services: www.territoryairservices.com.au, Arafura Aviation: www.arafuraaviation.com.au, ChartAir: www.chartair.com.au; and Hardy Aviation: www.hardyaviation.com.au
WHEN: 9 am–4 pm Monday to Friday. Closed for holidays in July and the Christmas period.
PERMITS: Permits are required to visit the Tiwi Islands. They are free. Apply at: www.permits.tiwilandcouncil.com www.ankaaa.org.au/art-centre/jilamara-arts-crafts-tiwi-islands

Keringke Arts

Keringke Arts is located in the remote Arrernte community of Santa Teresa, 80 km south-east of Alice Springs. In Eastern Arrernte the community is known as *Ltyentye Apurte*, meaning 'stand of beefwood trees'. The country is rich in rock art, artefacts and ceremonial sites. *Keringke* means 'kangaroo tracks'. It is the Dreaming story of Kathleen Wallace, the custodian of Keringke Arts and one of its senior and most well-known artists. The kangaroo came from the south-east and created a rock hole in the desert. Known also as *Keringke*, the rock hole is a scared site with great significance to many Arrernte people.

The art centre was established in 1987 after a 9-week fabric-painting course was run in the community. The following year the women exhibited their work at the Australian Bicentennial Craft Show; a first for Aboriginal artists. In 1989 the Keringke Art Centre was built. The artistic style of the Santa Teresa women is unique and is now referred to as

Keringke Style. The artists use bright colours and dynamic patterns and shapes to represent their desert country and culture, and pay close attention to detail in their works. Their work includes canvases, silk prints, ceramics and furniture. It is represented in many collections nationally and internationally.

WHERE: Santa Teresa, 80 km south-east of Alice Springs. Driving to Santa Teresa from Alice Springs takes 1½–2 hours. The road is open year round. However, it is unsealed and 4WD is recommended.
WHEN: 9 am–4 pm Monday to Thursday; Friday by appointment only. Please contact the art centre before visiting.
CONTACT: 08 8956 0956; www.keringkearts.com.au

Maningrida Arts and Culture

Located on traditional Kunibidji country in Arnhem Land, Maningrida Arts and Culture represents the artists from an area of 7000 sq km of land and sea. This encompasses more than 100 clan estates and more than 12 distinct languages, including the Kunibidji, Kunbarlang, Nakkara, Burarra, Gun-nartpa, Gurrgoni, Rembarrnga, Eastern Kunwinjku, Djinang, Wurlaki and Gupapuyngu people.

The art from the centre conceptually displays the natural and spiritual worlds, with a focus on the country itself and the ancestral beings, such as Ngalyod, the Rainbow Serpent; Yawkyawk and jin-Merdewa, the female water spirits; and Namorrorddo, a spirit being.

Artists use materials sustainably harvested from their clan estates, including ochres and pigments; the bark, wood and roots of various tree species; feathers; and the wax from bush honey. Fibre work from the region has always been highly regarded. It comes in decorative, ceremonial and sculptural forms, including conical fish traps, baskets, string bags, dilly bags, mats and ceremonial regalia. Artists are also known for their bark paintings, *yidakis*, sculptures and prints. Acclaimed senior artists continue to expand their artistic narratives across new mediums, while new artists continually emerge and become nationally and internationally celebrated.

WHERE: Maningrida community, 500 km east of Darwin; 300 km north-east of Jabiru. Air North operates flights to Maningrida from Darwin twice daily. The drive to Maningrida is via Gunbalanya. The road is unsealed so 4WD is recommended; it is generally only accessible in the Dry season, from June to November.
WHEN: 9 am–4 pm Monday to Friday, excluding public holidays.
PERMITS: Permits for Maningrida are free but must be obtained from the Northern Land Council prior to travel. For more details and applications, visit: www.nlc.org.au/articles/cat/permits
CONTACT: 08 8979 6100
www.maningrida.com

Djómi Museum

This Djómi museum at Maningrida Arts and Culture houses an extremely valuable and unique cultural collection, with local, national and international significance. The collection has mainly grown through acquisitions from Maningrida Arts and Culture and donations from private collections and people who worked in Maningrida, dating back to the 1940s. The museum includes the works from generations of prominent artists, both deceased and still active today, including bark paintings, sculptural works, and weavings. It also houses artefacts and other items of material culture, as well as photographs documenting the historical life and culture of the region. The museum is a fantastic way to learn about the history and the cultural practices of the Maningrida area.

WHEN: By appointment only. Contact Maningrida Arts and Culture.
CONTACT: 08 8979 6100
www.bawinanga.com/what-we-do/arts-culture/djomi-museum

Maruku Arts

Maruku Arts is a collective of about 900 artists from 20 Anangu communities across Central Australia. *Maruku* means 'belonging to black', referring to the ownership and operation of the arts collective by these communities. Maruku Arts is a very accessible way to engage in authentic Anangu culture from across the Central Desert of Australia. It consists of a warehouse in the Mutitjulu community, a retail gallery at Uluru–Kata Tjuta National Park Cultural Centre, and a market stall in the Yulara town square. The main works are paintings and *punu*, wooden carvings.

THINGS TO DO: Maruka Arts runs 90-minute dot-painting workshops twice daily at the Yulara town square. A local Anangu artist and an assisting interpreter teach visitors about traditional Anangu culture, art, symbols and the Pitjantjatjara language. Visitors can apply this knowledge to create a piece of their own.

Maruku Arts offers dot-painting workshops

WHERE: Uluru–Kata Tjuta Cultural Centre. The 450 km drive to Uluru–Kata Tjuta from Alice Springs takes about 5 hours via the Stuart and Lasseter hwys. These are entirely sealed roads, so a 4WD is not required. Jetstar and Virgin Airlines fly from Sydney directly to Uluru; Jetstar has 4 return services from Melbourne Tullamarine each week. Workshops are held in Yulara town square.
WHEN: 7.30 am–5.30 pm Monday to Friday; 9am–5 pm Saturday to Sunday. Dot-painting workshops: April–September: 11.30 am–1 pm and 2 pm–3.30 pm; October–March: 10.30 am–12 pm and 1.30 pm–3 pm.
COST: For the workshops: adult: $69; child 5–15 years: $35; family (2 adults, 2 children): $195.
CONTACT: 08 8956 2558; www.maruku.com.au

Merrepen Arts Centre

Merrepen Arts opened in 1986 and is now a well-established art centre. It supports 20 to 80 artists who work traditionally and also in contemporary mediums that provide new platforms to express traditional stories. Merrepen Arts is located in the community of Nauiyu (pronounced new-yoo), in the Daily River region. While the land is the traditional country of the Malak Malak people, local people now mainly belong to the Ngan'gi language group, which is made up of the two closely related Ngan'gikurrungurr and Ngen'giwumirri languages. There are 10 minority language groups also still in use, including Malak Malak, and Pidgin or Creole is spoken throughout. The art centre has taken its name from the Merrepen palm tree, which local women use to make their dilly bags, mats and fishnets.

Artists here have become particularly well known for their etchings and award-winning screen-printed textiles. In 2013, Marita Sambono's *Fog Dreaming* design was interpreted into a dress that won the national Myer Fashions on the Field prize at the Melbourne Cup, bringing Merrepen art to national acclaim. In 2014, Kieren Karritpul's textile design, *Yerrgi*, won the Youth Award at the 31st National Aboriginal and Torres Strait Islander Art Awards (NATSIAA). Other renowned artists, such as Aaron McTaggart, whose painted and etched glass mural is displayed at the Darwin International airport, and Gracie Kumbi and Miriam Rose Ungunmerr-Baumann, are also producing world-class designs and paintings. Artists from Merrepen also produce fibre work and artefacts. The Merrepen Arts Festival is a highlight on the annual calendar in this area.

WHERE: Nauiyu community, next to the picturesque Daly River. From Darwin, the scenic drive to Merrepen Arts is 230 km and takes approximately 2½ hours. Drive south from Darwin on the Stuart Hwy to Adelaide River. Turn right onto Dorat Rd, just after the Adelaide River bridge. Follow Dorat Rd for approximately 30 km then turn right onto Daly River Rd. Follow this road all the way to the Merrepen Art Centre at Nauiyu. The road is sealed and is easily accessible for most of the year, although care should be taken in the Wet season (November– April) as the region is susceptible to flooding.
WHEN: 9 am–5 pm Monday to Friday; 9.30 am–4.30 pm Saturday. The centre is open June–September only.
PERMITS: No permits are required to visit the Nauiyu community.
CONTACT: 08 8978 2533
www.merrepen-arts.squarespace.com

Merrepen Arts and Music Festival

The vibrant Merrepen Arts and Music Festival is held annually, usually in early June, and celebrates the culture and arts of the beautiful Daly River region. The small population of Nauiyu triples in size as visitors from Australia wide and beyond travel to the community to watch traditional music and dance performances, and to see the celebrated art of the region. The art program is a massive drawcard for visitors, with limited-edition prints launched and sold, an art sale all weekend, and artist Q&A forums and workshops. On the Saturday night a concert is held on the banks of the picturesque Daly River, with a fashion show, unique cultural performances and some of the Top End's favourite bands.

COST: Festival entry is free. Concert: $20 per adult; $10 concession; free entry for anyone under 18.
www.merrepenfestival.com.au

Milingimbi Art and Craft Centre

The Yolŋu artists of Milingimbi Island (off the coast of Arnhem Land) and its regional homelands create unique fibre works including pandanus weavings of dilly bags, mats and fish trap forms, bark paintings, ceremonial poles and carvings. They also create sculptures and works on canvas. The artists use art to express their rich culture, which is a connection of land, sea, song and ceremony. With more than 150 artists from 12 clan groups, art from Milingimbi is highly regarded around the world.

WHERE: Lot 53 Gadupu Rd, Milingimbi via Winellie. Milingimbi community is 15 km from the mainland and 500 km east of Darwin. The art centre is located on the foreshore of the community facing the Arafura Sea. Access to the island is by air or sea. Fly Tiwi operates a daily service from Monday to Friday to Milingiumbi from Darwin. Charter flights are also available.
WHEN: 9 am–4 pm Monday to Friday.
PERMITS: Permits are required to visit the Milingimbi community. For information, see the Northern Land Council website: www.nlc.org.au/articles/cat/permits
CONTACT: 08 8987 9888; www.milingimbiart.com

Mimi Aboriginal Arts and Crafts

Mimi Aboriginal Arts and Crafts houses a collection of artwork from an extensive 380 000 square km area. This includes Arnhem Land, the entire Katherine region, the

Tanami Desert and parts of the Kimberley. Mimi is named after the Mimi Spirits, from the Dreamtime. Many still inhabit Arnhem Land, and while some are said to be dangerous and must be avoided, many are harmless and can be heard calling in the night.

WHERE: 6 Pearce St, Katherine. Katherine is an easy 3-hour drive from Darwin along the Stuart Hwy.
WHEN: 8.30 am–4.30 pm Monday to Friday; other times by appointment only.
CONTACT: 08 8971 0036; www.mimiarts.com

Munupi Art Centre

Munupi is located on the north-west coast of Melville Island, in the Tiwi Islands. It grew from the merger of the Yikikini Women's Centre and Pirlangimpi Pottery. Today it celebrates Tiwi culture through a range of traditional and contemporary mediums.

Art at Munupi is inspired by the lush environment of the Tiwi Islands, as well as the creation stories and culture of its people. Tiwi culture is very rich, with traditional hunting, gathering and ceremonial events occurring daily, and the art reflects this lifestyle. Artists use ochre, gouache and acrylic paint and are celebrated for the diversity of their works. These include painting, pottery, weaving, carving, screen prints, lino printing and textile work.

Although Munupi Arts is separate from Jilamara Arts, the two centres work closely together and a visit to both is recommended when visiting Melville Island.

WHERE: The Garden Point community on the north-west coast of Melville Island. It is approximately 125 km from Darwin and 30 minutes by air. Fly Tiwi runs two flights on weekdays between Darwin and Garden Point, and one per day on weekends. For more information visit: www.flytiwi.com.au/gardenpoint. Munupi is 1 km from Garden Point airport. Other air charter services include Territory Air Services: www.territoryairservices.com.au; Arafura Aviation: www.arafuraaviation.com.au; ChartAir: www.chartair.com.au; and Hardy Aviation: www.hardyaviation.com.au
PERMITS: Permits are required to visit the Tiwi Islands. They are free. Apply at www.permits.tiwilandcouncil.com
CONTACT: 08 8978 3975; www.munupiart.com

Ngurratjuta Iltja Ntjarra Many Hands Art Centre

Ngurratjuta Iltja Ntjarra Many Hands Art Centre supports new, emerging and well-established contemporary Aboriginal artists from Central Australia. The art centre is a place for Arrernte artists to come together and paint, sharing new techniques, ideas and stories and in doing so preserving their ancient culture.

Ngurratjuta Iltja Ntjarra has a particular emphasis on supporting the artists of the Hermannsburg school, who paint in the watercolour tradition of their famous grandfather and relative, Albert Namatjira. Namatjira painted in the 20th century and was famous for painting his native desert country in western-style watercolour paints. He is arguably one of the most celebrated Australian artists of the 20th century. He passed his unique style onto his children, who have since taught their children, creating a legacy of outstanding watercolour artists from the Central Desert region. The Hermannsburg school artists are a living part of history.

Town-based artists also come to the centre to work on their paintings. A visit to the centre is a chance to see a wide range of artworks and to meet the artists. It is also a unique way to learn about Central Australian Aboriginal culture and art.

WHERE: 29 Wilkinson St, Alice Springs, approximately a 15-minute walk from the centre of Alice Springs town.

WHEN: 9 am–5 pm Monday to Friday. Artists paint on site 10 am–3 pm Mondays to Thursdays.
CONTACT: 08 8950 0908
www.manyhandsart.com.au

Nyinkka Nyunyu Art and Culture Centre

This art centre offers an insight into the culture of the Aboriginal people of the Tennant Creek region. It includes an art gallery with changing exhibitions showcasing the art movement of Tennant Creek, a gallery shop, an Aboriginal plants and bush-tucker garden, and a cafe.

WHERE: Paterson St (Stuart Hwy), the main road running through Tennant Creek. Tennant Creek is 500 km north of Alice Springs.
WHEN: October to April, 9 am–5 pm Monday to Friday; 10 am–2 pm Saturday and Sunday; May to September, 8 am–6 pm Monday to Saturday; 10 am–2 pm Sunday. Closed 25 December–2 January and Good Friday.
COST: There is an entry fee for the museum/gallery, but entry to the gardens, cafe and shop is free. Guided tours around the centre cost $15 per adult.
CONTACT: 08 8962 2699
www.nyinkkanyunyu.com.au

Outstation Art

Outstation Art was established in 2008 and supports artists working in rural art centres in the Tiwi Islands, Arnhem Land, the Western Desert, the Kimberley and Central and South Australia. It encourages the presentation and promotion of Indigenous art, ensuring ethical work practices are maintained through close connection to artists and the communities. Outstation embraces a broad range of works, from traditional media, such as bark paintings, hollow logs and weaving, to contemporary visions in fibre art, photography, soft sculpture and acrylic paintings.

In February each year Outstation holds a 'Rising Stars' exhibition to promote emerging Aboriginal artists. Each year in August they also present *Salon des Refusés*, which showcases works submitted to the NATSIAAs but not shortlisted for the award.

WHERE: 8 Parap Place (upstairs, entry via Gregory St), Parap, Darwin. Outstation is located in Parap's gallery precinct. The area is also home to the famous Parap markets, held every Saturday. Parap is a short drive from the city and close to the Museum and Art Gallery of the Northern Territory. The local bus route 4 (Monday to Sunday), route 6 (Monday to Friday), and route 10 (Monday to Sunday) leave frequently from the Darwin Bus Interchange in the city.
WHEN: 10 am–1 pm Tuesday; 10 am–5 pm Wednesday to Friday; 10 am–2 pm Saturday. Closed Sunday and Monday.
CONTACT: 08 8981 4822
www.outstation.com.au

Papunya Tjupi Aboriginal Arts

Papunya is a small Aboriginal community, formed in the late 1960s from the removal and displacement of Aboriginal people from their land. It is made up of Pintupi, Luritja, Warlpiri, Arrernte, and Anmatyerr peoples. The community is famed as the birthplace of the Western Desert dot-painting movement. In the early 1970s the school teacher encouraged the locals to paint a traditional mural on the walls of the school. The murals inspired a large art collective in the community and in 1972 the artists, original entirely men, successfully established their own company, Papunya Tula Artists Pty Ltd.

Traditionally the people of the Western Desert painted traditional stories in the sand or on the body for ceremonial purposes. The artists adapted their cultural practices to remove sacred symbols and monitor ancestral designs, and also to paint in the western style with acrylic paint and a hard surface. They brought the art of the Western Desert into national and international acclaim.

In the 1980s the Pintupi artists returned to their homelands further west and continued painting for Papunya Tula Artists at art centres established in Kintore and Kiwirrkura. The current art centre at Papunya, Panunya Tjupi, was established in 2007 and supports 100 artists from Papunya and its surrounding art stations. Many of these artists are descendants of the original artists in the Papunya movement and continue to work in the high standards of their forefathers, while carving out their own unique identity in the world of contemporary Aboriginal art. Art remains an important part of the community and connection to the land.

WHERE: Papunya is 250 km north-west of Alice Springs. From Alice Springs, Papunya is a 3-hour drive via the Larapinta and Namatjira Tourist Route. A 4WD is required.
PERMITS: Permits are not required for day visits. Visitors are welcome to visit the art centre but it is necessary to make an appointment.
CONTACT: 08 8964 7141; www.tjupiarts.com.au

Papunya Tula Artists

Papunya Tula Artists are renowned for their innovative work with the Western Desert art movement. The gallery in Alice Springs represents the Aboriginal artists who are originally from Papunya and the Western Desert region. This includes Pintupi, Luritja, Warlpiri, Arrernte, and Anmatyerr peoples.

WHERE: 63 Todd Mall, Alice Springs.
CONTACT: 08 8952 4731; www.papunyatula.com.au

Tangentyere Artists

Tangentyere Artists celebrates the complex cultural diversity of Central Australia. It represents the residents of various Alice Springs town camps, who came from many traditional lands across the desert. The centre aims to share the stories from the town camps. Despite sometimes difficult conditions, the camps are important places that also have many positive aspects. The art is diverse, representing various traditional stories and using a range of styles. Today, Tangentyere is comprised of approximately 400 artists.

WHERE: 16 Fogarty St, Alice Springs.
CONTACT: 08 8951 4232
www.tangentyereartists.org.au

Telstra NATSIAA

The National Aboriginal and Torres Strait Islander Art Award (NATSIAA) is Australia's most prestigious Indigenous art award. It celebrates the significant contribution of Indigenous artists from around the country and working in a range of traditional and contemporary mediums.

Originating in 1984, the NATSIAAs provide a platform that deepens the understanding of Indigenous culture. The awards are now an important event on Australia's cultural calendar and attract a wide audience of keen observers. They are delivered and exhibited by the Museum and Art Gallery of the Northern Territory (MAGNT).

The Telstra Art Award, worth $50 000, is presented to the artist of the work deemed by the judges as the most exceptional across all categories. The Telstra Emerging Artist Award, worth $5000, is awarded to an artist within their first 5 years of practice who has not exhibited in a major institution. Prizes of $5000 are awarded in another 5 categories, including the Telstra Bark Painting Award, the Telstra General Painting Award, the Telstra Works on Paper Award, the Wandjuk Marika Memorial Three-Dimensional Award and the Telstra Multimedia Award. The award ceremony is held in mid-August, but the work of all shortlisted finalists is displayed at MAGNT until late November.

CONTACT: Museum and Art Gallery of the Northern Territory 08 8999 8264; www.magnt.net.au/natsiaa

Tiwi Design

Tiwi Design promotes, preserves and enriches the culture of the Tiwi people, and supports some 100 local artists. The art centre opened in the late 1960s with exhibitions of wood-block prints. This style of art was a natural link to the traditional techniques of woodcarving. Within a year, the wood-block designs were transferred to silk screens, and textile printing became a major medium of the artists. By the mid 1970s, Tiwi Design artists were creating a wide range of art and craft, including bark and canvas ochre paintings, ironwood carvings, screen-printed fabrics, ceramics, bronze and glass sculptures, pandanus weaving, and limited-edition prints. Today the art centre comprises a pottery studio, screen-printing studio, carver's shelter, a painting studio, plus a retail gallery and administration centre. The work of the artists is as diverse now as it has always been at Tiwi Design.

WHERE: Tiwi Design is located in the community of Wurrumiyanga, on the south-eastern corner of Bathurst Island, 80 km north of Darwin. Fly Tiwi operates a daily, 30-minute flight to Bathurst Island from Darwin. For more information and bookings, visit: www.flytiwi.com.au. On Thursdays, Fridays and Sundays, SeaLinkNT ferries depart from Cullen Bay, Darwin, for Wurrumiyanga in the morning and return in the afternoon. Return ferry prices: adult: $120; child: $65; concession: $90: family (2 adults, 3 children): $320. The trip is 2½ hours each way. For more information see: www.sealinknt.com.au/ferry
PERMITS: Permits are essential; apply on the Tiwi Land Council website: www.tiwilandcouncil.com/permits/index.htm
CONTACT: 08 8978 3982
www.tiwidesigns.com

Tiwi Design Tours

Visitors can immerse themselves in the culture of the Tiwi Islands on this cultural walking tour. It begins with a traditional welcome ceremony at Tiwi Designs, followed by morning tea and a tour of the museum, which showcases the culture and history of the Tiwi people. After lunch at Tiwi Designs, a unique screen-printing session with a local artist gives visitors the chance to create their own piece of art. The tour includes a return ferry from Darwin to Bathurst Island.

WHERE: From the ferry landing, the tour walks up to Tiwi Design for a traditional welcome ceremony and morning tea.
WHEN: Tour departs Cullen Bay at 8 am and returns 5.45 pm. Tours run Thursdays and Fridays April–December; there are additional tours in the peak season of June–August.
COST: Adult: $345; child: $295; seniors: $325.
www.sealinknt.com.au/tours/tiwi-by-design

Tjanpi Desert Weavers

Tjanpi Desert Weavers is an Indigenous social enterprise that enables the Indigenous women of Australia's remote Central Desert to earn a regular income from their fibre art. The enterprise was formed by the Ngaanyatjarra Pitjantjatjara Yankunytjatjara Women's Council (NPYWC) in 1995, and now represents more than 400 Aboriginal women from 26 remote western and central desert communities covering an area of approximately 350 000 sq km.

Tjanpi, which means 'wild harvested grasses', is harvested and woven by the women, and then decorated with emu feathers, painted seedpods and coloured raffia. The pieces are beautiful, intricate and whimsical, ranging from conventional basket designs to quirky, colourful animals, teapots, and even life-sized figures of people. In 2005 the Tjanpi Desert Weavers earned national and international fame when a group of weavers from Blackstone, 450 km south-west of Alice Springs, won first prize at the NATSIAAs for their woven model of a Toyota 4WD.

Tjanpi has a public gallery in Alice Springs, and regularly exhibits work in various galleries across Australia. They also run public weaving workshops.

WHERE: 3 Wilkinson St, Alice Springs.
WHEN: 10 am–4 pm Monday to Friday.
CONTACT: 08 8958 2377
www.tjanpi.com.au

Top: (From left) Mary Katatjuku Pan, Ilawanti Ungkutjuru Ken, Niningka Lewis, Imiyari Frank and Tjunkaya Tapaya of Tjanpi Desert Weavers

Bottom: Paint your own designs at Top Didj Cultural Experience and Art Gallery

Top Didj Cultural Experience and Art Gallery

Top Didj has been offering their authentic Aboriginal Cultural Experience since 2000, and is now also the home of the Katherine Art Gallery. Indigenous artists and guides run the 2-hour-long Aboriginal Cultural Experience, teaching guests about local Indigenous cultures, as well as traditional skills such as boomerang throwing and painting. All the artists and guides working at Top Didj are locals to the Katherine and Red Centre regions.

The Katherine Art Gallery, opened in 1997, showcases works that reflect the cultures of the Jawoyn, Dagoman and Warlpiri peoples, Traditional Owners of the lands surrounding Katherine, as well as works by artists from Arnhem Land and the Kimberley. The gallery holds a range of artworks across many mediums, including traditional artefacts and didgeridoos.

WHERE: Cnr Gorge and Jaensch rds, Katherine. Katherine is located 300 km south of Darwin when travelling along the Stuart Hwy and is accessible by car. There are three main roadside stops between Katherine and Darwin where visitors can restock and refuel. Katherine is also a major stop on both Greyhound bus and Ghan rail trips through central Australia, and is accessible by air with Airnorth.
WHEN: The Aboriginal Cultural Experience runs at 9:30 am and 2:30 pm daily from May to October.
COST: Adult: $75; child 3–15 years: $47. Bookings can be made by phone or by the booking form on the website. Top Didj requires a minimum of 24 hours' notice for all bookings.
CONTACT: 08 8971 2751; 0414 888 786
www.topdidj.com

Walkatjara Art Centre

Walkatjara is the Mutitjulu community's art centre, located in the Cultural Centre at Uluṟu. The vibrant paintings depict the stories of the

A<u>n</u>angu Traditional Owners of the area. At the art centre visitors can see artists at work and learn about their culture and stories.

WHERE: The Cultural Centre in the Uluru–Kata Tjuta National Park.
WHEN: 8.30 am–4.30 pm daily.
CONTACT: 08 8956 2537
www.walkatjara.com

Warlukurlangu Artists Aboriginal Corporation

Warlukurlangu is a vibrant and active art centre that supports artists from the remote Tanami Desert communities of Yuendumu and Nyirripi, and neighbouring communities. These are the traditional lands of the Warlpiri people. *Warlukurlangu* means 'belonging to fire', and refers to the Fire Dreaming site near Yuendemu. The art centre was established in 1985 and today includes more than 600 artists. They are recognised for creating some of the finest contemporary art in Australia and the world, using coloured acrylic paint to translate traditional cultural designs and stories. Warlukurlangu is also well known for its wide selection of outstanding limited-edition prints.

WHERE: Ral Ral Ave, Yuendumu, 290 km north-west of Alice Springs. From Alice Springs, drive north on the Stuart Hwy for 25 km, before turning west onto the Tanami Rd. The road is sealed most of the way, but unsealed for the final 110 km; 4WD is recommended. Rain can greatly affect the condition of the road. Check conditions before driving.
WHEN: 9 am–4 pm Monday to Friday. Weekends by appointment only.
PERMITS: Day visitors do not require a permit. Any longer stays require a permit, which can be obtained from the Central Land Council at www.clc.org.au. Please contact the art centre before visiting.
CONTACT: 08 8956 4133
www.warlu.com

Yarrenyty Arltere Artists

Yarrenyty Arltere is a town camp within Alice Springs that is associated with the Dog Dreaming of the Arrente people. Both Arrente and Luritja people live there.

Yarrenyty Arltere Artists was an arts training project established in 2000 to combat the chronic social issues faced by residents in the camp. The project quickly became a vibrant hub for the community, rebuilding cultural strength and creating economic opportunities for the people. In 2008 it was established as an Indigenous-owned-and-managed enterprise. The artists have gained national and international acclaim for their soft sculptures. This practice sees recycled woollen blankets dyed with local plants, scrap metal collected from around Alice Springs, and feathers, beads and hand embroidery made into a various quirky sculptures of spirits, figures and animals.

Yarrenyty Arltere artists won the Telstra National Aboriginal and Torres Strait Islander Art Award 3D Award in 2013 and 2015, and the Vincent Lingiari Art Award in 2016. Artists were also highly commended in the 2012 NATSIAA 3D award and the 2013 WA Indigenous Art Award.

WHERE: Larapinta Valley town camp, Blain St, Alice Springs.
CONTACT: Art Centre Manager: yalc.art@tangentyere.org.au
www.yarrenytyarltereartists.com

2

WESTERN AUSTRALIA

Dancers at the Mowanjum Festival

FESTIVALS

Mowanjum Festival

Hosted by the Mowanjum Art and Culture Centre, the Mowanjum Festival celebrates the culture of the Ngarinyin, Worrorra and Wunambal peoples. Held each year in July, the one-night spectacular is one of the largest cultural celebrations in WA and attracts visitors from Australia wide. Open to the general public from 2 pm, the festival includes a variety of free workshops in the afternoon, including painting, didgeridoo playing (for men only) and boab-nut carving, followed by corroborees featuring performers from throughout the Kimberley. The art gallery stays open until 9 pm and food, drinks and local bush tucker are available.

WHERE: Mowanjum Aboriginal Art and Culture Centre, 12 km from Derby, 3 km along the Gibb River Rd.
WHEN: July; check the website for details.
COST: Tickets are available at the gate; adult: $20; child $10.
CONTACT: 08 9191 1008
www.mowanjumarts.com

NATIONAL PARKS

The WA Parks and Wildlife Service manages more than 100 national parks in the state. In addition to the parks included here, visitors can find out about the many others at: parks.dpaw.wa.gov.au

Karijini National Park

Set in the Hamersley Range in the heart of the Pilbara, the vast Karijini National Park is an ancient landscape of massive mountains and steep escarpments cut by spectacular gorges more than 100 m deep. Within these sheer-sided chasms hide crystal-clear rock pools, cascading waterfalls and lush vegetation.

ABORIGINAL CULTURAL HERITAGE: The Traditional Owners of the Hamersley Range are the Banyjima, Kurrama and Innawonga people. Aboriginal sites more than 20 000 years old have been found here, many of which are still significant to the local Aboriginal community. The park was first known as Hamersley Range National Park, but this name was changed in 1991 in favour of the Banyjima word for the range, Karijini.

NATURAL FEATURES: While much of the southern part of the park is inaccessible, it is the famous gorges in its northern section that attract visitors. Chasms as deep as 100 m scour a steep escarpment, exposing dominant layering and sediments dating back millions of years.

Each gorge has its own particular features. Nestled between the walls of Dales Gorge and shaded by lush vegetation are Fern Pool and Circular Pool, separated by the park's only permanent waterfall, Fortescue Falls. Circular Pool is surrounded by beautiful sunken gardens. Kalamina Gorge and Pool is the most accessible gorge. At Hamersley Gorge a wave of tectonic rock acts as a backdrop to a swimming hole and natural spa. Joffre Gorge boasts a natural amphitheatre created by an unusual curved wall and,

Top: Hiking through breathtaking gorges in Karijini National Park

Bottom: The pools at the base of Dales Gorge are an incredible place to cool off

after rain, a 100 m waterfall. Oxer Lookout is above the pool where the Joffre, Hancock, Weano and Red gorges join. Many of these gorges are relatively easy and safe to enter, but some are best undertaken with a guide.

Karijini National Park also contains the two tallest mountains in Western Australia: Mt Meharry at 1250 m; and Mt Bruce, known as Punurrunha by the Aboriginal people, at 1234 m high. A climb to the summit of Mt Bruce gives a panoramic view of the Hamersley Range.

The dusty red earth of the hills, ridges and plateaus of Karijini is covered with spinifex and porcupine grass, punctuated by eucalypts such as the drought-resistant snappy gum (*Eucalyptus brevifolia*), with its twisted white trunk. Low mulga woodlands are found on the lower slopes and valley plains. The wildflowers that bloom here vary with the seasons. July to October is the best time to see floral displays, when countless everlastings carpet the landscape, along with the ubiquitous purple–pink mulla mulla. Within the gorges are luxuriant ferns thriving on moist rock ledges and reed-lined pools of water surrounded by river red gums, white-barked gums and cadjeputs. The latter, also known as weeping paperbark (*Melaleuca leucadendra*), are covered with fragrant creamy white flower spikes in spring. Native rock figs (*Ficus platypoda*) grow in seemingly impossible positions on the rock faces of the gorges; birds that eat the fruit leave undigested seeds on the rock ledges, where they germinate in small pockets of soil and leaf debris. The roots of the fig then stretch downwards to reach water, sometimes as far as 10 m below.

Two of the smallest creatures in the park build homes that are a feature of Karijini – look out for the huge termite mounds and, on stony slopes among the spinifex, the rock piles of the rare western pebble-mound mouse. This tiny marsupial uses stones to build a small volcano-like crater for its nesting chamber. These laboriously constructed stone piles serve as entrances to a system of burrows underground. Within, the nesting chambers are lined with leaves and other plant debris. Mounds can cover areas of up to 9 sq m. This little creature is just one of the many species of native rodent to reside in the national park.

Other mammals in Karijini include red kangaroos, euros, rock wallabies, dingoes, echidnas and bats. The park also boasts a variety of birds, which are drawn to the waterholes. Spinifex pigeons, distinctive for their sandy coloured crests, fly between the rocks and through the grasses, and wedge-tailed eagles are a common sight soaring high up on the thermals created by the warm air rising from the surrounding plains. Reptiles abound, with geckos, goannas, dragons and legless lizards scurrying about or lazing on rocks, and pythons and other snakes are common but not necessarily sighted.

THINGS TO DO: This is a park for wilderness adventurers, nature photographers and keen bushwalkers.

BUSHWALKING: Karijini offers plenty of marked walking trails ranging from easy to difficult. These include the Gorge Rim Trail (2 km, 2 hours return, easy), which winds from Circular Pool Lookout along the edge of Dales Gorge. A steep trail (800 m return, 2 hours, medium difficulty) descends from Dales Gorge carpark to Fortescue Falls, which provides the perfect spot for a dip. A steep descent, followed by a walk along the gorge floor will take you to Circular Pool (800 m return, 2 hours, difficult), which is framed by lush green ferns.

At Kalamina Gorge an easy 30-minute return walk that leads to the gorge's lush, shaded pool can be extended into a 3-hour return walk through the gorge. The trailhead carpark for the walk to Kalamina Gorge has an information board, tables and toilets. Hancock Gorge walk is through a steep narrow gorge takes you down to Kermit's Pool (1.5 km return, 3 hours, medium difficulty).

Mt Bruce (Punurrunha) summit walk (9 km return, 5 hours, difficult) is recommended for fit and experienced walkers only. The summit offers good views of the national park and along the way there are interpretive signs giving information about Aboriginal heritage, flora and fauna. There are also giant termite mounds in this area. If you are contemplating any of the longer hikes, you must notify a ranger before starting out. Regardless of the length of the walk, remember that the gorges can be extremely hazardous.

SCENIC VIEWS: There are lookouts over most of the gorges, which then lead on to walking trails. A good place to get your bearings is Oxer Lookout, which is an easy 30-minute return walk from the Weano carpark. The lookout has breathtaking views down a 100 m drop to Junction Pool, the confluence of four gorges – Weano, Red, Knox and Joffre. At Joffre Gorge, rock steps take you down to a lookout overlooking a spectacular curved waterfall, which forms a natural amphitheatre. The 300 m walk down into Knox Gorge to the lookout is best undertaken in the early morning or late afternoon, to witness the full play of light on the view.

SWIMMING: The pools of water in the gorges provide delightful places for a refreshing swim. However, some of the deep pools that remain shaded can be extremely cold, especially between April and September. Take care, as hypothermia can occur; wetsuits are recommended. When swimming in gorges or rivers, watch out for submerged hazards. Most of the gorges have picnic areas.

THE KARIJINI VISITOR CENTRE: Located on Banyjima Dr, the visitor centre is a good place to start any visit to this national park. It offers displays about the flora, fauna and geology of the area, and about the local Aboriginal people and their culture. The design of the building represents a goanna moving through the country; the animal is highly symbolic to the local Aboriginal people. The tail represents their history, the centre or stomach their law, and the head represents the future direction of the Traditional Owners. The high, weathered steel walls of the centre mimic the sheer-sided gorges that are a feature of the park. The building is designed to withstand the fires that are a regular occurrence in the region.

WHERE: 75 km east of Tom Price. All park roads are suitable for conventional vehicles and caravans. Roads within the park are generally in good condition but heavy rains can result in track closures. To check road conditions in the park contact the visitor centre.

CAMPING AND ACCOMMODATION: There are two campsites within the park, each with pit toilets, picnic tables, water, solar showers and gas barbecues. Bush camping is not allowed. The nearby town of Tom Price offers a range of accommodation from camping and caravan sites to motels.

COST: Park entry and camping fees apply in the national park, payable either on-site at the entrance stations or by the self-registration system or to campground hosts.

CONTACT: 08 9189 8121
parks.dpaw.wa.gov.au/park/karijini

Purnululu National Park

Purnululu National Park lies deep in the rugged east Kimberley region, protecting one of the world's natural wonders, the Bungle Bungle Range. The remarkable tiger-striped, beehive-shaped rock domes have become, somewhat belatedly, one of the iconic images of the Australian outback, and are appreciated worldwide for their exceptional beauty. The region also holds sacred Aboriginal Dreaming stories and a rich culture that has maintained connections to this land for at least 20 000 years.

Purnululu National Park was declared a World Heritage area in 2003, in recognition of it being 'the most outstanding example of cone karst in sandstones anywhere in the world' and for its 'superlative natural beauty and aesthetic importance'. The dramatically sculptured rocks are hailed as being unrivalled in their scale, extent, grandeur and diversity of form anywhere in the world. They undergo remarkable seasonal variation in appearance, including striking changes in colour following rain. The adjacent conservation area is a buffer zone established to protect the park's World Heritage values.

Today, the local Aboriginal people maintain a strong connection and association to the ancient landscape, which holds the stories of their Dreaming. In the Kija Aboriginal language, *purnululu* means 'sandstone'. Australia is pursuing an additional World Heritage nomination of Purnululu for the remarkable Aboriginal cultural traditions in the area.

The ancient Bungle Bungle Range was the Kimberley's best-kept secret until the early 1980s, known only to local Aboriginal people and a few pastoralists. In 1885 gold was discovered at Halls Creek and the subsequent gold rush brought miners to the region. European graziers followed in the 1880s, marking the beginning of a 150-year period of land erosion. In 1967, the government resumed the leases as part of an erosion-control program throughout the Ord River catchment area. However, it was not until the early 1980s when film-maker Guy Baskin included aerial footage of the Bungle Bungles in his television series 'Wonders of Western Australia' that Australians became aware of this 350-million-year-old natural treasure in the outback. In 1987 the area was gazetted as a national park.

ABORIGINAL CULTURAL HERITAGE: The area is traditionally the land of the Kija people of the eastern Kimberley region, and their neighbours the Jaru, a group belonging to the Desert region. The Kija people put up fierce resistance to the pastoralists. They killed the cattle (livestock numbers on the Ord River grasslands had reached 50 000 by 1902) and in retaliation there were brutal massacres of local Aboriginal people and punitive police raids. At the height of the violence, many of the Kija took refuge in the Bungle Bungles. They used notched tree trunks to scale the cliffs and pulled these makeshift ladders up afterwards to prevent pursuit. To try to stop the livestock killing, the government provided some refuges and food, but did not stop the land and cultural dispossession, which continued into the 1970s.

Today, descendants of the park's Traditional Owners live in population centres such as Halls Creek and Warmun. The people of Warmun have worked extensively on language and literacy programs for schools and have produced a large amount of teaching material. Some help manage the national park, with a number of Aboriginal people employed as rangers and guides.

The history of the Jaru following white settlement mirrored the history of the Kija

Top: Echidna Chasm in the western section of the Bungle Bungle Range, Purnululu National Park

Bottom: The striking forms of the Bungle Bungle Range are refelected in the waters of Piccaninny Creek

described above. Most of the people lived and worked on pastoral properties in the area until 1968, when the introduction of award wages resulted in Aboriginal workers being forced to leave. Many moved to Halls Creek.

Aboriginal rock art adorns some shelters, caves and gorges in the park, with depictions of crocodiles and fish, as well as hand stencils. There is no public access to these sites. There are also many Aboriginal burial sites but these, too, are closed to the public. Living Area leases in the national park for some Traditional Owners have been signed recently with the Purnululu Aboriginal Council.

The relationship of the Indigenous people to the land has been highlighted by the renowned paintings of the Warmun artists. This group emerged in the 1970s, painting ceremonial boards using natural ochres of brown, black and yellow defined by white and black dots. Warmun Art Centre was established in 1998 to represent the Warmun artists and market their work in Australia and overseas. The most famous of the Warmun artists are Rover Thomas and Queenie McKenzie.

NATURAL FEATURES: The national park has four major ecosystems: the Bungle Bungle Mountain Range, a plateau that dominates the centre of the park; wide sand plains surrounding this plateau; the Ord River valley to the east and south of the park; and limestone ridges and ranges to the west and north of the park.

The Bungle Bungle Range is a deeply fissured plateau that rises more than 200 to 300 m above the surrounding plain. It is distinguished by great cliffs on its western edge that are cut by seasonal waterfalls and pools, numerous narrow gorges, deep gullies, and beehive-shaped domes of rock on its southern edge. Some 350 million years ago geological activity caused uplifts that formed the ranges to the north and west, and then erosion by creeks and rivers resulted in the transportation of sand and rocks. The rocks were strewn at the edge of the cliffs but the sand was carried further, gradually hardening over time to form sandstone channels. Over the last 20 million years further uplift and erosion of the sandstone has created the range's distinctive domes, some rising up to 300 m high. The sandstone is so fine that it crumbles when touched. The dark bands are the more porous layers of rock, where the presence of moisture has encouraged the growth of dark coloured algae. The less porous layers of the domes are coated with iron oxides that stain the surface orange. These thin layers of black lichen (*Microthelia arterrina*) and orange silica cover and protect the sandstone, giving the domes their distinctive horizontal black-and-orange banding. While sandstone towers are known in other parts of the world, the features of the Bungle Bungles are unrivalled.

Of the many gorges in the range, Cathedral Gorge is perhaps the most awe-inspiring. It is a natural amphitheatre, a quiet place surrounded by sheer rock walls, with a sliver of blue sky above and a still pool of water below.

The vegetation in the park is diverse, closed forests in the park's valleys and gorges change to open forests and woodlands in drier areas. Within the deep valleys and gorges various palms thrive, along with orchids and delicate ferns. A total of 653 plant species have been recorded in the national park, including 17 different types of fern.

Located in an area where the desert meets the tropics, Purnululu has animal species that typify both environments. There are 41 mammal, 149 bird, 81 reptile, 12 amphibian and 15 fish species. In the drier areas on the plateau reptiles are common, with monitors (including Gould's goanna) and skinks blending in with the colours of their surroundings. Mammals include the short-eared rock wallaby, which roams the grasslands and also ventures into the rocky hills and gorges searching for seeds. The northern nailtail wallaby inhabits the open woodlands, moving onto the grasslands at night to feed.

In the sheltered valleys and damper areas you may glimpse frogs, pale field-rats and the large-footed myotis, a species of bat that roosts close to water – it has exceptionally large feet, up to 14 mm long.

Of the large numbers of birds found in the park, many are migratory species, such as the rare grey falcon, a beautiful white and grey raptor that nests in tall eucalypts overlooking watercourses. More commonly seen in the park are the gorgeous blue and green rainbow bee-eaters and flocks of colourful budgerigars.

THINGS TO DO: This remote wilderness offers quiet pleasures such as birdwatching. The only means of access into the gorges is by foot so walking is the main activity. You cannot climb the domes.
BUSHWALKING: Cathedral Gorge walking trail (3 km return, 1–2 hours) is mostly easy, but has a few short difficult sections, with some rock ledges, waterholes and stony depressions to be negotiated. At the wide still pool at the end of the trail, look for animal tracks near the water's edge. Piccaninny Gorge walking trail (30 km return, 2 days, moderate–difficult) requires an overnight camp. You must register with the ranger before setting out and again on your return. You must be self-sufficient, carry plenty of water, and a fuel stove for cooking (no campfires allowed). From the Piccaninny Gorge carpark, the short Domes walk (1 km circuit, easy) leads through sandstone towers.

On the northern side of the park, Frog Hole Trail (1.4 km return, 1–2 hours, moderate–difficult) leads to a small seasonal pool at the base of the Bungle Bungle Range. After rain a waterfall drops over 100 m into the palm-fringed pool, which is home to a number of frog species. Echidna Chasm Trail (2 km return, 1–2 hours, easy–moderate) involves some rock scrambling and clambering over several large boulders. The chasm is narrow and is not for the claustrophobic; at its narrowest part the walls are over 100 m high and barely an arm's width apart, and it ends at a sheer rock face. The challenging Mini Palms Trail (5 km return, 3 hours, easy–difficult), leading to a scenic amphitheatre of palms, begins easily then narrows and becomes closed in and walkers have to clamber over boulders and 'squeeze' between rocks.

The Walanginjdji Lookout, a short walk from the ranger's station (500 m return, 30 minutes), provides panoramic views of the western side of the Bungle Bungles. Sunset is the best time for viewing, when the setting sun intensifies the vibrant colours of the range.
PHOTOGRAPHY: The best times of the day for photography are early morning and late afternoon, when the rays of the fading sun cast a red glow across the landscape, producing a striking richness of colour in the sandstone.
SCENIC FLIGHTS: A scenic flight from within the park, or from Halls Creek, Kununurra or Warmun, is the best way to gain a perspective of the massive size and spectacular scenery of the Bungle Bungle Range. Both helicopter and fixed-wing aircraft operate flights. Contact Slingair Heliwork WA: 08 9169 1300.
WHERE: 300 km south of Kununurra. The road into the park from the main highway is the very rough Spring Creek Track and is accessible by 4WD only; 53 km along it is an intersection known as 'Three Ways', with a ranger base and information shelter. Kununurra to the ranger station takes 5 hours travelling time; from Halls Creek allow 4 hours.
WHEN: The park is only open between April and the end of December (weather permitting).
CAMPING: There are two camp sites, both with toilets, untreated water and fireplaces. Camping fees apply. Campers must be fully self-sufficient, bringing in all supplies and water. The nearest supplies available are from Warmun on the Great Northern Hwy.
COST: Park entry fees apply.
CONTACT: 08 9168 7300
parks.dpaw.wa.gov.au/park/purnululu

TOURS AND STAYS

Brian Lee Hunters Creek Tagalong Tours

Brian Lee is a Bardi man from the Dampier Peninsula in the Kimberley region. His people have been a part of the land and sea for thousands of years. On his half-day tour around the turquoise waters of Hunters Creek, Brian shares his wisdom and experience as a Traditional Owner, teaching visitors about his country and culture, and offering an insight into the lives of the Bardi people. Visitors also learn about the region's fascinating history, traditional bush tucker and traditional crabbing and fishing methods. The tour concludes with a traditional seafood lunch over an open fire with the catch of the day.

WHERE: Kooljaman.
WHEN: Tours depart from Kooljaman at 8:30 am.
REQUIREMENTS: Guests must use their own 4WD.

Kooljaman at Cape Leveque offers 4WD hire. Also bring a hat, swimwear, sunscreen and drinking water.
COST: Adult: $98; child: $45. Personalised full-day tours can also be arranged: adult: $150; child: $75.
CONTACT: 08 9192 4970
www.brianleetagalong.com.au

Bundy's Cultural Tours

Bundy is a Bardi man and he offers a range of informative tours on his beautiful traditional homeland. They include the Bush Tucker walk: sample seasonal fruit and learn about local bush tucker, bush medicines, enjoy the breathtaking scenery and learn about the seasons as told by the Bardi people. The tour departs Kooljaman at 8:30 am and runs for 1 hour. Adult: $45; child: $25.

Night fishing tour: as the sun sets, join Bundy and his mob for an amazing and unique night fishing experience. Guests need to drive their own 4WD. Wear reef shoes or old sandshoes. Adult: $80; child: $40.

Spear-making tour: Bundy and his family teach guests the ancient art of spear making using local materials, and share the history of the Dampier Peninsula and the Dreamtime stories of the Bardi people. Visitors learn how to spear fish and possibly catch lunch. A 4WD is essential, as well as reef shoes or sand-shoes, water and sun protection. The half-day tour departs Djarindjin at 8:30 am. Adult: $80; child: $40.

Personalised half and full-day tours are also available, and can include bush-tucker walks, spearfishing and unique fish-poisoning lessons. This traditional fishing method temporarily immobilises fish to enable Bardi people to collect the quantity that is required.

WHERE: Kooljaman at Cape Leveque
CONTACT: 08 9192 4970
www.bundysculturaltours.com.au

Top: Fresh seafood cooked by Brian Lee of Tagalong Tours

Bottom: Learn about the Bardi people of the Dampier Peninsula with Indigenous guides at Cape Leveque

Bungoolee Tours

In the inspiring landscape of the Banuba country of the Kimberley, Dillon Andrews and his family run tours on their traditional lands. Through Bungoolee Tours, he shares his knowledge and powerful spiritual connection to the land. In addition to the Aboriginal cultural significance of the area, the tours give visitors insights into the history, geography, topography, and biology of this region. For prices, itineraries and bookings contact Bungoolee Tours.

WHERE: Bungoolee Tours are based in Fitzroy Crossing.
CONTACT: 08 91915355
www.bungoolee.com.au

Imintji Campground and Art Centre

Camp at the foot of King Leopold Range with the local custodians of the land, the Imintji people. The wilderness camp is well located for visits to Bell Gorge, Tunnel Creek, Windjana Gorge and surrounds, and offers spectacular escarpment views. The camp-grounds are a great stopover point or base, while exploring the Kimberley region. Imintji Art Centre has a range of art and crafts by local artists on display and for sale.

WHERE: Imintji Roadhouse, Gibb River Rd, Kimberley.
WHEN: Campground: May to October, the Dry season; bookings recommended. Imintji Art Centre: 10 am–4 pm; if the art centre is closed inquire at the community store.
CONTACT: 08 9191 7227; 08 9191 7699
imintji.com.au

Kepa Kurl Tours

Kepa, meaning 'water', and *kurl*, meaning 'boomerang', is the local Noongar Aboriginal name for Esperance, translating to 'where the water lies like a boomerang'. Kepa Kurl runs eco discovery tours of this pristine coastline, providing visitors with a high-quality and informative cultural experience. The Noongar people have maintained their rich culture in this area for thousands of years. Learn about their hunting and gathering techniques, visit the naturally rugged coastline and see some of the most southern Aboriginal rock art. Tours range from half days to overnight stays; they can be personalised to suit individual needs and can include coastal or rock-art excursions. All tours include a full cultural commentary, Dreamtime stories, and tasting of seasonal bush foods. The tour cost includes the entry fee to national parks. Most tours also offer a billy tea and damper morning tea. For prices, itineraries and bookings contact Kepa Kurl Tours.

WHERE: Kepa Kurl Tours are located in the Esperance Museum Village, cnr Dempster and Kemp sts, Esperance.
CONTACT: 08 9072 1688
www.kepakurl.com.au

Kimberley Coastal Adventure

This tour begins in Broome with a spectacular scenic flight to Cape Leveque, followed by an adventure where visitors experience Bardi culture with Bundy. The tour is peronalised and can include traditional spear making and spearfishing, a tasting of seafood cooked over the fire, Dreamtime and cultural storytelling, and a bush-tucker walk. Activities depend on the season and the daily tides. Guests are returned to Broome by plane via a different scenic route.

WHEN: The tour, including flights to and from Broome, is 5 hours.
COST: $595 per person (no children's rates available). Maximum: 4–5 people.
CONTACT: Book with King Leopold Air: 08 9193 7155
www.kingleopoldair.com.au

Kooljaman at Cape Leveque

Kooljaman is the Bardi Aboriginal name for Cape Leveque, in the remote far northern reaches of the Kimberley region, on the Dampier Peninsula. It is also the name of the resort that is owned and operated by the Traditional Owners of the land, the Bardi and Jawi people from the nearby Aboriginal communities of Djarindjin and Ardyaloon. To some people Kooljaman is seen as a luxury resort, as the Traditional Owners have taken care to ensure the resort showcases their country in its natural, unspoilt beauty. Others see it as a wilderness camp; off the grid and sustained by solar power and local bore water. However you see it, staying there is a unique experience in some of the most incredible and isolated country in the world.

The beaches of the Kooljaman are endless stretches of fine white sand and clear, turquoise waters. Accommodation is designed to capture the rugged beauty of the Bardi Jawi country and reflect the traditional values of caring for country. Guests can enjoy fishing, swimming, snorkeling, mud crabbing, charter-boat trips, scenic flights, whale watching, bird spotting, or just relax. Unique tour opportunities are also available.

WHERE: Cape Leveque.
CAMPING AND ACCOMMODATION: Options range from deluxe safari tents, to cabins, to beach shelters and camping, to suit all budgets and itineraries.
CONTACT: 08 9192 4970
www.kooljaman.com.au

Koomal Dreaming Tours

Josh Whiteland takes guests on cultural tours based throughout the Wadandi and Bibbulman country of the Busselton, Dunsborough and Margaret River areas of south-west WA. Wadandi and Bibbulman are two language groups of the Noongar people, whose country stretches from Kalbarri to Esperance. Josh is a Wadandi custodian, and *Koomal*, the Wadandi word for 'brushtail possum', is his totem. He has a deep connection to country and passion for his culture, and he is committed to sharing his knowledge with visitors. Koomal Dreaming Tours offer guests the opportunity to taste native foods and discover bush medicine, animals and plants, and learn about the ancient Dreaming spirits and culture of Wadandi and Bibbulman people. Tours include: Ngilgi Cave cultural tour; Twilight Didgeridoo cave tour; Aboriginal food, culture, cave and didge tour; as well as customised tours.

WHERE: Yallingup Caves Rd, Yallingup.
CONTACT: 0413 843 426
www.koomaldreaming.com.au

Lombadina

The Lombadina community is situated at Cape Leveque on the Dampier Peninsula. It is the country of the Bardi people, who are saltwater people. The ocean has shaped their culture and they maintain a pivotal connection to it. Lombadina offers guests a unique chance to experience the saltwater life of the Bardi people. Guided tours include: traditional mud crabbing; Ancient Footprints tour; Bardi Country tour; whale watching; Lombadina community tour; and half or full-day fishing charters. In addition to the numerous guided tours, guests can enjoy the beautiful beaches, walk, relax and interact with the local people. The art and craft centre is a great place to check out traditionally and locally made carved pearl shell, trochus bangles, and pearl and ebony pendants, along with silk-screen prints, carved bowls, boomerangs and shields.

The community has a general store open Monday to Friday, and a bakery with fresh wood-fired bread baked Monday, Wednesday and Friday.

Top: Kooljaman at Cape Leveque offers guided fishing and mud-crabbing tours

Bottom: Josh Whiteland, owner–operator of Koomal Dreaming, runs foodie tours and bush-food walks

Kayaking off the Dampier Peninsula with people from the Lombadina community

WHERE: Lombadina Aboriginal Corporation, Lombadina.
ACCOMMODATION: Options range from budget to deluxe.
COST: Tour prices vary. Lombadina can transfer guests to and from the following destinations: Broome: $130 one way, $260 return. Kooljaman: $44 one way, $55 return. Airstrip: $15 one way, $20 return. All flights require a minimum of 3 people.
CONTACT: 08 9192 4936
www.lombadina.com

Narlijia Cultural Tours

In the Yawuru language of the Western Kimberley area, *Narlijia*, means 'true for you'. This name refers to the authenticity of Narlijia Cultural Tours, run by passionate Yawuru man, Bart Pigram. Born and bred on his traditional country in Broome, Bart has a deep knowledge of his saltwater lifestyle, and shares his Aboriginal perspective with his guests. His stories are rich and fascinating, often drawn from his family's long tradition in the local pearling and music industry. Bart's tours are unique and personable.

WHERE: Narlijia Cultural Tours are based in Broome.
CONTACT: 08 9195 0232
www.toursbroome.com.au

Ngurrangga Tours

The Pilbara Aboriginal culture and country are as unique as they are ancient. The Aboriginal people have inhabited this region in north-western WA for more than 40 000 years.

Clinton Walker is a Ngarluma and Yindjibarndi man from the Pilbara region. He was brought up learning the traditional ways of his people and now provides unique tours to share some of his knowledge with others. Clinton takes visitors to some of the Pilbara's most stunning locations for an opportunity to see the world's largest outdoor rock-art gallery, learn about traditional bush medicines and foods, and traditional stories and songs.

WHERE: Ngurrangga Tours is based at 42 Roe St, Roebourne.
COST: Day trips start from: adult: $160; child: $80; overnight stays begin at: adult: $600; child: $275.
CONTACT: 08 9182 1777
www.ngurrangga.com.au

Njaki Njaki Tours

Mick Hayden delivers at authentic Aboriginal experience with his walking tours of the Njaki Njaki Nyoongar country of Merredin Peak and the surrounding reserve. As a Traditional Owner, Mick shares the wisdom of his culture and country with Aboriginal Dreamtime stories and tells visitors about bush tucker and Aboriginal tools and artifacts at sites of significance for the Njaki Njaki people. Njaki Njaki Tours can also cater to school groups and personalised tours.

WHERE: Merredin, in the central wheatbelt, halfway between Perth and Kalgoorlie.
COST: Tours range from: adult: $70; seniors: $55; child 10–17 years: $40 for the 2-hour Merredin Peak tour to the Moulyk Dreaming tour: 7–8 hours: adult: $150; seniors: $120; child 10–17 years: $100.
CONTACT: Mick Hayden: 0407 984 470
www.njakinjaki.com.au

Poornarti Aboriginal Tours

These tours offer unique experiences in Noongar country in the south-west of WA. They are run by Joey Williams, a Noongar Elder and Law man. He is passionate about sharing the ancient knowledge of his people and strives to create cultural connections and environmental awareness. To the Noongar people, the land is their *Boodja*, or mother, and they hold a deep connection to the country. Day tours, overnight camps and personalised tours are available.

CONTACT: 0415 840 216; 0412 786 588
poornarti.com.au

Wuddi Cultural Tours and Cultural Centre

Wuddi Cultural Tours and Cultural Centre offer tours around the local area, visiting mostly untouched sites and imparting valuable knowledge of the Traditional Owners of the lands through storytelling, demonstrations and hands-on experiences. Visitors learn the history of the region at the Cultural Centre before heading out for a 2-hour, half-day or full-day adventure. Owners Grant and Anne Riley run this small but impressive business and have set up the centre with gardens, arte-fact and artwork displays and a souvenir shop.

TIPS FOR VISITORS: All tours can be booked ahead of time, but Grant and Anne try their best to accommodate last-minute and same-day bookings as well. Please note that Wuddi accept cash and cheque payments only.
WHERE: 22 Harvey St, Dumbleyung.
CONTACT: 0476 646 766
www.wudditours.com

Wula Guda Nyinda Eco Adventures

Join Darren 'Cape' Capewell, a descendent of the Nhanda and Malgana people, as he shares his land, ocean and spirit of country in his award-winning tours around the Shark Bay area. *Wula Guda Nyida* means 'you come

On tour with Wula Guda Nyinda Eco Adventures

Top left: Bush food found on a foraging tour

Top right: Tour guide and guests at Shark Bay

Bottom right: Kayaking on Big Lagoon, Francois Peron National Park

this way', referring to the Aboriginal tradition of sharing stories, not only between different generations but different cultures as well. Darren's tours inspire visitors to see the country from a new perspective – through the lens of the Aboriginal culture, history and tradition.

To the Traditional Owners, Shark Bay is known as *Gutharraguda*. The area is renowned for its crystal-clear turquoise waters, impressive wildlife such as manta rays, dugongs and dolphins, and beautiful country. Experience this remarkable beauty up close and learn how the Aboriginal people have connected to it and cared for it for thousands of years. Tours include the full-day Kayak and Wildlife Adventure; day tours of the spectacular Hamelin Pool Stromatolites or Francois Peron National Park; the Didgeridoo Dreaming Night tour; and various camping tours.

CONTACT: 0429 708 847; 0432 029 436
www.wulagura.com.au

Wundargoodie Aboriginal Safaris

See the ancient beauty, mystery and diverse culture of the Kimberley through the eyes of the Traditional Owners, Colin and Maria. They have a deep affinity and love for their homeland, and a passion to share the rich culture and history of their people. Their tours traverse the brilliant landscape of the Kimberley while steering clear of the usual tourist spots. Discover gorges, swim in unspoilt rock holes, camp under the stars, and learn about ancient Aboriginal rock art. They also offer the women-only Kimberley Spiritual Experience tour where visitors learn about Aboriginal culture from Aboriginal women.

WHEN: Tours are offered in April to September
CONTACT: 1707 Great Northern Hwy, Wyndham; 0429 928 088.
www.wundargoodie.com.au

ART GALLERIES AND CULTURAL CENTRES

Kepa Kurl Art Gallery and Gift Shop

Located in Esperance Museum Village, the Kepa Kurl Art Gallery supports and promotes local artists. Paintings displayed in the gallery are available for purchase. See also Kepa Kurl Eco Tours listed in the Tours section above.

WHERE: Esperance Museum Village, cnr Dempster and Kemp sts, Esperance.
WHEN: 9 am–4:30 pm daily, October to April and all school and public holidays; 10 am–4 pm May to September.
CONTACT: 08 9072 1688
www.kepakurl.com.au/art.html

Maalinup Aboriginal Gallery

In the Wardandi language from the Busselton area, *maali* means 'black swan' and *up* means place of. Located in the picturesque Swan Valley, Maalinup is the place of the black swan. The gallery is unique to Perth, offering traditional and contemporary artworks, cultural activities, talks and performances. Maalinup specialises in art from the south-west of the Perth area, with works by many celebrated local artists including Naomi Grant, Deborah Bonar, Sheila Humphries, Phillip Narkle and Greg Flahey. Cultural activities include a night-time corroboree with dance, stories and a gourmet 3-course bush-food dinner, a bush-tucker talk and tastings, and a local history, culture and weaponry talk, and more. These activities can be tailored to suit the needs of groups, with prices available on request.

WHERE: 10070 West Swan Rd, Henley Brook.
WHEN: 10 am–5 pm daily; closed Christmas Day, Boxing Day, New Year's Day and Good Friday.
CONTACT: 08 9296 0711; 0411 112 450
www.maalinup.com.au/contact-us

Mangkaja Arts Resource Agency

Mangkaja Arts was established in the late 1980s as a space for local people to paint their histories, personal stories and bush trips. Today the centre functions as a fine art gallery, specialty store and studio space. It represents artists across four language groups within the Fitzroy Valley region: Bunuba and Gooniyandi of *Martuwarra* (river country), and Walmajarri and Wangkajunga from the *Jilji* (sand-hill country of the Great Sandy Desert).

The artists of Mangkaja are distinguished by a style that is uninhibited and lively in its use of colour. While they share land, history and culture, they have various backgrounds and upbringings from the river and desert country. The coming together of a variety of individuals leads to a unique diversity in the artworks, each with distinct influences and vibrant styles. While artists at Mangkaja are best known for their acrylic work on canvas and paper, they also work in printmaking, carving, basket weaving and traditional artefact making.

The art centre has produced many prominent artists, such as Wakartu Cory Surprise (1929–2011), Janangoo Butcher Cherel (1920–2009), Paji Honeychild Yankarr (c.1912–2004), Boxer Yankarr (1930–1995), Nyirlpirr Ngalyaku Spider Snell, Ngarralja Tommy May, Janyka Ivy Nixon (1935–2004), Mawukura Jimmy Nerrimah, Jikila Nada Rawlins and Sonia Kurarra, who are celebrated for their contribution to contemporary Aboriginal art.

WHERE: 8 Bell Rd, Fitzroy Crossing.
WHEN: 11 am–4 pm Monday to Friday.
CONTACT: 08 9191 5833
www.mangkaja.com

Martumili Artists

Martumili Artists was established by the Martu people from the communities of Parnpajinya (Newman), Jigalong, Parnngurr, Punmu, Kunawarritji, Irrungadji and Warralong. These artists are the Traditional Owners of 13 million hectares of land, which traverses the Pilbara region. The country is scattered with significant landforms such as *jila* (waterholes), *jurnu* (soaks), *tuwa* (sand hills) and *warla* (lakes), which hold the age-old stories of the *Jukurrpa* (Dreaming).

Martumili Artists supports the work of established and emerging artists working typically in painting, woodcarvings and artefacts. The artists use bright colours and distinctive shapes and patterns to tell the stories of their ancestors and create striking and unique works. In more recent years, the fibre work of the Martu women has diversified, and includes beautiful, colourful woven baskets. Martu people use their art, and the way it is sold and exhibited, to keep their culture strong and independent in its own right. The artwork is of a very high quality and the cultural significance of the works is undiluted and authentic.

WHERE: East Pilbara Art Centre, Newman Dve, Newman.
WHEN: 10 am–4 pm Monday to Friday; outside of business hours by appointment – please call ahead.
CONTACT: 08 9175 1020
www.martumili.com.au

Mowanjum Art And Culture Centre

The Mowanjum Art and Cultural Centre is the creative home of the Worrorra, Ngarinyin and Wunumbal language groups, of the Mowanjum community just outside the township of Derby. These three clans

Namarali Wandjina spirit design by artist and Worrorra cultural leader Donny Woolagoodja of Mowanjum displayed in the opening ceremony of the Sydney Olympics in 2000

are custodians of the Wandjina law and iconography. The Wandjina spirit has captured the attention of researchers, collectors and the general public alike, and is recognisable throughout the world. A huge Namarali Wandjina, designed by Worrorra cultural leader Donny Woolagoodja, featured in the opening ceremony of the spectacular Sydney Olympics in 2000. The Mowanjum Art and Cultural Centre ensures the preservation and continuation of the Wandjina culture.

The community collection at the art centre contains artworks, materials, photographs and recordings important to the cultural heritage of the Worrorra, Ngarinyin and Wunumbal groups. The artists exhibit their work in a range of mediums including traditional carving and painting, as well as the more contemporary art forms of wood-block and screen printing, to keep the heritage alive.

The art centre holds exhibitions, workshops and community projects, as well as the annual Mowanjum Festival, one of Australia's longest running Indigenous cultural festivals.

WHERE: Gibb River Rd, Derby.
WHEN: 9 am–5 pm Monday to Friday all year; also 10 am–3 pm Saturday and Sunday in the Dry season, May to October.
CONTACT: 08 9191 1008
www.mowanjumarts.com

Warakurna Artists

At the base of the spectacular Rawlinson Ranges in the Gibson Desert, in the Ngaanyatjarra lands of WA is the remote community of Warakurna, which has a long history of artistic expression. The art centre is the energetic, creative and happy hub of the community, where people, young and old, paint the stories of the Tjukurrpa, traditional law and culture and their desert home. The young people learn from their Elders, and their rich culture is alive and strong. Opened in 2005, the art centre studio's supports artists living in Warakurna and the nearby community of Wanarn. Paintings are vibrant and diverse, and unique to each artist.

WHERE: Warakurna community is approximately 330 km from Uluru, near the border with NT.
CONTACT: 08 8955 8099. Contact the art centre to request permission to visit.
warakurnaartists.com.au

Waringarri Aboriginal Arts

Waringarri Aboriginal Arts is set in the heart of the Miriwoong country in the Kimberley, and celebrates the unique culture and country in this region. The art centre was established in the late 1970s, and now supports more than 100 artists from the township of Kununurra and its surroundings. Miriwoong land stretches across a large area, which straddles the WA and NT border and includes Kununurra, Lake Argyle, the Keep River and the Ord River Irrigation area. In the *Ngarranggarni*, or Dreaming, spirits roamed the land and created the natural features of the landscape, imparting a deep spirituality within the country. Aboriginal people have significant cultural responsibilities to care for this country. Artistic expression, particularly painting, communicates this knowledge and ensures culture remains strong.

The Waringarri Aboriginal Arts centre is an environment of collaborative creativity, where the rich Miriwoong culture is alive and growing, shared between the artists, the community and visitors alike. Artists work in a range of mediums, including painting, printmaking, woodcarving, boab engraving, sculpting and textile art.

The art centre offers a range of authentic cultural tours led by local Miriwoong guides. They range in duration from 1 hour to 5½ hours and in price from $55 to $225 for an adult. Bookings well in advance are essential for all tours. Contact Waringarri for more information and bookings.

WHERE: 16 Speargrass Rd, Kununurra; a 2-minute drive from the centre of Kununurra.
WHEN: 8:30 am–4:30 pm Monday to Friday; also 10 am–2 pm Saturday, May to September.
CONTACT: 08 9168 2212
www.waringarriarts.com.au

Warlayirti Artists Aboriginal Corporation

The small Aboriginal community of Wirrimanu sits on the edge of the Great Sandy and Tanami deserts. It is part of the *Luurna Tjurkurpa*, or Kingfisher, Dreaming and is a ceremonial hub for several clan groups from the Western Desert and Kimberley regions. Warlayirti Artists Aboriginal Corporation was established in the 1980s to keep the rich culture of this community alive. Today it supports approximately 200 artists from the communities of Wirrimanu, Mulan and Kururrungku, including some of Australia's most highly regarded and well-known Aboriginal artists.

The artists of Warlayirti mainly belonging to the Kukatja, Walmatjarri, Ngarti, Jaru, Wangkatjunga, Pintupi and Warlpiri language groups, and work in a range of traditional and contemporary art styles. While they have gained a reputation as producers of unique and vibrant paintings, they also produce original etchings, film, photography and music. In addition to the gallery and painting studio, Warlayirti Art Centre includes a large culture gallery, archive and new media centre.

WHERE: Wirrimanu (Balgo) community is accessible off the Tanami Track, which runs between the Stuart Hwy in the NT and the Great Northern Track in WA. The Tanami Track starts approximately 20 km north of Alice Springs and 17 km south-west of Halls Creek, and then after the turn-off to Wirrimanu (Balgo) the access road is 31 km. The drive is 3½ hours from Halls Creek and 9 hours from Alice Springs. 4WD recommended.
WHEN: 10 am–4 pm Monday to Friday. Weekends and other times by appointment only. Contact the art centre prior to visiting, including during the week.

PERMITS: Only required for overnight stays.
CONTACT: 08 9168 8960
www.balgoart.org.au

Warmun Art Centre

Warmun Art Centre is owned and governed by the Gija people of northern WA. It was established in 1998 and now represents almost 60 established and emerging artists. The current artists maintain many of the traditions initiated by previous artists, and in doing so they conserve the culturally significant knowledge systems and traditions of the Gija people. The Warmun Artists are among some of Australia's leading contemporary Aboriginal artists, and their work is exhibited nationally, in flagship art institutions such as the Art Gallery of Western Australia, Art Gallery of New South Wales, the National Gallery of Australia and National Gallery of Victoria, and internationally.

Warmum Art Centre includes a gallery and an art studio. The gallery displays many contemporary Gija artworks and is one of the Kimberley region's most significant attractions. Each year thousands of visitors come to engage with Gija culture.

WHERE: 200 km south of Kununurra. From Warmun Roadhouse, take the Great Northern Hwy southwest for 2 km. Turn left at the 'Warmun Art Centre' sign, follow the road over the bridge and up a small rise, then veer right to the front of the gallery.
PERMITS: Warmun Art Centre is part of an Aboriginal community. Visitors need a verbal permit to enter, which can be arranged by calling the gallery.
CONTACT: 08 9168 7496
warmunart.com.au

Yamaji Art

Yamaji Art is an emerging, contemporary Aboriginal art centre on Yamaji land in Geraldton. Yamaji country covers nearly one-fifth of the state of WA, and includes coastal, regional and remote areas. The culture of the Yamaji remains strong today and the stories of their Dreaming continue to shape their laws, customs and lives.

Servicing a broad area of Yamaji country in the mid-west region of WA, Yamaji Art mainly represents the Amangu, Nhanagardi, Naaguja, Badimaya, Wajarri and Wilunyu language groups. The artwork celebrates the huge diversity within this region, showcasing a range of styles in various mediums including painting, textiles, weaving, printmaking, design and performance. The art centre has an exhibition gallery, a sales outlet and an artist studio and workshop.

WHERE: 205 Marine Tce, Geraldton.
WHEN: 9 am–4 pm Monday to Friday. Weekends by appointment.
CONTACT: 08 9965 3440
www.yamajiart.com

PLACES

Roelands Village

Situated 2 hours from Perth, Roelands Village was originally known as Roelands Mission, used to house Aboriginal children who had been forcibly removed from their homes from the 1940s to the 1970s. Today, it is run by the former 'Mission kids' and has become a place of healing. The Village comprises 500 acres of farmland and bushland, grows citrus fruit and bush tucker, and offers accommodation, conference and catering facilities. You can book any of the 15 nicely furnished houses, one with wheelchair access.

WHERE: 575 Seven Hills Rd, Roelands.
WHEN: Extended stays, conference facilities and catering available on request.
COST: Contact Roelands Village directly for information.
CONTACT: 08 9726 3606
www.roelandsvillage.com.au

3

NEW SOUTH WALES

FESTIVALS

Yabun Festival

Held every year on Australia Day or Survival Day, 26 January, Yabun Festival is a celebration of Aboriginal culture on a day that signifies for many Aboriginal people the beginning of the invasion of their country. The festival started in the inner-city suburb Redfern in 2003 as way for Aboriginal people to be together for Survival Day. It is now Sydney's largest Survival Day event and a beautiful community gathering where people from all backgrounds come together. *Yabun* is a Gadigal word meaning 'music to a beat' and the festival is filled with live music from the morning to the evening, with performances by Aboriginal artists and a corroboree ground with traditional dancing, as well as more than 100 stalls selling food and merchandise, and the Speak Out Tent where Aboriginal community members conduct a panel discussion. In Jarjum's Tent there are children's activities and Aboriginal Elders read to them and tell stories. This is a great way for visitors to experience Aboriginal culture, especially on such a significant day in Aboriginal and Australian history.

WHERE: Victoria Park, cnr Parramatta and City rds, Camperdown, Sydney.
WHEN: Annually on 26 January, 10 am–7 pm.
COST: Free admission.
CONTACT: 02 9384 4000; yabun.org.au

SPORT

The Harvey Norman Rugby League All Stars Match

This is a must see for all Rugby League fans and anyone who enjoys watching great sport. The Harvey Norman Rugby League All Stars Match is a spectacular celebration of Rugby and Aboriginal and Torres Strait Islander culture. The match features the Indigenous All Stars versus the World All Stars. Both teams play with vigour and passion, making it one of the most significant NRL (National Rugby League) matches in the season. With traditional Aboriginal dancing before the match, the atmosphere of the All Stars Match will excite even those spectators who have never watched a NRL match before. It is essential to book tickets early so check the website to find out when they will go on sale

WHERE: The venue changes yearly; in 2017 the game was held in Newcastle.
WHEN: Usually held in the second week of February. Details about the date, location and ticket prices will be available on the website in the weeks leading up to the game.
allstars.nrl.com

NATIONAL PARKS

The NSW National Parks and Wildlife Service manages more than 870 national parks and reserves in the state, covering over 7 million hectares of land. In addition to the parks included here, visitors can find out about the many others at: www.nationalparks.nsw.gov.au/visit-a-park

Bundjalung National Park

Bundjalung National Park, on the north coast of NSW, is one of the most beautiful national parks in Australia, with its scenic coastlines and lush bushland. It stretches north from Iluka to Evans Head, and meets the Pacific Ocean on the east. The park is in the land of the Bundjalung people.

ABORIGINAL CULTURAL HERITAGE: This park is one of a group where the Bundjalung people's native title rights have been recognised and is one of four determinations of native title rights in NSW. Native title rights come from the Bundjalung people's traditional laws and customs and legally recognises their connection to country. This means that these lands will continue to be places of Indigenous ceremony, learning and inspiration for generations to come.

Dreamtime stories tell of how animals helped to shape the land. At the centre of the Bundjalung beliefs is the battle between the Goanna and the Snake. They formed the Evans River as they fought, creating the headland coast known today as Evans Head.

The Gummigurrah area in the park was once used as a winter camp for the Bundjalung people and the remains of a midden can be seen near the end of the Gummigurrah walking track, located close to the Evans Head entrance.

WHERE: The closest town is Evans Head.
WHEN: Open all year round, however can be subject to closure due to bad weather or danger of fires. The New South Wales National Parks and Wildlife Service recommends visiting during spring, as this is whale-spotting season. Winter can be nice to escape the scorching summer heat, and it can still be warm enough to swim.
CAMPING: There are two campgrounds, Black Rocks, with 52 sites, and Woody Head, with 94 sites. The rates and availability of sites at the Black Rocks and Woody Head campgrounds are displayed when making an online booking. Black Rocks: www.nationalparks.nsw.gov.au/camping-and-accommodation/campgrounds/black-rocks-campground; Woody Head: www.nationalparks.nsw.gov.au/camping-and-accommodation/campgrounds/woody-head-campground
COST: $8 per vehicle per day. Visitors planning to go to a few national parks in NSW can purchase an All Parks Pass. For details see: www.nationalparks.nsw.gov.au/visit-a-park/parks/bundjalung-national-park/visitor-info#Fees-and-passes
CONTACT: Clarence North Area: 02 6641 1500; 8.30 am–4.30 pm Monday to Friday. Alstonville: 02 6627 0200; 8.30 am–4.30 pm Monday, Tuesday, Thursday and Friday; closed for lunch 12–1 pm.
www.nationalparks.nsw.gov.au/visit-a-park/parks/bundjalung-national-park

Kosciuszko National Park

Located in the Snowy Mountains, Kosciuszko National Park boasts Australia's largest and highest continental mountain, Mt Kosciuszko. With 7 adventure-filled areas within the park, visitors who love the outdoors will never be idle here.

ABORIGINAL CULTURAL HERITAGE: The park is in the lands of the Ngarigo people, around Cooma, and the Bidawal people, from around Bombala. Today there are many people living in south-eastern Australia who have traditional connections to the Australian Alps. Aboriginal campsites dating back 20000

years have been found within the valleys of the Snowy Mountains and along the upper Snowy River, and prehistoric burial sites are also found in the Snowy Mountains. In 2011, a memorandum of understanding was signed by Tumut Brungle Gundagai Area Aboriginal community and NPNSW to ensure that the local Aboriginal community is involved in the management of culturally significant areas of northern Kosciuszko National Park.

WHAT TO DO: The Thredbo-Perisher area is the gateway to Mt Kosciuszko. It is ideal in winter for visitors who love to ski and snowboard in the fresh snow. Lower Snowy River area allows visitors to camp beside the Snowy River and explore the area by walking, cycling or horse riding. Khancoban area is perfect for visitors who enjoy fishing and hiking. Selwyn area is where visitors can find the family-friendly Selwyn Snow resort. Yarrangobilly area has incredible caves and thermal pools. Tumut area is full of walking trails and waterfalls. Visitors can also participate in water sports at the Blowering Dam. High Plains area is ideal in summer to explore the walking trails and gorges. Located on the north-east side of Kosciuszko National Park, it is the perfect place to camp in summer.
WHERE: Snowy Mountains. For the many entrances to the park check the website.
WHEN: All year round. Some roads and trails may be closed due to park maintenance or poor weather conditions.
COST: The cost for each of the seven areas differs depending on the season (winter or summer), and visitor's intentions (i.e., camping, skiing, trail walking, driving, etc.). For the full range of fees, see the websites:
Thredbo-Perisher: www.nationalparks.nsw.gov.au/visit-a-park/parks/thredbo-perisher-area
Lower Snowy River: /www.nationalparks.nsw.gov.au/visit-a-park/parks/lower-snowy-river-area
Khancoban: www.nationalparks.nsw.gov.au/visit-a-park/parks/khancoban-area
Selwyn: www.nationalparks.nsw.gov.au/visit-a-park/parks/selwyn-area
Yarrangobilly: www.nationalparks.nsw.gov.au/visit-a-park/parks/yarrangobilly-area
Tumut: www.nationalparks.nsw.gov.au/visit-a-park/parks/tumut-area
High Plains: www.nationalparks.nsw.gov.au/visit-a-park/parks/high-plains-area
CONTACT: Snowy Region Visitor Centre, 49 Kosciuszko Rd, Jindabyne; 02 6450 5600; 8.30 am–5 pm daily; closed Christmas Day.
www.nationalparks.nsw.gov.au/visit-a-park/parks/kosciuszko-national-park

TOURS

Aboriginal Blue Mountains Walkabout

Located about 2 hours west of Sydney, the Blue Mountains is one of the largest national parks in NSW. Local Darug man, Evan Yanna Muru, owns and operates the Blue Mountains Walkabout guided tours. Evan is a member of the Darug clan and a fully accredited wilderness guide, having worked for the Blue Mountains National Park and Wildlife Service as an Aboriginal Discovery Ranger.

On the tour, visitors have the opportunity to connect with Aboriginal country and culture in a deep and meaningful way. The bushwalk goes for 2 hours and covers 3.5 km. Visitors will see incredible sandstone caves, rock pools, waterfalls and rainforests, and Evan will point out and explain the significance of scared areas and sites along the way. After the walk visitors will spend the next 4 hours taking part in activities that offer insights into the ways the custodians of the land, the Darug people, traditionally used and cared for the land.

Visitors should bring lunch, water, rain jacket if rain is expected, swimmers are optional though highly recommended, water shoes, jacket as the area can be cooler than Sydney even in summer, sunscreen and hat, camera, and importantly a bag for any rubbish.

Top: Evan Yanna Muru running the Aboriginal Blue Mountains Walkabout Tour

Bottom: Summer scenery in the Snowy Mountains, Kosciuszko National Park

The tour is suitable for anyone 7–70 years of age, who is in good health; reasonable fitness and mobility are required as it is medium grade walk and medium gradient track.

WHERE: The tour starts and finishes in the Blue Mountains on the Faulconbridge railway station platform. Visitors can get there via train or car. Those travelling by car will find free parking along Railway Avenue. Those travelling by train can come from Sydney (1 hour 20 minutes) or Katoomba (30 minutes). At Sydney's Central Station trains leave from the country platforms.
WHEN: 10:50 am–4:30 pm. Tours are run all year round; the walkabout route changes depending on the season. In summer the route will accommodate to the hot weather and rest stops will be included to keep visitors cool; in winter the tour will include warm rest stops in the caves with a fire.
COST: $95 per person. Payments available online or in cash on the day. No refunds or bad-weather cancellations. Limited to 10 people per walkabout group, bookings are essential.
CONTACT: 0408 443 822
www.bluemountainswalkabout.com

Dreamtime Southern X

Operating out of central Sydney, Dreamtime Southern X is owned and run by Aunty Margret Campbell, an Indigenous woman who was raised in Dunghutti country on the north-east coast of NSW. Margret was educated from age 5 in her traditional custodianship, the Baranbyatti Mirra Buuka (Dreamtime Southern Cross), and encapsulates the living wisdom of her ancestors' Dreamtime. Margret has had a long career as an accredited teacher and has applied this knowledge to Dreamtime Southern X, which offers the The Rocks Dreaming Aboriginal Heritage Tour for individual tourists. The tour departs daily at 10 am from Cadman's Cottage and makes a total of 7 stops at significant sites during a 90-minute walk around The Rocks. Tours give insights into the ancient heritage of the Aboriginal people of Sydney Harbour and their use of and connection to the Harbour's waterways and foreshores.

WHERE: Cadman's Cottage, 110 George St, The Rocks, Sydney.
COST: The Rocks Dreaming Aboriginal Heritage Tour: adults: $44; children: $32. Tours must be booked in advance by phone or on the website.
CONTACT: 02 9517 4390; 0428 661 019
www.dreamtimesouthernx.com.au

Top right: On a bushwalk with Kane Ardler, Booderee National Park

Bottom left: Aunty Margret Campbell, owner–operator of Dreamtime Southern X, running The Rocks Dreaming Aboriginal Hertiage Tour

Bottom right: Tour guide Harry Nanya pointing to uncovered bones in Mungo National Park

Galamban Extraordinary Aboriginal Experiences (Booderee National Park)

Galamban owners Markeeta, Julie and Clive are the Traditional Owners of the Booderee National Park area and are passionate about preserving and promoting their heritage and the knowledge of their ancestors through art. Galamban operates out of the Aboriginal community at Wreck Bay and offers visitors a wide variety of bushwalks focussing on nature and wildlife, and cultural programs that include fire-side storytelling and weaving workshops, as well as children-specific lessons designed to awaken a curiosity and respect for the diverse wildlife of the region.

In 2014 Galamban was awarded the New South Wales South Coast Tourism Awards Gold Medal for Excellence in Indigenous Tourism, and received international acclaim at the Virgin Holidays Responsible Tourism Awards in London where, in partnership with Booderee National Park, it won the category of Best Conservation of Cultural Heritage in 2010.

WHERE: Dhugan Close, Wreck Bay Aboriginal community. The community is located on the Bherriwerri Peninsula, the southern arm of the Jervis Bay territory; about 2 km south of the Jervis Bay airport and 6.6 km by car from Jervis Bay village.
CONTACT: 02 4442 1117
www.galamban.net

Harry Nanya Tours

Harry Nanya is a Paakantyi man from the ancient Lake Mungo area. Lake Mungo is a part of the Willandra Lakes system, which was listed as a World Heritage site in 1981. Now it is acknowledged to be one the oldest places for human occupation in the world, dating back around 60 000 years. The lakes dried up approximately 18 000 years ago. Its shores, known as 'The Walls of China' or 'Lunette' for the 30 km crescent shape of the sand dunes, shows clear evidence of the campfires of the Aboriginal people as they sat around the once-full lake. Harry has been taking visitors on day tours and sunset tours of this region for the past 20 years. Some of the significant sites that his tour visits include a 2km walk around the Walls of China, the Lake Mungo information centre, historic woolshed, and Mungo Lookout, where visitors can look out over Lake Mungo.

WHERE: Tour pickups are from Wentworth NSW, or Mildura VIC; or visitors can drive their own vehicle.
WHEN: November to March daily; closed Christmas Day and New Year's Day. All-day tours take about 8 hours.
COST: Prices vary and a family discount is offered (2 adults, 2 children). Bookings are essential.
CONTACT: 03 5027 2076
harrynanyatours.com.au

Jibbon Aboriginal Carvings Tour – Sydney Coast Walks

The Jibbon Aboriginal Carvings Tour is an Aboriginal heritage and cultural discovery tour run by Sydney Coast Walks, a family-owned tour operator that has been in business since 2009. The 5 km-long Jibbon guided walk departs from Bundeena ferry wharf and follows the coastal track to Jibbon Beach through Australia's oldest national park, Royal National Park, and back to Bundeena on a return track and takes 3 hours to complete. During the walk, guests will learn about the Dharawal people, the Traditional Owners of the land, as well as seeing 3000-year-old shell middens, 1000-year-old rock engravings and even get the chance to forage for, taste and smell traditional bush foods and medicines used by the Dharawal people for thousands of years. The track is in good condition with minimal elevation and only a few stairs, making for a pleasant walk along the isolated and peaceful stretch of coast.

TIPS FOR VISITORS: Guests should wear comfortable walking shoes and, as the walk takes place along the coast, bring a hat, sunscreen and water.
WHERE: Tours depart from the Cronulla ferry wharf. Trains run from the centre of Sydney to Cronulla station, a 3-minute walk from the wharf. Cronulla ferry wharf is also accessible by car and free parking is available in the surrounding streets.
WHEN: Meet at 8:15 am for the 8:30 am ferry from Cronulla to Bundeena.
COST: First guest $397; each additional guest: $47. Morning tea, Royal National Park entry fees and the return ferry from Cronulla to Bundeena are included in the tour price.
CONTACT: 02 9188 7897
www.sydneycoastwalks.com.au/product/jibbon-aboriginal-carvings/

Kadoo Indigenous and Historical Tours

Kadoo Tours is owned and operated by Tim Ella, a member of the Yuin-Dharawal nation, and Grant Hyde, a local writer and historian. They offer a 90-minute walkabout cultural tour to Watsons Bay, which is a 10-minute ferry ride from the centre of Sydney, and a 2-hour Discovery cultural tour to historic La Perouse, 14 km from the city, as well as private walking tours. While each tour is different, all visitors will have the opportunity to walk along the coastline and through the surrounding bush, try bush tucker, learn about Gadigal culture, and be welcomed with a traditional ochre ceremony.

WHERE: For details about the meeting place for each tour and other information visit the website.
WHEN: Sundays and public holidays.
COST: Adults: $44; child 5–11 years: $32; family pass is available.
CONTACT: Grant Hyde: 0409 922 364
www.kadootours.com.au

Top: Jibbon Aboriginal Carvings Tour is a pleasant walk through Royal National Park

Bottom left: Dallas Kilponen running a tour through La Perouse with Kadoo Indigenous and Historical Tours

Bottom right: Thousand-year-old rock engravings seen on the Jibbon Aboriginal Carvings Tour

Top: Traditional smoking ceremony by Ngaran Ngaran in Narooma

Right: Glamping tents provided on Ngaran Ngaran's 2-day Djirranganj Dreaming Tour

Bottom: Guided tour of Mutawinjti National Park with Mutawintji Eco Tours

Mutawintji Eco Tours

Mutawintji Eco Tours is owned by the larger Tri State Safaris, which runs small-group tours through Mutawintji National Park led by accredited Aboriginal guides. Visitors will be shown around the national park and surrounding sites of significance in air-conditioned 4WDs, and can rest assured that all tours have been awarded Advanced Eco-Certification and emphasise leaving as little impact on the ecology of the region as possible. There are a variety of single- and multi-day tours to choose from, and guests also have the option of participating in a tour of their choice with their own vehicle through the tag-along options offered.

TIPS FOR VISITORS: Some tours include walking to reach some of the sites and although the pace is quite slow, the ground can be uneven. It is advised that guests wear sturdy, rubber-soled shoes and bring water, sunscreen and insect repellent.
WHERE: 422 Argent St, Broken Hill (office address).
CONTACT: 1300 688 225. Bookings should be made in advance. For details on specific tours and booking forms visit the website.
www.tristate.com.au/tours-old/mutawintji-eco-tours

Ngaran Ngaran Cultural Awareness

Ngaran Ngaran Cultural Awareness (NNCA) was established in 2011 and is an Aboriginal-owned and operated business and Tourism Australia accredited Indigenous Tourism Champion located on the NSW far south coast on Yuin country. Owner and operator Dwanye Bannon-Harrison created NNCA to pass on the legacies left to him by his family over 17 years of traditional teaching in Yuin country.

Ngaran Ngaran offers a range of workshops, performances and multi-day tours, including their ever-popular Gulaga Creation Tour, which gives participants a 2-night, fully guided walking tour departing from the Island View Resort in the Narooma region of the south coast. It includes traditional performances, ceremonies, a guided mountain hike up Gulaga Mountain, and meals.

Ngaran Ngaran have recently partnered with Tilba Lake Camp to create a 2-night glamping experience in their Djirranganj Dreaming Tour, offering participants a fully guided bus tour of the Yuin region, with traditional ceremonies, a fully guided tour of the Djirringanj Dreaming Trail, luxury accommodation in twin-share or solo glamping tents, and Indigenous-inspired meals served with ocean views.

WHERE: Narooma and the Tilba region are 4½ hours drive south of Sydney, or 3 hours drive east of Canberra. Bus transfers are available from the local Moruya airport as well as Sydney and Canberra airports at additional costs.
COST: Djirranganj Dreaming Tour: $800 per person; Gulaga Creation Tour: $605 per person. Ngaran Ngaran tours depart on set dates and advanced bookings are essential. Tour dates, booking forms and additional details can be found on the website.
CONTACT: 0408 272 121
www.ngaranaboriginalculture.com

Nura Diya – Taronga's Aboriginal Discovery Tour

Set in traditional Cammeraigal country, Taronga Zoo has many amazing Aboriginal stories to tell. *Nura Diya*, meaning 'this country or camp', takes visitors on a journey through Taronga. Developed with the local Indigenous community and led by an Aboriginal guide, visitors will hear the guide's own personal stories, and discover their important connections to the land, animals and nature. Visitors will see Australia's amazing animals in a new light, as they discover the binding relationships between flora and fauna and hear stories of the Dreaming, describing the creation of creatures and the landscape. They will also learn about the centuries-old traditional uses of plants for food and medicine, and enjoy interactive experiences with unique Australian wildlife.

WHERE: Taronga Zoo, Bradley's Head Rd, Mosman.
WHEN: Tours start at 9.45 am Monday, Wednesday, Friday; 1½ –2 hours duration.
COST: Adult: $99; child 4–15 years: $69. Bookings must be made 3 days in advance.
CONTACT: 02 9969 2777
taronga.org.au/taronga-zoo/tours/nura-diya

Royal Botanic Garden Sydney Aboriginal Heritage Experiences

In addition to the breathtaking views of the Harbour, the Royal Botanic Garden Sydney also offers immersive Aboriginal Heritage experiences, presenting the culture of the Traditional Owners of the Sydney city land area, the Cadigal people of the Eora Nation. Regular guided tours give visitors insights into the plants in the gardens and their significance for and use by the Cadigal people, as well as an opportunity to taste some of the fruits and herbs. Those wanting to learn the history of the Sydney region can walk along the Cadi Jam Ora (First Encounters) walk and read the information boards presented there, and see some of the plant life introduced by the First Fleet in 1788 in the First Farm Garden.

There are also occasional one-off Aboriginal cultural experiences and tours, such as bush-food foraging or artist workshops. These offer participants a deeper look at certain aspects of Aboriginal life and culture, and are advertised on the Royal Botanic Gardens website ahead of time.

WHERE: The Royal Botanic Garden Sydney are located in central Sydney. Aboriginal heritage tours depart from the Garden Shop inside the Gardens.
WHEN: The Royal Botanic Gardens Sydney open from 7 am daily but closing times change seasonally, details are available on the website or at the Gardens. Tours are run every Wednesday, Friday and Saturday at 10 am, departing from the Garden Shop.
COST: Entry to the Gardens is free; Aboriginal Heritage tours: adult: $40; children under 7 years: free.
CONTACT: 02 9231 8111
www.rbgsyd.nsw.gov.au

Sand Dune Adventures

Sand Dune Adventures offer quad bike and hummer tours of sand dunes in the Port Stephens area. Owned and operated by the Worimi Local Aboriginal Land Council, the company is a multi-award winning tourism operator based in Port Stephens. A number of tour packages are available, and quad bikes and safety gear come in both adult and child sizes. Visitors can choose from the 1½-hour hummer tour, or various quad bike tours ranging from 1–2 hours. On the tours visitors will explore the area, which is rich in shell middens, Aboriginal burial and tool making sites, shipwrecks and even WWII tank traps. Experienced guides ensure that visitors have a safe, informative, and enjoyable experience.

WHERE: 2163 Nelson Bay Rd, Williamtown (booking office).
WHEN: Hummer tours: Monday to Saturday; quad bike tours: Monday to Sunday.
COST: 1½-hour Hummer tour: adult: $55; child: $35; family (2 adults, 2 children): $155. Quad bike tours range from $110–$165 per adult; $65–$110 per child, depending on length. Book tours in advance; discounts are available on online bookings.
CONTACT: 02 4033 8808
www.sandduneadventures.com.au

Top: Tour the sand dunes outside Port Stephens on quad bikes with Sand Dune Adventures

Bottom left: Food foraged on the Aboriginal Bush Food Experience at the Royal Botanic Garden Sydney

Bottom right: Art produced during the Aboriginal Art Experience at the Royal Botanic Garden Sydney

Top: Visit Be-lang-le-wool (Clark Island National Park) to learn about the Indigenous coastal lifestyle

Bottom left: One of the crew of Tribal Warrior's tour boat, *Mari Nawi*

Bottom right: Man in traditional paint plays the didgeridoo in an Aboriginal cultural performance run by Tribal Warrior

Tribal Warrior

On a Tribal Warrior tour, visitors cruise the most beautiful harbour in the world aboard the *Mari Nawi* (Big Canoe), hear stories of the Cadigal, Guringai, Wangal, Gammeraigal and Wallumedegal people of Sydney Harbour and learn the Aboriginal names and meanings of significant Sydney landmarks, before stepping ashore on Be-lang-le-wool (Clark Island National Park). On the island, they are taken on a journey into the Indigenous coastal lifestyle, learning traditional fishing methods and food-gathering techniques, before participating in an exciting Aboriginal cultural performance.

COST: Adult: $60; concession: $45; children: $40. Price includes: 2-hour cruise with cultural commentary; tour on Clark Island National Park; cultural performance; tea and coffee. Tour needs a minimum 30, maximum 140 people in order to run.
WHERE: Departs from Eastern Pontoon, Circular Quay.
CONTACT: 02 9699 3491
www.tribalwarrior.org

ART GALLERIES AND CULTURAL CENTRES

Art Gallery of New South Wales

The Art Gallery of New South Wales in Sydney is one of Australia's leading public galleries. It displays both national and international art in its permanent galleries and in major exhibitions held throughout the year. The Art Gallery is proud of its strong collection of Aboriginal and Torres Strait Islander art, showcased in the Yiribana Gallery. *Yiribana* means 'this way' in the language of the Eora people and acknowledges that the Art Gallery stands on Gadigal land. The Yiribana Gallery celebrates Indigenous Australia's rich cultural heritage and contemporary expression, and artists from across Australia and the Torres Strait are represented here. The Yiribana Project Space houses a range of changing exhibitions. Visitors can also enjoy the Art Gallery's program of tours, lectures, performances and films, as well as its extensive educational program and activities for children.

WHERE: Art Gallery Rd, The Domain, Sydney.
WHEN: 10 am–5 pm daily; 10 am–10 pm Wednesday for Art After Hours. Closed Christmas Day and Good Friday.
COST: Free general admission. Some exhibitions are ticketed; check the website for details.
CONTACT: 02 9225 1700
www.artgallery.nsw.gov.au

Blak Markets

Blak Markets are Indigenous art and craft markets that are now run every few months at La Perouse and Barangaroo in Sydney. A feature of the markets are the many stalls selling artworks and craft created by Aboriginal artists from all around Australia. The markets start with a welcome to country and a smoking at 10 am. Throughout the day there are various workshops, such as making shell work and weaving, as well as Aboriginal dance performances, cooking demonstrations, and children's activities. Blak Markets is also a micro business hub for Indigenous businesses, providing economic development opportunities to Indigenous people. As well, Blak Markets trains and employs young Aboriginal people in barista, retail, food preparation and supervision, and they can then work in the pop-up coffee, food and retail stores at the markets.

WHERE: La Perouse and Barangaroo; also Blak Markets pop-up shops and online store.
WHEN: Blak Markets are held about 8 times a year. For market dates and addresses see Blak Markets' website.
CONTACT: 0427 824059
blakmarkets.com

Dunghutti-Ngaku Aboriginal Art Gallery

This proudly Aboriginal-owned art gallery in South Kempsey displays works from established and emerging artists from the local area and other regions. The gallery, designed by internationally renowned architect Glenn Murcutt, is located on the land of the Dunghutti people, on the mid-north coast of New South Wales. There are always changing exhibitions for visitors to see, and most of the art is available for purchase from the gallery and online. If purchasing online, shipping is available nationally and internationally.

WHERE: Kempsey Visitor Information Center, 62–118 Lachlan St, South Kempsey.
WHEN: 10 am–4 pm Tuesday to Sunday.
COST: Free admission.
CONTACT: 02 6562 1432
www.dnaag.com.au

Minjungbal Aboriginal Cultural Centre

The Minjungbal Aboriginal Cultural Centre, at the main entrance of Tweed Heads Historic Site National Park, gives visitors a unique insight into the local Aboriginal culture. Run by the area's Aboriginal community, it is a popular meeting place for Goori people and other Aboriginal peoples. It is also a popular destination for school excursions and for individuals who want to learn about local Aboriginal culture. In the centre there are museum exhibits, informative videos, Aboriginal art exhibitions, and sometimes there are outdoor performances of traditional dance and song.

Aboriginal guides offer tours through the museum and site, explaining the significance of its relics and sharing information about the local plants and animals. Visitors will gain an insight into what Aboriginal life was like when this area was an untouched paradise of natural forest and mangroves, and then learn about the cultural significance of the bora ring located on the Walk on Water walking track.

The centre is fully wheelchair accessible, and the amenities include picnic tables, barbecue facilities and drinking water. No pets or smoking allowed.

WHERE: Tweed Heads Historic Site, Kirkwood Rd, South Tweed Heads. It is accessible by bus, then a short walk from the bus stop at Tweed City Shopping Centre.
WHEN: 10 am–3 pm Monday to Thursday.
COST: Adult: $15; concession: $7.50.
CONTACT: 07 5524 2109
www.nationalparks.nsw.gov.au/things-to-do/visitor-centres/minjungbal-aboriginal-cultural-centre

DANCE

Bangarra

Dance is an important part of Aboriginal and Torres Strait Islander life. It is an ancient form of storytelling that connects people with their spirits, ancestors, community and traditional lands, and it is a vibrant part of Indigenous culture today.

Since it was founded in 1989, Bangarra has inspired audiences nationally and internationally. Its performances of powerful and emotive dance and music bring together the contemporary and traditional duality of Aboriginal and Torres Strait Islander culture. For the artistic director, Stephen Page, the dance company's relationship with Aboriginal and Torres Strait Islander communities and respected Elders remains at the heart of Bangarra. Stories for the company's productions are gathered from around the country and performed by highly skilled artists – each with their own proud Aboriginal

Top: *Dingo Family* by Mabel Ritchie, exhibited at Dunghutti-Ngaku Aboriginal Art Gallery

Bottom: *EORA-Bennelong* art installation, performed by Bangarrra Dance Theatre, projected on the south pylon of the Sydney Harbour Bridge during Vivd Sydney, 2017

and/or Torres Strait Islander background that drives their passion and influences their styles of dance.

Bangarra tours nationally in the major cities and in regional Australia, and also regularly tours internationally. Each production displays the wonderful diversity that is Aboriginal and Torres Strait Islander Australia.

CONTACT: 02 9251 5333
For dates, locations and ticket prices visit: www.bangarra.com.au

PLACES

Redfern

This inner-city suburb has long been home to Sydney's largest Aboriginal community. Redfern is a place that reflects the history of Aboriginal people: the dispossession, the discontent, the government policies, and the social and racial prejudices. However, it also represents the resilience and strength of the Aboriginal people.

Redfern is the cultural, economical, and political Indigenous epicentre for Indigenous people living in Sydney, where people gather for celebrations and protests. It is where the Redfern All Blacks, an Indigenous Rugby team, was established. In Redfern Park the then Australian prime minister Paul Keating delivered his national Redfern Park Speech that marked a pivotal moment in Australian and Indigenous Australian history. Keating gave the speech during the Year for the World's Indigenous People in 1992.

Redfern will always be a significant place for Aboriginal people. Today in the suburb there are sporting, legal, fitness and health, and support services that have been established by Aboriginal people, for the Aboriginal community. It is also a place for people of all backgrounds and from all walks of life to gather and celebrate life and culture together. The Yabun Festival was initially held at Redfern Park, but since its growth it has moved to the Victoria Park.

Visitors can walk through the streets of Redfern, respectful of the suburb's importance to the Indigenous people who live there, and take in the amazing artwork on many walls and public places, including the murals *40,000 Years is a Long Long Time (40,000 Years)*, *Welcome to Redfern/The Block*, *Mission Boy Dreams*, and the large mural of the Aboriginal flag at the site of the Redfern Aboriginal Tent Embassy.

WHERE: Redfern is a 15-minute drive or train trip from the centre of Sydney.

4
VICTORIA

FESTIVALS

Tanderrum

Tanderrum is a momentous and spectacular gathering of the five clans of the Kulin nation – Boonwurrung, Dja Dja Wurrung, Taungurung, Wathaurung and Woiwurrung. Each year it opens the Melbourne Festival, which means that the first words spoken in the festival come from the Traditional Owners of the land. Tanderrum celebrates '*Nugul-bulok. Ngarra. Nurru-nurru. Yinga*' – 'Stories. Dance. Ochre. Song', and pays respect to Victorian Aboriginal culture. The 5 clans come together in the centre of Melbourne to perform traditional dances for each other and for crowds of people from all over Australia and the world. A welcome to country ceremony is held and then the dancing begins. It is truly a sight to behold and an extremely significant traditional event. Tanderrum is facilitated by the Ilbijerri Theatre Company, Australia's leading and longest running Aboriginal and Torres Strait Islander theatre company.

Permission is required to film, photograph or record the ceremony.

WHERE: Tanderrum: Federation Square, cnr Flinders and Swanston sts, Melbourne; Ilbijerri Theatre Company: Meat Market, 5 Blackwood St, North Melbourne.
WHEN: Tanderrum: on the first day of the Melbourne Festival in October annually.
COST: Free.
CONTACT: Melbourne Festival: 03 9662 4242; Ilbijerri Theatre Company: 03 9329 9097
Tanderrum: www.festival.melbourne
Ilbijerri Theatre Company: http://ilbijerri.com.au

SPORT

Dreamtime at the G

Dreamtime at the G is held at the Melbourne Cricket Ground (MCG) during the Indigenous Round of the Australian Football League (AFL) season. Typically held in Round 10, in the last week of May, the Indigenous Round commemorates all the Indigenous players who have contributed to the hugely popular sport of football. It is way for all Australians to respect and pay tribute to the Indigenous presence within football and sport. The round itself is named in honour of Sir Doug Nicholls, an inspiring person and former football player who represented the spirit of reconciliation between Indigenous and non-Indigenous Australians.

While there are many games played in the Indigenous round, the match between Richmond and Essendon football clubs is the most highly anticipated. The day starts with the customary 'Long Walk' where attendees of the match walk from Federation Square, along Birrarung Marr to the MCG. The atmosphere is that of unity and excitement when Australians from all backgrounds take part in the Long Walk in commemoration of former Aboriginal Essendon football player, Michael Long, who walked to Canberra to protest for the human rights of Aboriginal and Torres Strait Islander people in Australia.

The game itself is opened with traditional dancing and a smoking ceremony conducted by local Wurundjeri Elders. If visitors enjoy sport and a great atmosphere, then Dreamtime at the G is the perfect way to see how sport can bring people together for a common cause.

WHERE: Melbourne Cricket Ground.
WHEN: Usually held in the last week of May; check the website for details about date, time, and cost of tickets.
COST: Ticket prices vary so check the website. Tickets can be purchased online at Ticketek, or at the games. Book early as tickets sell quickly.
www.mcg.org.au
Essendon Football Club: www.essendonfc.com.au/community/indigenous-programs/dreamtime-at-the-g
Richmond Football Club: www.richmondfc.com.au/tickets/dreamtime-at-the-g-ticketing

Harrow Discovery Centre and Johnny Mullagh Interpretive Centre

Harrow Discovery Centre presents the largely unknown story of the First Eleven: the first Australian international test cricket team to tour to England, which comprised of 13 Aboriginal men from the Jadawadjali, Gunitjmara and Wotjobaluk clans in south-western Victoria. Between May and October 1868, the team played 47 matches against English amateur teams, and also taught the traditional skills of their people in the heart of the Commonwealth. The story of these athletes has been told at the Harrow Discovery Centre (formerly the Johnny Mullagh Cricket Centre) since 2004 and is now being adapted into a stage play by Geoffrey Atherden of the Ensemble Theatre to be performed at the Sydney Opera House.

WHERE: 1 Blair St, Harrow.
WHEN: 9 am–9 pm daily.
CONTACT: 03 5588 1387
www.harrow.org.au

Photo of the First Eleven, Australia's first international test cricket team to tour to England

Top: Statue of Johnny Mullagh standing in the Harrow Discovery Centre and Johnny Mullagh Interpretive Centre

Bottom: The First Eleven team comprised of 13 Aboriginal men from south-west Victoria

NATIONAL PARKS

Parks Victoria manages an expanding and diverse estate covering more than 4 million hectares, or about 17 per cent, of Victoria, including 45 national parks. In addition to the Grampians National Park included here, visitors can find out about the many other parks at: parkweb.vic.gov.au

Grampians National Park

The Grampians National Park is a must see if visiting Victoria. The landscape is timeless, rugged and beautiful. The Grampians (Gariwerd) is and has always been a significant place for Victorian Aboriginal people, and their incredible rock art can be seen throughout the park, and at Bunjil's Shelter in particular.

ABORIGINAL CULTURAL HERITAGE: For the Aboriginal people of this area, Bunjil is an essential spiritual figure and the creator of life. Bunjil created the land, the trees, the people, the food and resources, the waterways, religion and Law. To see Bunjil's Shelter is to gaze upon rock art that is thousands of years old and yet the spirit and beliefs of Bunjil the creator are still evident in Victorian Aboriginal culture today. Many Victorian Aboriginal people continue to respect the stories and artworks about Bunjil that have been passed down through the generations and preserved in art galleries and museums.

THINGS TO DO: To discover more about the park's natural and cultural landscape and to gain the most up-to-date information about the Grampians, visit the Brambuk National Park and Cultural Centre. Visitors can go to the spectacular Gariwerd Dreaming Theatre and take in the interpretive displays at the centre. Cultural rangers take groups on bush-tucker walks and rock-art tours.

Top: Aerial views of Gariwerd, or the Grampians National Park

Bottom: The Brambuk National Park and Cultural Centre is a great gateway to the Grampians National Park

WHERE: The park is located in Western Victoria, 3-hour (260 km) drive from Melbourne; and 5-hour (460 km) drive from Adelaide. It is easily accessed from the villages of Halls Gap, Wartook and Dunkeld, and a scenic day trip from the regional towns of Hamilton, Horsham, Stawell and Ararat. The Brambuk National Park and Cultural Centre is located just south of the Halls Gap township.
WHEN: The Brambuk National Park and Cultural Centre: 9 am–5 pm daily; closed Christmas Day.
CAMPING: A variety of campgrounds are located in beautiful forest surroundings. All have basic amenities including pit toilets, fireplaces and picnic tables; they do not have power. Drinking water is not provided so bring your own. Book early during busy holiday periods.
COST: Park admission is free. For camping fees see: www.parkstay.vic.gov.au
CONTACT: 03 5361 4000
parkweb.vic.gov.au/explore/parks/grampians-national-park

Brambuk National Park and Cultural Centre

The Brambuk National Park and Cultural Centre is a great place to stop for information before visiting Gariwerd, or the Grampians National Park. Opened in 1990, the centre was the product of 10 years of work by the Aboriginal communities in the area to create a place to document, share and preserve the Indigenous cultures of the Gariwerd region. It is still fully Aboriginal-owned and operated.

WHERE: 277 Grampians Tourist Rd, 2.5 km south of the Halls Gap shops.
WHEN: 9 am–5 pm daily.
CONTACT: 03 5361 4000
www.brambuk.com.au

TOURS

Aboriginal Heritage Walk

The Aboriginal Heritage Walk takes visitors through the Royal Botanical Gardens, located in the heart of the city next to the Yarra River, opposite Birrarung Marr. Tours start at the visitors centre in the Melbourne Gardens, where Ben Church conducts a traditional smoking ceremony. Ben is the local Aboriginal guide and Aboriginal Programs Officer at the Royal Botanical Gardens. The tour teaches visitors about the type of foods Aboriginal people in Victoria traditionally ate, and the different and important functions of plants and trees in the gardens; which plants do what and which are medicinal. It is an important and fascinating experience for non-Indigenous people to see how the Indigenous people used the land in a way that didn't harm it or take from its resources. Ben also tells visitors how the five clans of the Kulin nation used natural materials such as wood and stones for various purposes, including as tools or weapons.

The Royal Botanical Gardens is a very peaceful and scenic part of Melbourne. Within its grounds, the Aboriginal Heritage Walk is an empowering and informative introduction to the presence and culture of Aboriginal people in Victoria.

WHERE: The tour start at the visitor centre, Melbourne Gardens, Royal Botanic Gardens.
WHEN: 11 am–12:30 pm daily except Saturdays, Christmas Day, New Year's Day.
COST: Adult: $35; concession and Friends' members: $29; child 5–17 years: $12. Bookings are essential.
CONTACT: 03 9252 2429
www.rbg.vic.gov.au/whats-on/aboriginal-heritage-walk

Bataluk Cultural Trail

The Bataluk Cultural Trail follows significant traditional routes used by the Gunai-Kurnai people for over 30 000 years. It was established by many Aboriginal organisations in the Gippsland region, including the Far East Gippsland Aboriginal Corporation, East Gippsland Shire Council, and Lake Tyers Aboriginal Trust. Together, the organisations identified places that are significant to the Gunai-Kurnai, the Traditional Owners of the East Gippsland and surrounding areas.

In this self-guided tour, visitors can use the maps and information on the Bataluk Cultural Trail website to go to some or all of the 11 significant sites. They are located throughout the vast Gippsland region, ranging from Won Wron State Reserve through to Sale, Stratford, Bairnsdale, Lakes Entrance, Orbost and Cann River. Visitors can drive from one end of the trail to the other, or select a range of sites and activities and design a route that suites their timeframe and interests.

WHERE: For a map of the trail visit the website. Bataluk Cultural Trail visitor information centres are located at Orbost, Lakes Entrance, Bairnsdale, Maffra, and Sale.
WHEN: Year round as this is a self-guided tour.
COST: There are no admission fees to the sites.
CONTACT: Krowathunkooloong Keeping Place Gippsland and East Gippsland Aboriginal Cooperative: 03 5152 1891. Bataluk Cultural Trail visitor information centres: Orbost: 03 5154 2424; Lakes Entrance: 03 5155 1966; Bairnsdale: 03 5152 3444; Maffra: 03 5141 1811; Sale: 1800 677 520.
www.batalukculturaltrail.com.au

Tower Hill Visitor Centre

Tower Hill is an important environmental and historical landmark near Warrnambool. The area is the result of a volcanic eruption that occurred on the site approximately 32 000 years ago, and ancient tools and artefacts of the Traditional Owners, the Gunditjmara Nation, have been discovered on the site since. In 1892, Tower Hill became Victoria's first national park.

The Tower Hill Visitor Centre is managed by WG Enterprises (formally Worn Gundidj Aboriginal Cooperative), formed in 1992 with a goal of supporting local Indigenous people by providing economic stability through employment and engagement in Indigenous-operated commercial enterprises. WG Enterprises offers guided tours, nature walks and twilight walks through the Tower Hill Reserve as well as school programs. The visitor centre and tours aim to educate visitors about the heritage of the reserve, its wildlife and environment.

WHERE: Great Ocean Rd, 10 minutes from Warrnambool.
CONTACT: 03 5561 5315. Bookings can be made through the website.
www.towerhill.org.au

ART GALLERIES, MUSEUMS AND CULTURAL CENTRES

Altair Fine Art Gallery

Altair Fine Art showcases artworks by highly acclaimed Indigenous artists, including Gloria Petyarre, Kevin Williams and Betty Mbitjana. The gallery was opened by Daniel Peers, voted Young Entrepreneur of the Year in the Wyndham Business Awards 2016, as a continuation of his parents' own business, Koorie Connections Altair, opened in 1994. Altair Fine Art emphasises fair treatment of Indigenous artists from all regions throughout Victoria, working across various mediums including painting, carving, pottery and photography.

WHERE: T3 Quay Bde, Wyndham Harbour, Werribee South. If travelling from the centre of Melbourne, Altair is a 30-minute drive along the M1 Freeway. Public transport is available via train to Werribee, followed by the local 439 bus, but the trip will take about 2½ hours from the Melbourne CBD.
WHEN: 11 am–5 pm Wednesday to Thursday; 11 am–5:30 pm Friday to Saturday; 11 am–5 pm Sunday.
CONTACT: 0432 036 166
www.altairfineart.com

Birrarung Marr

Winding along the Yarra River's north bank, next to Federation Square, Birrarung Marr is Melbourne's newest park. Open-air exhibitions in the park showcase Aboriginal and Torres Strait Islander art all year round. And a pathway winding through it is designed to symbolise the eel, an important traditional food source for Victorian Aboriginal people.

Often hosting major festivals, Birrarung Marr encapsulates what is means to be a multicultural society. The festivals commemorate many different cultures, from the annual Moomba festival to the Diwali festival. Additionally, each year before the Dreamtime at the G match, game attendees walk along Birrarung Marr together, showing their commitment to unity and reconciliation.

During a scenic stroll thought the park, visitors should stop to admire the five metal shields standing proudly in a semicircle, representing the five language groups of the Kulin nation: Boonwurrung, Dja Dja Wurrung, Taungurung, Wathaurung and Woiwurrung, commonly referred to as Wurundjeri.

WHERE: Batman Ave, Melbourne.
WHEN: All year round.
COST: Free.
CONTACT: 03 9658 9658
www.melbourne.vic.gov.au/parks

Top: Tour guide explains significance of the Aboriginal shields at Birrarung Marr

Bottom: Aboriginal rock carvings installation at Birrarung Marr in Melbourne

Bunjilaka Aboriginal Cultural Centre

The Bunjilaka Aboriginal Cultural Centre, located in the Melbourne Museum, draws on contemporary styles of learning to tell visitors about Victorian Aboriginal history. The centre also offers workshops and runs educational tours. It is perfect for visitors with children who want to learn about Victorian Aboriginal culture in an exciting and interactive way. The centre displays walls of artefacts and cases of possum-skin clothing, and projects videos showing the history of the political struggles that Victorian Aboriginal people have faced. There is also a Deep Listening Space where visitors can go to listen to the stories of Elders; these stories bring to life the artefacts on the walls. The cultural centre pays homage to important political figures such as William Barak, Sir Douglas Nicholls, and former St Kilda football player, Nicky Winmar.

WHERE: Melbourne Museum, Nicholson St, Carlton.
WHEN: 10 am–5 pm daily; closed Good Friday and Christmas Day.
COST: Entry to Melbourne Museum covers entry into Bunjilaka: Adult: $14. Free for children up to 16 years, concession holders, Museum members.
CONTACT: 03 8341 7777
museumsvictoria.com.au/bunjilaka

Narana Aboriginal Cultural Centre

A cultural centre located one hour from Melbourne, Narana offers guided and self-guided cultural tours, displays of artefacts and a cafe serving Indigenous-inspired meals. The onsite Cultural Exhibition Building and Art Gallery displays artworks by internationally acclaimed Aboriginal and Torres Strait Islander artists that are available for purchase. The site includes Australian wildlife such as wallabies and emus, and an adventure playground for children.

WHERE: 410 Surf Coast Hwy, 10 minutes from Geelong on the way to Torquay.
WHEN: 9 am–5 pm Monday to Friday; 10 am–4 pm Saturday.
CONTACT: 03 5241 5700; reception@narana.com.au
www.narana.com.au

Sandra Bardas Art Gallery

Sandra Bardas Art Gallery is associated with Worawa College, a primary and secondary boarding school for Aboriginal girls. The students come from all over Australia, and those who participate in art classes have the opportunity to showcase their work at the Sandra Bardas Art Gallery. The gallery also exhibits work from some of the students' communities.

Worawa College in Healesville is about 1 hour from Melbourne. Visitors can take in the views of the countryside on the drive there and enjoy their time in this unique gallery, which aims to empower young Aboriginal women. The gallery has an online shop and can ship worldwide.

WHERE: 60–80 Barak Lane, Healesville.
WHEN: By appointment only. Email: artgallery@worawa.vic.edu.au
CONTACT: 0498 967 292
www.worawa.vic.edu.au/2016/10/sandra-bardas-art-gallery

Top: Children enjoying the First Peoples Exhibition at the Bunjilaka Aboriginal Cultural Centre in Melbourne Museum

Bottom left: Works by Indigenous artists decorate the cafe at Narana Aboriginal Cultural Centre

Bottom right: Baby emus join one of Narana Aboriginal Cultural Centre's guided tours

Koori Heritage Trust

The Koori Heritage Trust is many things: it is a shop that stocks Aboriginal art from south-east Australia; it operates educational workshops for schools and workplaces; it is a safe space for Indigenous people to learn about culture; it offers basket-weaving workshops and yarning circles; it houses an archival collection of oral, photographic and written histories; and it has an art gallery, with exhibitions running year round. Also, information services are available via an online reference library that holds more than 4000 items.

The Koori Heritage Trust is filled with valuable information about Victorian Aboriginal people and their culture, land and history. It even offers family history tracing for Aboriginal people to find out where their families come from.

A visit to the Koori Heritage Trust is essential for anyone who wants to learn about Victorian Aboriginal culture, and leave with a beautifully handcrafted souvenir or two.

WHERE: Levels 1 & 3, The Yarra Building, Federation Square, cnr Swanston & Flinders sts, Melbourne.
WHEN: 10 am–5 pm daily. Closed on Victorian and national public holidays.
COST: Admission is free; fees apply for some educational workshops and basket-weaving workshops.
CONTACT: 03 8662 6300
kooriеheritagetrust.com.au

PLACES

Charcoal Lane

Adorning Charcoal Lane in Fitzroy, Melbourne, is an incredible mural painted by Aboriginal man Robert Young. The suburb of Fitzroy has long had a strong presence of Aboriginal people; it is a place where Aboriginal people have struggled over land rights with the Australian government; and the Fitzroy Stars, an Aboriginal football team, was founded there.

Charcoal Lane restaurant is a social enterprise operated by Mission Australia and dedicated to providing customers with native Australian foods served in restaurant quality meals. At Charcoal Lane Indigenous students who are obtaining hospitality qualifications, prepare and cook the food. The aim is to empower and generate economic independence for the young Indigenous students while inviting people from all backgrounds to taste Indigenous-inspired cuisine. Diners at Charcoal Lane enjoy delicious meals and increase their appreciation of the diversity and beauty of Aboriginal culture.

WHERE: 136 Gertrude St, Fitzroy.
WHEN: Tuesday to Saturday: lunch 12 pm–3 pm; dinner from 6 pm; closed on Victorian and national public holidays.
COST: See menu: www.charcoallane.com.au/menu
CONTACT: 03 9418 3400
www.charcoallane.com.au

Top: Children inspecting boomerangs at the Koorie Heritage Trust, Melbourne

Bottom: Just some of the modern, Indigenous-inspired food offered at Melbourne's Charcoal Lane

5 SOUTH AUSTRALIA

FESTIVALS

Survival Day Festival

Held on 26 January every year, this festival marks a time when the whole community celebrates the resilience of the Aboriginal and Torres Strait Islander people. It runs all day and includes live music from Aboriginal singer–songwriters, traditional dances, children's activities, arts and craft and food stalls, and the Tandanya Gallery pop-up store.

WHERE: Semaphore Foreshore, Adelaide.
CONTACT: www.tandanya.com.au

Tarnanthi Festival of Contemporary Aboriginal and Torres Strait Islander Art and Art Fair

Tarnanthi (Tar-nan-dee) Festival is presented by the Art Gallery of South Australia. The festival showcases aspects of the rich, diverse and ancient cultures of Indigenous Australia by providing the opportunity for significant and unique new works to be displayed. *Tarnanthi* means 'to emerge', like the sun at first light, and signifies new beginnings. It is a Kaurna word from the Traditional Owners of the Adelaide Plains, and refers to the festival's artistic vision of showing distinctive works that challenge existing notions of Aboriginal art. The inaugural festival in 2015 was extremely popular and successful, and provided a platform for artists to share their stories. Now the festival includes a series of exhibitions, an art fair, artists' talks, performances and events held in key cultural institutions in Adelaide.

WHERE: The Art Gallery of South Australia, North Terrace, Adelaide, and various partner locations around Adelaide city.
WHEN: Tarnanthi Festival of Contemporary Aboriginal and Torres Strait Islander Art and Art Fair are held annually in October. Tarnanthi at the Gallery runs from October until the end of January.
CONTACT: www.tarnanthi.com.au

NATIONAL PARKS

National Parks South Australia manages 22 national parks in the state. In addition to the ones included here, visitors can find out about the other parks at: www.environment.sa.gov.au/parks/Home

Coorong National Park

Coorong National Park is a long, narrow ribbon of saline wetlands, saltpans, coastal dunes and wild ocean beaches, stretching for 150 km along the Younghusband Peninsula on SA's mid-south coast. Its beaches face the blustery winds of the Southern Ocean but behind a chain of tussocky dunes is a sheltered sliver of shallow lagoons, which is an internationally recognised sanctuary for thousands of shorebirds.

ABORIGINAL CULTURAL HERITAGE: The rich landscape of the Coorong has been home to the Ngarrindjeri people for around 6000 years. They hunted kangaroos, wombats, snakes and goannas, and harvested fish and shellfish, and their fishing culture still flourishes in this environment of saltwater lakes and lagoons. The Ngarrindjeri people travelled along the lagoons in bark and reed canoes and made substantial shelters for protection from the wild, cold southerly weather. They originally came from an Aboriginal nation further up the Murray River near the Victorian border, before they moved into the coastal country. After Europeans arrived the Ngarrindjeri suffered disease followed by dispossession – smallpox decimating the population from more than 3000 to just 511 by 1874. Today, however, the Ngarrindjeri Aboriginal group is among the largest in southern Australia, with a strong, rich culture. The Coorong is archaeologically and culturally significant, with burial sites, shell middens, cooking ovens and campsites to be seen among the dunes.

THINGS TO DO: Visitors to the Coorong can learn about Ngarrindjeri culture and beliefs from gifted storytellers and guides based at Coorong Wilderness Lodge (08 8575 6001), and at Camp Coorong (08 8575 1557). Nature lovers and birdwatching enthusiasts can join a 4WD Coorong Nature Tour or one of Spirit of the Coorong's eco-cruises.

BUSH AND BEACH WALKING: Walks in the park are generally easy and fairly short. Lakes Nature trail (3 km circuit, 1 hour, easy) at Salt Creek passes various habitats from ephemeral salt lakes to sand dunes to stands of mallee. From the same carpark, Ngrugie Ngoppun, or 'good walk' (2.5 km, 1 hour, easy), links to a 27 km trail that leads to 42 Mile Crossing. The trail from Godfreys Landing, accessible

Top: Birds take off from the water on the Limestone Coast, Coorong National Park

Bottom: An emu stands in the Murray River, Coorong National Park

only by boat, heads from the lagoon to the ocean beach just south of the mouth of the Murray River. Chinamans Well trail (1.3 km, 1 hour, easy) leads to disused quarries, the ruins of a Chinese eating house and remains of an 1856 well; from Jacks Point carpark, a short stroll (10 minutes, easy) ends at a lookout over pelican breeding grounds.

CANOEING AND KAYAKING: Canoeing in the Coorong's sheltered waters is one of the best ways to explore the park's lagoons and islands. Some islands are protected bird-breeding habitats and must not be approached closer than 140 m.

FISHING: The northern Coorong lagoon is a great place to catch mullet, bream, salmon and flounder. Nets are best as the lagoon is shallow with rocky reefs that snag lines. There are boat-launching sites at Long Point and Parnka Point. Line fishing from the jetty at Long Point is worth a try and the kids are likely to catch carp from the jetties at Meningie. On the ocean beach there is excellent surf fishing for the Coorong's famous mulloway, as well as salmon, shark, whiting and flathead. A fishing licence is not required for recreational fishing in SA but bag and size limits apply. Contact PIRSA Fisheries: 08 8204 1370.

SCENIC VIEWS: There are many lookouts along the eastern side of the lagoon. In the north, Pelican Point offers good birdwatching; further south, Parnka Point has scenic views up and down the lagoons with the possibility of seeing a rare orange-bellied parrot; at Jacks Point pelican observatory there are high-powered binoculars to look over nearby breeding islands, home to pelicans and fairy terns.

WHERE: 200 km south-east of Adelaide; 61 km south-east of Meningie to Salt Creek (Tea Tree Crossing). From Adelaide drive via Princes Hwy through Meningie; from Mount Gambier drive via Princes Hwy through Kingston.

WHEN: Open 24 hours a day, 7 days a week. The park is closed on days of Catastrophic Fire Danger and may be closed on days of Extreme Fire Danger. Listen to the local radio station for the latest updates and information on fire safety.

CAMPING: There is a wide range of exciting camping options within the park; to see them all visit the website. Fees apply and bookings are essential.

COST: There is a vehicle entry fee, but entry to the park on foot or bicycle is free. If you plan to visit a few of SA's national parks the Park Pass is a cost-effective and time saving way to pay the vehicle entry fee. Camping fees apply.

Top: Sweeping views over Ikara–Flinders Ranges National Park from Bunyeroo Lookout

Bottom: 560-million-year-old red sandstone in Brachina Gorge, Ikara–Flinders Ranges National Park

CONTACT: Coorong National Park Information Office: 08 8575 1200; Natural Resources Centre, Mount Gambier: 08 8735 1177
www.environment.sa.gov.au/parks/find-a-park/Browse_by_region/Limestone_Coast/coorong-national-park

Ikara–Flinders Ranges National Park

Ikara–Flinders Ranges National Park is one of SA's most popular tourist destinations. The 95000 hectare park takes in rugged mountain ranges, dramatic gorges, peaceful creeks lined with river red gums, and an abundance of seasonal wildlife. It includes Heysen Range, Bunyeroo and Brachina gorges and the vast mountains that make up Ikara or Wilpena Pound. It is also renowned for its Aboriginal rock-art sites and a rich and well-preserved cultural heritage.

ABORIGINAL CULTURAL HERITAGE: The Traditional Owners of the land on which the park is located, the Adnyamathanha people, have a connection to the land that goes back many thousands of years. They co-manage the park together with representatives from the Department of Environment, Water and Natural Resources. While the Traditional Owners are very proud to show off its cultural treasures, including ancient rock paintings and engravings, they do ask for all visitors to show the utmost respect for these culturally significant places to assist in protecting them for future generations.

Things to do

BUSHWALKING: There are numerous walking trails in the park. Those with cultural significance include: Sacred Canyon walk (500 m, 30 minutes return, easy), from the Sacred Canyon carpark follow a short, gum-lined creek to an ancient rock-art site found on sandstone walls. The art depicts animal tracks, people and waterholes. The best time to visit is during the soft morning or afternoon light as some paintings are weathered and hard to see. Arkaroo Rock walk (3.1 km circuit, 2 hours return, moderate) to the Akaroo rock shelter, a significant cultural site for the Adnyamathanha people. The site features ochre and charcoal rock paintings of the Yura Muda or the Dreaming for Ikara. While paintings are best seen in morning light, at sunset there are spectacular views of the Chace Range. Living with Land walk (1 km, 2 hours return, easy) from the Old Wilpena Station is a self-guided walk that reveals the pastoral heritage of the Aboriginal people and the European settlers from remote and isolated areas of the Flinders Ranges. A fee applies for this walk. St Mary Peak Hike, Ngarri Mudlanha (14.6 km direct route, 6 hours return, challenging; 21.5 km loop route, 9 hours return, challenging), the highest peak in the Flinders Ranges, is central to the Adnyamathanha creation story. The peak is 1171 m above sea level and rewards hikers with spectacular 360° views of the ranges, salt lakes and surrounding plains. Due to its cultural significance the Traditional Owners ask that visitors do not climb to the summit. The walk begins at the trailhead at the Wilpena Visitor Centre complex. The trail is closed over summer from December to February. For more walks contact the park directly.

CYCLING: The park offers fantastic mountain-bike opportunities for visitors, which take in some of the most stunning scenery of the park. The Mawson trail is a long-distance cycling trail that includes spectacular views as it traverses the park. Contact the visitor centre for more information about the bike cycle loops.

SCENIC DRIVES: Several spectacular scenic drives are on offer in the park. Highlights include the Brachina Gorge Geological trail, which passes through 130 million years of the earth's history over a 20 km distance. Signs along the way provide information about the formation of the ranges, past climates and the evolution of early life forms.

WHERE: Ikara–Flinders Ranges National Park is in the central Flinders Ranges, approximately 450 km north of Adelaide. From Adelaide, take one of many routes to Hawker, and then follow signs to Wilpena. All public roads within the park are accessible by 2WD vehicles, caravans and trailers. However, caution is advised on unsealed roads, which may be affected by changing weather conditions throughout the year.

WHEN: Open 24 hours a day, 7 days a week. The park is closed on days of Catastrophic Fire Danger and may be closed on days of Extreme Fire Danger. Listen to the local radio station for the latest updates and information on fire safety.
CAMPING: Several campgrounds provide a base from which visitors can explore the park and take in the landscape. Many sites cater for vehicle-based camping, while others are only accessible by foot. Fees apply and you must book in advance.
COST: There is a vehicle entry fee, but entry to the park on foot or bicycle is free. If you plan to visit a few of SA's national parks the Park Pass is a cost-effective and time saving way to pay the vehicle entry fee. Camping fees apply.
CONTACT: Natural Resource Centre, Port Augusta: 08 8648 5300; Wilpena Visitor Centre: 08 8648 0048, open 8 am–5 pm daily.
www.environment.sa.gov.au/parks/find-a-park/Browse_by_region/flinders-ranges-outback/ikara-flinders-ranges-national-park

Wilpena Pound Resort

The only accommodation located within the Ikara–Flinders Ranges National Park, Wilpena Pound Resort was purchased in 2012 as a joint venture by Indigenous Business Australia (IBA) and the Adnyamathanha Traditional Lands Association (ATLA), to provide a sustainable economic future for the local Adnyamathanha people. The resort offers a number of activities to visitors to Adnyamathanha Country, including Aboriginal culture walks, 4WD tours, and scenic flights around the park and over Lake Eyre. Accommodation ranges from hotel rooms to luxury safari tents and camping grounds; check the website for details.

WHERE: Ikara–Flinders Ranges National Park is located 429 km north of Adelaide and accessible by car or scenic flight transfer (must be arranged in advance). Buses run from Adelaide to the town of Hawker, with transfers available from Hawker to the resort if booked in advance.
WHEN: 7 am–6 pm daily (reception); 8 am–6 pm daily (visitors centre and general store).
BEST TIME TO VISIT: Partial park closures are implemented during the summer months. Check the resort website for changes to activities.
CONTACT: Resort reception: 08 8648 0004; reservations: 1800 805 802; campground bookings: 08 8648 0048
www.wilpenapound.com.au

TOURS

Aboriginal Cultural Tours SA

A tour operator located on Adjahdura Land on the Yorke Peninsula, Aboriginal Cultural Tours is run by Quenten Agius, who is a Traditional Owner, and chairperson and Senior Heritage Monitor for the Adjahdura Narungga Heritage group. The lands are significant cultural sites for Aboriginal communities in the area and were the site of the Point Pearce Aboriginal Mission, built in 1867. The township still survives and, unlike most missions, Point Pearce is remembered by local Elders as an Aboriginal sanctuary.

Aboriginal Cultural Tours SA offers 10 single- and multi-day bush, coastal and combination tours through Ngadjuri country and Adjahdura land, and has a focus on supporting local businesses, accommodation providers and produce. The company has won 29 global, national, state and regional awards and is an 8-time Australian Tourism awards finalist.

WHERE: 46 Maitland Rd, Point Pearce.
CONTACT: 0429 367 121: tours@adjahdura.com.au
www.aboriginalsa.com.au

Top: Guests gather around a campfire at Wilpena Pound Resort

Bottom: Quenten Agius, owner–operator of Aboriginal Cultural Tours SA, is a Traditional Owner of the lands surrounding Point Pearce

ART GALLERIES AND CULTURAL CENTRES

Art Gallery of South Australia

The Art Gallery of South Australia houses one of the most important collections of Aboriginal and Torres Strait Islander art in the country. As well as its outstanding permanent collections, the gallery has a calendar of exciting temporary exhibitions and events throughout the year, including the Tarnanthi Festival and educational programs for school children, many focusing on Indigenous art.

WHERE: North Terrace, Adelaide.
OPEN: 10 am–5 pm daily; closed Christmas Day.
COST: General admission is free. Some exhibitions are ticketed, see the gallery's website for more details.
CONTACT: 08 8207 7000
www.artgallery.sa.gov.au

The Art Gallery of South Australia in Adelaide houses important Aboriginal and Torres Strait Islander art collections

Arts Ceduna

Arts Ceduna sells artworks by more than 100 artists from the far-west region of SA. The artists from this region have strong ties to their country and the influence of the environment is clearly seen in their work. Surrounding Ceduna is the largest untouched mallee and spinifex country to the north, ancient rock formations, such as the Gawler Ranges, to the east, the pristine waters of the Great Australian Bight to the south, and the vast Nullabor Plains to the west. This diverse country accounts for the equally diverse and unique range of artworks displayed and sold at Arts Ceduna.

WHERE: Ceduna Arts and Cultural Centre, 2 Eyre Hwy, Ceduna. Ceduna is located 786 km north-west of Adelaide on the Eyre Peninsula. Bus services operate between Adelaide and Ceduna in both directions 4 times a week: www.premierstateliner.com.au; Rexair operates daily flights between Ceduna and Adelaide: www.regionalexpress.com.au/home.aspx
CONTACT: 08 8625 2487
www.artsceduna.com.au

Living Kaurna Cultural Centre

The Kaurna (pronounced Garna) people are from the Adelaide Plains area in SA. The Living Kaurna Cultural Centre (LKCC) is a community-based centre which ensures that the Kaurna culture, along with its unique Dreaming story, is passed from generation to generation. The centre is located at the Warriparinga wetlands, which have been a gathering place for the Kaurna people for thousands of years. As well as a cultural and community hub for the Kaurna people, the LKCC is open to visitors. The centre includes an art gallery of original Kaurna works, such as paintings, woven baskets and woodcarvings, and a heritage display of the key dates in Kaurna history from pre-settlement to today. Additionally, the centre offers cultural tours and workshops.

WORKSHOPS: The range of workshops includes: Warriparinga bush tucker; a history and music workshop; weaving workshop with the Southern Elders Weaving Group; and a 90-minute art workshop run by the artist in residence. See the centre's website for details.
WHERE: Warriparinga Way (off Sturt Rd), Bedford Park, Adelaide.
WHEN: 10 am–4 pm Monday to Friday.
CONTACT: 08 8357 5900
www.marion.sa.gov.au/lkcc-tours-and-workshops.

Kuju Aboriginal Arts

Kuju Aboriginal Arts showcases Indigenous art from Port Lincoln and the Wangka Wilurrara region. The works exhibited come from a range of artists and reflect the culture, stories and lifestyle of the region. Local artists explore traditional and contemporary mediums, giving the artworks a unique look. Kuju is Aboriginal-owned and operated, and strives to provide artists with a source of income and a level of economic independence.

WHERE: 30 Ravendale Rd, Port Lincoln. The coastal city of Port Lincoln is located on the south-east point of the Eyre Peninsula in SA.
WHEN: 9 am–4.30 pm Monday to Thursday; 9 am–4 pm Friday.
CONTACT: 08 8682 6677
www.placc.com/contacts.htm

Tandanya National Aboriginal Cultural Institute

Tandanya is the oldest Aboriginal-owned and managed multi-arts centre in Australia and features traditional and contemporary Aboriginal and Torres Strait Islander visual and performing arts. In the Kaurna language *Tandanya* means 'place of the red kangaroo', referring to the centre's location on Kaurna land, within the location of the traditional Red Kangaroo ceremony. Several gallery spaces display about 12 exhibitions annually, which seek to reflect the vibrant and diverse culture existing within Aboriginal and Torres Strait Islander communities. Throughout the year Tandanya also hosts community events and festivals, including Survival Day in January and the Spirit Festival in March.

WHERE: 253 Grenfell St, Adelaide.
WHEN: 10 am–5 pm Monday to Saturday.
COST: The visual arts program includes free and ticketed shows.
CONTACT: 08 8224 3200
www.tandanya.com.au

APY Lands

The Anangu Pitjantjatjara Yankunytjatjara (APY) Lands occupy 103 000 sq km in the isolated far north-west of SA. The Pitjantjatjara, Yankunytjatjara and Ngaanyatjarra Anangu people are the Traditional Owners of these lands. The Pitjantjatjara people are from the central and western sections of the APY Lands, extending into the Central Australian deserts of the Northern Territory. The Yankunytjatjara people have their origins in the central and eastern sections of the land. There are 11 Aboriginal communities in the area as well as several homelands of various sizes.

Art centres in the communities of the APY Lands are Aboriginal-owned and governed. They promote the cultural development and artistic excellence of local artists through career development, various educational opportunities and training, and support the ethical creation and sale of Indigenous art. They help to create widespread financial gain for families in the communities and homelands, and build the capacity for the Anangu people to take positive control of their

Aboriginal paintings, sculptures and ceremonial poles on display at Tandanya National Aboriginal Cultural Institute

lives. The art from the remote APY Lands Indigenous communities reflects the rich cultural heritage and strong connections the people have to country in this area.

The artworks from the region are highly regarded in the Australian art scene. In 2017 there were 25 nominations for APY artists in the Telstra National Aboriginal and Torres Strait Islander Art Awards (NATSIAA), the most prestigious Indigenous art prize in the country. Two APY artists were named as finalists in the 2017 Archibald Portrait Prize, worth $100 000. Also, Peter Mungkuri, from Indulkana, won the inaugural Hadley's Art Prize, the world's richest landscape art award, worth $100 000. APY Land artists have also won or been shortlisted for the Hazelhurst Art on Paper Award, the John Fries Award, the Ramsay Prize and the John Sulman Prize.

TIPS FOR VISITORS: When going to any part of the APY Lands visitors must follow the protocol of the Traditional Owners.

No alcohol or drugs are permitted on the Lands.

The Pitjantjatjara and Yankunytjatjara women dress conservatively, usually in long skirts and blouses, and take great offense at inappropriate, skimpy clothing. In view of this, men and women should dress modestly.

Do not take photographs without explicit permission

Do not visit homes or off-road areas without explicit permission

There are cultural protocols following the death of a community member: do not say the person's name and do not ask questions about them. The community store and offices may close for a period of time following a death.

Please arrange your visit in a formal way by letter so that your visit is expected.

Road safety is important and drivers are advised to take extreme caution when driving on the APY Lands because of the urgent need for maintenance of the roads. In addition to the hazards presented by washouts, corrugations and dips, the roads are mainly unfenced and wandering feral animals, such as donkeys and camels, present a danger.

WHERE: Access to the APY Lands is via the Stuart Hwy. Extreme caution is advised when driving there due to unsealed roads and wandering feral animals such as donkeys and camels.
PERMITS: Permits are required by all visitors to go onto any part of the APY Lands. Permit application forms can be found online and must be submitted to the APY Lands permit officer. The fee is $22 for adults; $11 for students. Visit www.anangu.com.au/permits.html
BEST TIME TO VISIT: The weather in Australia's Central Desert regions is one of extremes, with very cold winters and hot summers. Autumn, from March to May, is the one of the best times to visit. The days are warm and the nights are cool, with average temperatures between 12 and 27°C.
CONTACT: Umuwa, PMB 227 via Alice Springs, Northern Territory, 0872 (although the APY Lands are in South Australia the postal address is for the Northern Territory); 08 8954 8111
www.anangu.com.au

Iwantja Arts

Iwantja Arts is named after Iwantja Creek where the Indulkana community was first formed. The history of Iwantja Arts is rich in printmaking. In the early 1980s two artists travelled to Canberra campaigning for funding to establish a printmaking workshop and painting studios. Many of the early limited-edition prints from Iwantja Arts are now held in the South Australian Museum in Adelaide and the National Gallery of Australia in Canberra. Today, the centre supports artists working across a range of mediums, both individually and collaboratively. It is a not-for-profit, Aboriginal-owned and run centre aiming to provide opportunities, training and career development for artists.

WHERE: Indulkana community is close to the Stuart Hwy, approximately 575 km south of Alice Springs. It sits in a small ridge on the edge of the Indulkana Ranges.
WHEN: Contact Iwantja Arts to enquire about making an appointment to visit.
CONTACT: Iwantja Arts, Indulkana community, APY Lands, PMB 8 via Alice Springs, NT 0872; 08 8670 7722; www.iwantjaarts.com.au

Mimili Maku

Mimili Maku Art Centre is named after the witchetty grub, *maku*, which is found in the Acacia Kempeana roots. The Maku Tjukurpa is the witchetty grub song line, a story of great cultural and historical significance in this area. Artworks feature the traditional narrative, imagery and symbols, juxtaposed with abstract designs and bold colours.
The complex depiction of country and the Maku Tjukurpa is of particular interest to art collectors nationally and overseas. The art centre involves and supports artists from the Mimili community and well as Perentie Bore, Wanmara, Blue Hills and Sandy Bore homelands in the surrounding area.

WHERE: Mimili is about 645 km south of Alice Springs. It lies at the base of the Everard Ranges.
WHEN: To make an appointment to visit Mimili Maku Arts please contact the manager: info@mimilimaku.com

CONTACT: Mimili Maku, PMB 252 Mimili community via Alice Springs, NT 0872; 08 8956 2984
www.mimilimaku.com

Tjala Arts

Tjala Arts is one of the 10 largest Australian Aboriginal art centres. Founded by local women of the Amata community in 1997, the art centre now includes both male and female artists and has been described as the heartland of the Amata community. The works have a strong focus on *Tjukurpa*; the stories, law and dreaming of the region. *Tjala* means 'honey ant' in Pitjantjatjara. The ant is both a traditional bush food and the Tjukurpa creation story for the Amata area. Tjala Arts is renowned for a diverse range of styles, including rich colours and energetic brushstrokes. Artists work across a variety of media, including traditional woodwork, sculptural fibre weaving, acrylic painting on linen, and for some of the younger artists more contemporary mediums such as film and photography.

WHERE: The Amata community is approximately 115 km due south of Uluru, and 14 km south of the NT border, in SA. It is located on the western side of the Musgrave Ranges.
WHEN: To make an appointment to visit Tjala Arts please contact: info@tjalaarts.com.au
CONTACT: Tjala Arts, PMB 261 via Alice Springs, NT 0872; 08 8956 2899
tjalaarts.com.au

The Tjatu Gallery

Tjatu Gallery is a partnership between Mimili Maku, Iwantja Arts and Marla Travellers' Rest. *Tjatu* means 'together' in Yankunytjatjara. The partnership enables the artworks, and the various stories told through them, to be displayed in a gallery space that is more easily accessible to tourists than some others in the APY Lands. In the future the gallery plans to hold artists' talks and meet-the-artist markets to provide a direct link between tourists, passersby and visitors to the Aboriginal people of these remote areas. Art prices range from AUD $100 to $500.

WHERE: Marla is a small service town on the Stuart Hwy, 159 km south of the NT border and 676 km north of Port Augusta. It offers a range of facilities for travellers including accommodation, a restaurant, bar, service station and supermarket.
WHEN: To make an appointment to visit Mimili Maku Arts please contact the manager: info@mimilimaku.com
PERMITS: No permit is required to go to Marla or the Tjatu Gallery as they are on the Stuart Hwy.
CONTACT: Mimili Maku, PMB 252 Mimili community, via Alice Springs, NT 0872; 08 8956 2984
www.mimilimaku.com/home/tjatu-art-gallery

Tjungu Palya

Tjungu Palya means 'good together', and the art centre is the result of the collaboration of artists from the Nyapari community and the neighboring homelands of Kanpi and Watarru. Founded in 2006, the art centre is now a dynamic and innovative space supporting the many local artists through various mediums.

WHERE: Nyapari is located at the base of the Mann Ranges, 20 km south of the NT border and about 450 km south of Alice Springs.
WHEN: To make an appointment to visit Tjunga Palya please contact: info@tjungu.com
CONTACT: Tjungu Palya, Nyapari community, APY Lands, PMB 126 via Alice Springs, NT 0872; 08 8956 7111
www.tjungu.com

6
QUEENSLAND

FESTIVALS AND FAIRS

Laura Dance Festival, Cape York

The Laura Dance Festival is a celebration of Aboriginal culture held in Western Yalanji country in North Queensland. It is also a vibrant and unique way for tourists to experience this ancient and ongoing culture through powerful performances of the songs and dances of many Indigenous nations from the Cape York region. This biennial festival, which runs over the weekend that marks the end of June and start of July, is one of Queensland's largest cultural gatherings. It has attracted crowds of visitors from Australia and around the world for the last 25 years.

WHERE: Held 15 km south of Laura, at the Ang-Gnarra Festival Grounds, or meeting grounds, of Cape York.
WHEN: The next festival will be in June 2019. Bookings are essential.
CAMPING: The festival sets up a campground for visitors, with facilities including showers and toilets, and a range of stalls selling food and crafts.
COST: Approximately $100 per person; additional charges for camping.
CONTACT: 0407 481 931
www.lauradancefestival.com

Cairns Indigenous Arts Fair

The Cairns Indigenous Arts Fair is one of the most highly acclaimed art festivals in Northern Queensland. It is the perfect family event that caters to all interests; with food, fashion, dance and music programs, and theatre, there is plenty to see, eat and watch over the three-day celebration of Aboriginal and Torres Strait Islander culture.

The art fair is also a world-renowned, ethical market place for buying art created by Indigenous Queensland artists. Visitors have the opportunity to meet many of the artists, which leads to a better understanding and appreciation for the artworks. Buyers can learn about the stories that have influenced and inspired the artworks they have purchased, or admired. The vision of the art fair is to generate economic empowerment for the artists. Cairns Indigenous Art Fair Pty Ltd is a not-for-profit organisation that operates on a fair-trade policy, with proceeds going to the artists to continue to support their individual development and production of art.

The festival has been a great success since it started in 2009, and provides Australians and overseas visitors with the chance to join in the celebration of the culture and creativity of the Indigenous people of Queensland.

WHERE: Cairns Cruise Liner Terminal, Corner Wharf and Lake sts, Cairns.
WHEN: Held every year over a weekend in the middle of July.
COST: Admission to most events is free admission; some are ticketed. Check the website for information about program events and ticket sales.
CONTACT: 07 4050 7712
ciaf.com.au

MARINE AND NATIONAL PARKS

Great Barrier Reef Marine Park

The Great Barrier Reef is one of the seven natural wonders of the world. Stretching for more than 2300 km along the Queensland coast and covering 35 million hectares, it features brilliantly coloured corals living beneath aquamarine waters, a profusion of tropical islands and a wealth of marine creatures and birdlife. The Great Barrier Reef

Crowds watch a dance performance at the Cairns Indigenous Arts Fair

Top: Aerial views of the reef formations on the Great Barrier Reef

Bottom: A clownfish hides in an anemone in the Great Barrier Reef

was designated as a World Heritage area in 1981, and was the first coral reef ecosystem in the world to receive this status. It is the world's largest and most famous coral formation.

The Great Barrier Reef is the leading tourist attraction in Queensland. and one of the world's foremost tourist destinations, particularly for diving and snorkelling. Breathtakingly beautiful just below the surface of the water, the Reef has a complex ecosystem – more than 1500 species of fish coexist with 4000 species of molluscs, 400 species of sponge and over 400 species of hard corals, as well as sea turtles, manta rays, sharks, dolphins and whales. Extensive seagrass beds provide a home for the threatened dugong; threatened green and loggerhead turtles nest on islands in the Reef; and humpback whales migrate there to give birth. Birdlife is also abundant, and hundreds of species nest in the Reef islands.

Aboriginal and Torres Strait Islander peoples are the Traditional Owners of the Great Barrier Reef region, and there are significant cultural sites on many of its islands. The strong ongoing links between the Traditional Owners and their sea country was recognised in the Great Barrier Reef's World Heritage listing and contributes to its Outstanding Universal Value. The cultural and ecological knowledge of the Traditional Owners will be essential to delivering the Reef 2050 Plan, which is the blueprint for protecting and managing the Reef and designed to be implemented in a collaborative partnership. The Plan was released by the Australian and Queensland governments in 2015, and a statement from the Department of Environment and Energy noted that, 'With input from scientists, communities, Traditional Owners, industry and non-government organisations, a key principle of the Plan is developing the Reef's resilience in the face of a variable and changing climate.' Australians and people all around the world are gravely concerned for the health of the Reef, and UNESCO has identified that climate change is a challenge to the Reef now and will be increasingly so over the next few decades.

Scattered throughout the Reef are more than 900 islands, many of which are protected as national parks. Each of the Reef's island national parks provides very different experiences for visitors. Some offer luxury resort-style accommodation with a range of recreational activities; others are remote and rugged with bush camping only (dozens of islands in these national parks permit camping). There are islands with strong Aboriginal cultural links, and islands that provide important breeding grounds for birds.

SOUTHERN REEF ISLANDS: The southern part of the reef stretches from just north of Hervey Bay to the southern reaches of the Coral Sea, north of Yeppoon. Access to the islands in this area is from the major population centres of Gladstone and Yeppoon, east of Rockhampton, and various smaller places along this coast.

ISLANDS OF THE WHITSUNDAY COAST: Off the central Queensland coast from south of Mackay to Bowen are hundreds of islands, many grouped together and protected under national park status. The main access is by boat from Mackay in the south and Shute Harbour or Airlie Beach in the north. Airports are at Mackay, Proserpine and Hamilton Island.

TROPICAL NORTH ISLANDS: The islands in this region lie offshore from just south of Townsville to Cape York. They are generally accessible from the main population centres of Townsville and Cairns, both of which have major airports. Cairns has an international airport and services a range of tours to the outer reef.

The Queensland Parks and Wildlife Service (tel: 13 74 68) together with the Great Barrier Reef Marine Park Authority (07 4750 0700) are responsible for managing the Reef and associated island national parks along its length.

PLANNING YOUR TRIP TO THE GREAT BARRIER REEF

When planning your visit to the Reef you will find useful information on the Great Barrier Reef Marine Park Authority site: gbrmpa.gov.au/visit-the-reef To find out about the national parks in the area visit: www.npsr.qld.gov.au/parks

The Cairns Visitor Centre provides information about Indigenous-owned and operated Reef tours: 07 4036 3341; www.cairnsvisitorcentre.com

To read the UNESCO World Heritage listing for the Reef visit: whc.unesco.org/en/list/154

The Queensland Parks and Wildlife Service manages over 300 national parks in the state. In addition to the ones included here, visitors can find out about the other parks at: www.npsr.qld.gov.au

Chillagoe–Mungana Caves National Park

The rugged Chillagoe–Mungana Caves National Park is rich in natural and cultural heritage. Its outstanding features include spectacular limestone caves, small galleries within the caves of Aboriginal rock art engraved in the ancient limestone, jagged limestone outcrops, and a historically significant mining site.

There are many walking trails to explore, such as the Balancing Rock track that leads to some majestic caves. The Royal Arch track, an easy 9 km walk, passes through the Wullumba rock-art site. More challenging tracks include the Pompeii Cave track (which hosts a colony, or cloud, of bats), and the Bauhinia Cave track. Ranger-led tours take groups into the fascinating and stunning limestone caves, or visitors can go on self-guided tours with the assistance of the Discovery Guide, which can be downloaded from the NPRS website.

WHERE: About 215 km, or 3 hours drive, west of Cairns. The Hub, 21-23 Queen St, Chillagoe.
WHEN: The Hub: 8 am–3.30 pm daily.

ACCOMMODATION: Camping is not permitted in the park, however there is accommodation located in the nearby town of Chillagoe.
COST: Free admission to the park. For fees and bookings for the ranger-guided tour contact The Hub. Vehicle permits required to drive into the park.
CONTACT: The Hub: 07 4094 7111; Queensland Parks and Wildlife Service: 13 74 68
www.npsr.qld.gov.au/parks/chillagoe-caves

Great Sandy National Park

Great Sandy National Park comprises of two parts. Cooloola is on the coast between Rainbow Beach in the north and Noosa Heads in the south. K'gari (Fraser Island) takes in nearly all of the world's largest sand island, north of Rainbow Beach. The famous coloured sands, pristine blue water, plentiful marine life, and lush rainforests are some of the features visitors will find at Great Sandy National Park, one of Queensland's largest national parks.

ABORIGINAL CULTURAL HERITAGE: Aboriginal people have lived in the Great Sandy area for at least 5000 years according to archaeological evidence, but they may have been there far longer. The Butchulla people lived on K'gari (Fraser Island) and the nearby mainland. Their heritage sites of spiritual, social and archaeological significance are found on the island, as well as their middens, artefacts, scarred trees and campsites. The Butchulla led a complex, self-sufficient way of life intrinsically connected to the seasons, the land, and life on it and in the surrounding ocean. Soon after European settlement of the area in the 1840s the Indigenous people were forced off their land, and by the late 1800s their lifestyle had been destroyed and the Aboriginal people from around the region were relocated to a mission on Fraser Island. Today, descendants of these people who live in the area are

Top: Spectacular limestone formations in Chillagoe–Mungana Caves National Park
Bottom: View from Carlo Sand Blow near Rainbow Beach in Great Sandy National Park

working to protect and share their culture and way of life, which is so closely tied to this beautiful and bountiful natural environment.

WHERE: Cooloola lies between Noosa Heads and Rainbow Beach. Noosa Heads is about 155 km (about a 3-hour drive) and Rainbow Beach is about 240 km (about a 3-hour drive) north of Brisbane. Fraser Island is about 300 km north of Brisbane and 15 km off the coast of Hervey Bay and Maryborough.
CAMPING: There is an exciting range of camping options in the park. Visit the websites below for details.
COST: Driving on the beaches and some inland sand tracks requires a Vehicle Access Permit (VAP). The cost of the VAP depends on which area of the Great Sandy National Park. Camping fees also apply.
CONTACT: 13 74 68
www.npsr.qld.gov.au/parks/cooloola
www.npsr.qld.gov.au/parks/fraser

TOURS AND TOURIST CENTRES

Adventure North Australia

Adventure North Australia has been operating out in the Daintree region of north-east Queensland since 2004, and developed its Bama Way Aboriginal Tours in 2007 in partnership with several Indigenous-owned tour companies and cultural centres. Tours run by Adventure North are created in partnership with, and guided by Traditional Owners of the lands and immerse visitors in the natural and cultural beauty of the area. Guests can choose from 1- and 2-day Daintree Dreaming or Dreamtime Walk tours, a 2-hour coastal walk along Cooya Beach, or 30-minute walking tours to Bloomfield Falls. All tours have an emphasis on the rich Aboriginal cultures of the area and guides provide demonstrations, teach traditional skills and share their cultural knowledge.

TIPS FOR VISITORS: Bookings for all tours can be made through the website. All tours include walking, sometimes on uneven ground, so guests are advised to wear appropriate clothing and bring water and sunscreen.
WHERE: 36 Aplin St, Cairns (Adventure North tourism office).
CONTACT: 07 4028 3376
www.adventurenorthaustralia.com/the-bama-way/

Currumbin Wildlife Sanctuary

Located at Currumbin on the Gold Coast, just one block away from the beach, the Currumbin Wildlife Sanctuary makes a perfect day for families with children or nature-loving adults, with all manner of animals and reptiles to see, from the ever-smiley quokka to Tasmanian Devils, capybaras and even crocodiles. The sanctuary is committed to rescue and conservation projects and to providing their live-in friends with an experience as enjoyable as the one they offer visitors. There are regular live performances, including the Aboriginal Dance Show, on daily at 3:15 pm, for which Currumbin Wildlife Sanctuary have partnered with the Jellurgal Aboriginal Cultural Centre from nearby Burleigh Heads. The performance celebrates the culture of the Yugambeh people, Traditional Owners of the Gold Coast region.

TIPS FOR VISITORS: While you're here, head up to Burleigh Heads to check out the Jellurgal Aboriginal Cultural Centre, Tours and Information Hub at 1711 Gold Coast Hwy, just 8 minutes away by car or 14 minutes on the route 700 bus.
WHERE: 28 Tomewin St, Currumbin. The sanctuary is a 10-minute drive by car or bus from the Gold Coast airport, on the Gold Coast Hwy, or the route 700 bus will take you straight to the sanctuary.
WHEN: 8 am–5 pm daily; except Christmas Day and Anzac Day.
COST: Tickets are available at the sanctuary or online; a range of ticket options is available.
CONTACT: 07 5534 1266
www.currumbinsanctuary.com.au
www.jellurgal.com.au

Top left: Men in traditional body paint lighting a fire at Currumbin Wildlife Sanctuary

Top right: Walking through mangroves on Advenuture North Australia's Daintree Dreaming Tour

Bottom: Giving spearfishing a try during the Daintree Dreaming Tour

Ingan Tours

Ingan Tours is an Aboriginal-owned tour company in Tully, North Queensland. It is owned and run by the Grant family who are Janbanbarra Jirrbal people from the Davison Valley region situated halfway between Cairns and Townsville. They offer the Spirit of the Rainforest tour, which takes visitors into the Tully Valley to the beautiful Echo Creek Falls. Aboriginal guides will interpret the environment along the walking track and show you the forest through their eyes.

The Ingan Yunba tour includes a rainforest walk and a swim in the crystal clear waters of Echo Creek. The Indigenous Guided Kayak tour includes a 4-hour guided kayak ride down Bulgan Creek where visitors can experience the serenity of Tully's freshwater eco-systems. Visitors will learn about the rain-forest plants and animals found along Bulgan Creek. While there is a stopover for tea and damper, visitors should bring their own lunch and water bottle, and appropriate footwear such as water shoes.

All Ingan tours give visitors the opportunity to experience the traditional lands of the Jirrbal people with experienced Aboriginal guides.

WHERE: Ingan Tours is based at 5 Blackman St, Tully. Details of the pickup point are provided once a tour is confirmed.
WHEN: Tours will not operate during particularly bad weather conditions or flooding.
COST: For tour prices, dates and times check the website.
CONTACT: 07 4068 0189
www.ingan.com.au

Top: Ingan Tours offer exciting river kayaking experiences
Bottom: Tasting coconuts and other bush foods on tour with a Kuku Yalanji Traditional Owner

Journey into Olkola Country

Over six days, visitors have an incredible opportunity to experience the rugged wilder-ness of Olkola country in Cape York Peninsula through a safe and expertly guided tour operated by Intrepid Travel. It is the harmonious combination of exploring nature and learning about Aboriginal culture that makes this tour unforgettable and special. The Traditional Owners are willing to share their ancestral lands with visitors who are eager to learn about the richness of Aboriginal culture. With more 1 million hectares of biodiverse savannah woodlands, river systems, lagoons and rocky escarpments to explore, visitors will walk and drive through places of great significance for the Olkola. Basic camping facilities are provided along with breakfast, lunch and dinner. This tour offers a unique cultural and travel experience.

TIPS FOR VISITORS: The tour does not require a high level of fitness.

Visitors must be respectful of the experience and open to learn about Aboriginal culture.

There is no wifi or phone coverage.

WHERE: The tour starts and ends in Cairns and travels up to the town of Laura in Cape York Peninsula and on to Olkola country.

WHEN: Tours run from late August through to early September.

COST: From $2845 for 6 days.

CONTACT: 1300 797 010
www.intrepidtravel.com/au/australia/journey-olkola-country-105262

Kuku Yalanji Cultural Habitat Tour

Beautiful Cooya Beach (Kuyu Kuyu), a 15-minute drive north of Port Douglas, is the traditional fishing grounds of the Kuku Yalanji people and home to Kuku Yalanji Cultural Habitat Tours. Both the Coastal Beach and Mangrove tour and the Coastal Beach Night Time walk focus mainly on fishing. A Kuku Yalanji Traditional Owner will meet visitors at their traditional homeland on Cooya Beach where they continue to practice their cultural activities and maintain their cultural heritage. After explaining the importance of this country, guides will introduce guests to their traditional fishing activity of spear throwing and handling as it is still practiced here today. Visitors can try their hand at fishing with a spear, and learn about traditional medicinal and food plants along the way. In the night tour, visitors can walk or row into the waters to fish.

The Tradition Owners, the Kuku Yalanji people, operate and conduct the tours, providing visitors with the opportunity to see how the Kuku Yalanji people have hunted for thousands of years, and how they have mastered and adapted to using technology to continue hunting.

WHERE: Cooya Beach, Mossman.

WHEN: Coastal Beach and Mangrove tour: starts 9.30 am and 1.30 pm daily; Coastal Beach Night Time walk: 7.30 pm–9.30 pm.

COST: Coastal Beach and Mangrove tour: adult: $75; child 4–14 years: $45; Coastal Beach Night Time walk: $75 per person; boat rowing: $150 per person.

CONTACT: 07 4098 3437
www.kycht.com.au

Mossman Gorge Centre and Ngadiku Dreamtime Walks

The Mossman Gorge Centre is a wonderful starting point from which to visit Mossman Gorge and the Daintree rainforest. The centre contains an Indigenous art gallery, gift shop, the Mayi Cafe and Restaurant, and runs guided and self-guided walks through the surrounding world heritage-listed rainforest. The Mossman Gorge Centre is committed to limiting the damage that can be caused by tourism. An example of how they are achieving this is through their low-emission shuttle bus, which departs every 15 minutes and transports visitors from the centre to the heart of Mossman Gorge and back for a

Top: Mungalla station homestead, where historic artefacts from the surrounding area are on display

Bottom: Visitors to Mossman Gorge can join a guided Ngadiku Dreamtime walk through the rainforest

small cost, eliminating unpoliced car traffic through the area.

Ngadiku (Nar-di-gul) means 'stories and legends from a long time ago' in local Kuku Yalanji language. The Indigenous people from the Mossman Gorge area in North Queensland offer visitors a unique experience, guiding them on the Dreamtime Gorge Walk where the local people have exclusive access to Kuku Yalanji land. The walk starts with a smoking ceremony then winds through stunning rainforests, visiting culturally significant sites and special places, passing traditional bark shelters and walking over cool clear streams. The Indigenous guide demonstrates traditional plant use, identifies bush foods and medicines, and shares the Kuku Yalanji people's stories about the rainforest and explains their special relationship with this unique tropical environment. At the end of the tour, guests are invited to enjoy bush tea and damper.

WHERE: Mossman Gorge Centre, 212 Mossman Gorge Rd, Mossman; 77 km from Cairns; 20 km from Port Douglas.
WHEN: Ngadiku Dreamtime Walk: 10 am, 11 am, 12 pm, 1 pm, 3 pm daily from April to March. Duration: approximately 1½ hours. Mossman Gorge Centre: 8 am–6 pm daily; closed Christmas Day.
COST: Adult: $68; child 5–15 years: $34; family pass (2 adults, 2 children): $169.
CONTACT: For enquiries about the Mossman Gorge Centre and about the Ngadiku Dreamtime Walk: 07 4099 7000.
www.mossmangorge.com.au/experience/dreamtime-walks

Mungalla Aboriginal Tours

The Nywaigi people are the Traditional Owners of the lands around Ingham in North Queensland. On the day-long Mungalla tours, visitors learn about the rich culture and history of the Nywaigi, and hear about the often brutal conflict between the Aboriginal people and the European settlers who shaped the destiny of North Queensland, and witness the birdlife of the area. In 2016, 204 different species of birds were recorded in this area, with 118 species recorded in one day. The tours start and finish at the grand Mungalla station homestead, where visitors can see historic artefacts and try their hand at throwing a boomerang. Then, the tour goes by bus to the original homestead where the guide shares stories of the first European settler on Mungalla in 1882, James Cassady, and rich and fascinating stories of the Nywaigi people and the beautiful tropical area that is their land. Depending on the tour, visitors can enjoy a country BBQ lunch or a Kup murri dinner, where the food is cooked in the ground.

The Mungalla Aboriginal Business Corporation and its parent body, The Nywaigi Aboriginal Land Corporation, which holds the title Mungalla station, are committed to improving the economic and social position of the Nywaigi people. They are working to achieve these aims by sharing the history of Mungalla station and its stunning environment though these fascinating tours.

WHERE: Mungalla Station is located outside of Ingham, 128 km north of Townsville.
WHEN: See website for details.
COST: Standard tour: adult: $70; child: $35; premium tour, with BBQ: adult: $95; child: $50; Deluxe tour, with Kup murri dinner: adult:$120; child: $60.
CONTACT: 07 4777 8718
www.mungallaaboriginaltours.com.au

Pamagirri Aboriginal Experience at the Woodward Family RainForeStation

The Pamagirri Aboriginal Experience is hosted by the Woodward Family's RainForeStation, a tourism destination that has been in operation for 40 years. As well as Pamagirri, the park operates the Koala and Wildlife Park, the Army Duck Rainforest tour, Bush Tukka walks and a host of other things to do and see.

The Pamagirri Aboriginal Experience tells the story of the Dreamtime and the traditions and customs of the Pamagirri people, the Traditional Owners of the Kuranda rainforest. The experience is conducted by Pamagirri guides a few times a day and takes about 1 hour. It includes the Dreamtime Walk, a 30-minute walk giving insights into the customs of the Traditional Owners, taken either before or after the show. There are other Dreamtime activities on offer, which guests can experience for a small cost. Further details and show times are displayed on the website.

WHERE: Kennedy Hwy, Kuranda. The RainForeStation is accessible by shuttle bus from Kuranda Village at $12 return for adults and $6 return for children. Alternatively, there is parking on site if arriving by car.
WHEN: 9 am–4 pm daily; except Christmas Day.

A Pamagirri man plays the didgeridoo at the Pamagirri Aboriginal Experience

COST: Prices vary for the different attractions and are displayed on the website.
CONTACT: 07 4085 5008
www.rainforest.com.au

Riverlife Mirrabooka

At Riverlife Mirrabooka, visitors can sit outside by the river at Kangaroo Point, Brisbane, and watch performances by the Yuggera Aboriginal Dancers, who have performed for audiences around Australia and internationally. There are also opportunities for visitors to get involved and participate in traditional song and dance passed down over many generations, learn traditional fire-starting techniques and boomerang throwing, taste Indigenous bush tucker, or paint a boomerang. Also, listen to musicians playing Aboriginal instruments and gain insights into Aboriginal life and history through fascinating and educational talks. Riverlife Mirrabooka is perfect for visitors who enjoy learning through interactive experiences.

Riverlife Mirrabooka is in the Queensland Tourism Awards Hall of Fame for the Best Indigenous Product in Queensland, Australia.

WHERE: Naval Stores, Kangaroo Point, Brisbane.
WHEN: 12 noon Thursday; 7 pm Saturday; subject to minimum numbers. The event runs for 1½ hours.
COST: $35–$95 per person. Bookings are essential.
CONTACT: 07 3891 5766
www.riverlife.com.au

Straddie Adventures

Straddie Adventures is owned and operated by Traditional Owners of Quandamooka (Stradbroke Island). Owner Mark Jones is passionate about sharing his 'Kulcha' with visitors and passing down the invaluable knowledge he has received from his predecessors to new generations, and Straddie Adventures is a registered Authentic Aboriginal Cultural Experience. Mark offers kayaking, sandboarding and 4-wheel driving experiences from 2 hours up to many days, all with a cultural element. There are also combo packages available, such as the 5-hour long Sandboard & Kayak Kulcha Experience, or the 2-day Kayak & 4WD Safari. Children can participate in all the tours as well, and ticket prices for tours and packages vary depending on age.

WHERE: 34 Dickson Way, One Mile, Stradbroke Island.
CONTACT: 0433 171 477
www.straddieadventures.com.au

Tjapukai

Tjapukai, in Cairns, was established in 1987 by a group of creative people including David Hudson, a Ewamain man who was brought up among the Djabugay people. Their aim then, and now is to celebrate the culture and traditions of the local Djabugay people and provide employment opportunities for their people as they share their culture with others.

Tjapukai is located on large grounds next to Skyrail Rainforest Cableway at Caravonica (Cairns) and includes a cultural centre, restaurant and retail gallery. Tjapukai performers, from the centre, are in demand nationally, and took part in the Welcome Ceremony for the Sydney Olympic Torch in 2000 and in the successful bid for the Gold Coast to host the Commonwealth Games in 2018. Tjapukai is one of the largest Indigenous employers for a tourist enterprise in Australia, and was selected winner of the Qantas Award for Excellence in Aboriginal and Torres Strait Islander Tourism in the 2017 Queensland Tourist Awards.

Perhaps the most impressive thing about a visit to Tjapukai is that two very different experiences are offered, depending on the time you arrive; Tjapukai by Day and Tjapukai

Top left: Tjapukai performers from Cairns are acclaimed nationally

Top right: Sandboarding with Straddie Adventures on beautiful Quandamooka (Stradbroke Island)

Bottom: Kayaking through the remains of a ship wreck off the coast of Quandamooka

by Night. During the day, the park is full of interactive cultural experiences to give visitors an insight into the lives and culture of the Tjapukai people. There are corroboree celebrations, fire-making ceremonies, cooking demonstrations, art classes and bush-food walks, as well as a buffet lunch served at the Flame Tree Restaurant. By night, guests can participate in the Night Fire, where you will meet the Bama, the Indigenous rainforest people, and be linked to their traditional lands through face painting and be able to join in a corroboree celebrating the Dreamtime stories and learn songs in traditional languages as part of the Rainbow Serpent Circle. During the evening, dinner is served at the Flame Tree Bar and Grill, after which the evening winds down with a casual getting-to-know-you session around the campfire with the Tjapukai warriors.

WHERE: 4 Skyrail Dr, Caravonica (Cairns); see the website for information about public transport from Cairns.
WHEN: Day: 9 am–4.30 pm; night: 7 pm–9.30 pm.
CONTACT: For all information, including event costs and to make bookings: 07 4042 999: bookings@tjapukai.com.au
www.tjapukai.com.au

Walkabout Cultural Adventures

Owned by Juan Walker, a descendant of the Kuku Yalanji people, Walkabout Cultural Adventures was created in 2008. Juan is passionate about sharing the stories, history and culture of the Kuku Yalanji country, located between Port Douglas and Cape Tribulation. Walkabout offers tours primarily within the Daintree, Cap Tribulation, Mossman and Cooya Beach areas. The daily tours are either full- or half-day, and guests can choose from cultural or sightseeing experiences. While the tours are run in groups, there are also private personalised tours available where guests can choose which sites and experiences they would like to explore.

TIPS FOR VISITORS: As some tours include water-based activities, it is a good idea to bring shoes appropriate for walking in water (reef walkers, etc.) along with swimwear, a towel, sunscreen, a hat and insect repellent.
WHERE: Guests staying in Port Douglas (1 hour north of Cairns), Mossman and the Daintree will receive transfers to and from their accommodation. Those staying elsewhere should make their own way to Mossman for collection, although arrangements can sometimes be made for transfers from other towns at an extra cost.
WHEN: Tours run daily.
CONTACT: 0429 478 206
www.walkaboutadventures.com.au

A small tour group learns about traditional life on the coast of Kuku Yalanji country

Top left and right: Guests on guided tours of the rainforest and the coast with Walkabout Cultural Adventures

Bottom: Visitors learning about Kuku Yalanji country on a Cultural Interpretive walk

ART GALLERIES

Janbal Gallery

Janbal Gallery, located on Kuku Yulanji country in Mossman, just north of Cairns is run by local Aboriginal artist Brian 'Binna' Swindley and is named after his late mother, acclaimed Aboriginal artist Shirley 'Janbal' Swindley, whose name referred to the rare Blue Quandong that grows in the Mossman region. The gallery exclusively showcases hand-painted originals, completed on site by Binna himself, including didgeridoos and artefacts. Brian's Aboriginal name *Binna* means 'hearing impaired', pointing to the severe hearing impairment that he was born with. Binna has taught himself to speak and lip read, and runs daily, hour-long private art classes for visitors, during which he talks about his culture and the legacy his mother left him. The private classes give guests the chance to paint either canvasses or boomerangs and can be booked on the website.

WHERE: 5 Johnston Rd, Mossman, 1 hour north of Cairns when driving along the Captain Cook Hwy.

Janbal Gallery hosts art classes for visitors with owner–operator Brian 'Binna' Swindley

WHEN: 9 am–5 pm Monday to Friday (gallery); classes: 9 am and 3 pm Monday to Friday.
CONTACT: 07 4098 3917. Due to Binna's hearing impairment, it is preferred that enquiries be made by email: info@janbalgallery.com.au
www.janbalgallery.com.au

Queensland Art Gallery and Gallery of Modern Art (QAGOMA)

These galleries are one institution, QAGOMA, located on two sites in the Cultural Precinct of South Bank, across the river from the centre of Brisbane. Their combined vision is to be the 'leading institution for the contemporary art of Australia, Asia and the Pacific', and the Asia Pacific Triennial is one way they achieve it. This major exhibition, held in both galleries, displays works across many mediums by Aboriginal and Torres Strait artists as well as artists from other countries and cultures in Asia and the Pacific.

The permanent collection and annual calendar of temporary exhibitions and events also celebrate the art and culture of Aboriginal and Torres Strait Islanders. GOMA had a focus on collecting and displaying contemporary Indigenous art, while the Queensland Art Gallery shows and collects traditional Indigenous works as well. Throughout the year GOMA's Children's Art Centre runs a dynamic and fun free program for kids that parents will enjoy too.

Tourists can spend the day visiting the two galleries, dining in their cafes and restaurants, and sitting by the river and smelling the flowers of the frangipani trees that grow along its banks.

WHERE: Stanley Place, Cultural Precinct, South Bank, Brisbane.
WHEN: 10 am–5 pm daily; from 12 noon Anzac Day; closed Good Friday, Christmas and Boxing Day.
COST: Entry to QAGOMA is free. Some exhibitions and special events have an entry fee.
CONTACT: 07 3840 7303; www.qagoma.qld.gov.au

7 TASMANIA

FESTIVALS

Nayri Niara Good Spirit Festival

The Nayri Niara Good Spirit Festival is held on Bruny Island every 3 years over a weekend in April. It aims to bring people from all backgrounds together to celebrate Aboriginal culture in a safe and supportive environment. Various ceremonies are held during the festival, as well as live music performances and contemporary celebrations of culture and diversity. Many different social enterprises run stalls over the weekend and feature music, food, weaving and arts and crafts. The focus of the festival is on creating positive social change and bringing joy to the festival participants.

TIPS FOR VISITORS: Temperature and weather conditions on Bruny Island can change quickly and dramatically. Visitors should dress accordingly and bring adequate supplies of water. Drinking alcohol and drug use is not permitted at the festival. Camping is not available. A ferry service operates; for more information on getting there visit: www.nayriniaragoodspirit.com/getting-here
WHERE: Great Bay, Bruny Island.
WHEN: Held towards the end of April every 3 years; the most recent festival was held in 2017.
COST: Most of the festival events are free, however some may charge admission. Information about the program and ticket sales is released closer to the event date.
CONTACT: Ruth Langford, 0481 120 880
www.nayriniaragoodspirit.com

WORKSHOPS

Tasmanian Aboriginal Corporation for Women's Art and Craft

Formed in 1977, the Tasmanian Aboriginal Corporation for Women's Art and Craft provides a safe space for Tasmanian Aboriginal people to learn about their culture and art. The corporation also offers workshops for visitors to learn about the histories and intricacies of ancient and contemporary Tasmanian Aboriginal arts and crafts practices. The workshops cover practices from all over Tasmania, including the other islands in the Bass Strait, King Island and Cape Barren Island.

WHERE: 163 St John St, Launceston.
COST: For workshop fee visit: www.aboriginalartdirectory.com/shop/community-centre/tasmanian-aboriginal-corporation-for-womens-art-and-craft.php
CONTACT: 03 6334 9378
www.tacwac.yolasite.com

NATIONAL PARKS

Parks and Wildlife Tasmania manage 19 national parks. In addition to the ones included here, visitors can find out about the many other parks at: www.parks.tas.gov.au

TIPS FOR VISITORS: When visiting any of Tasmania's stunning national parks, always bring warm, rainproof and windproof clothing, no matter what time of year it is. It snows in Tasmania during winter and temperatures can also drop quickly and dramatically at other times of the year. Heavy snowfalls occur even in December, in summer.

Pack adequate food and water.

When driving between sunrise and sunset, watch out for wildlife crossing the roads.

All Tasmanian national parks require a Parks Pass. For the cost of the pass see: www.parks.tas.gov.au/?base=914

Some Tasmanian national parks are serviced by public transport. For contact details see: www.parks.tas.gov.au/index.aspx?base=5766

Cradle Mountain–Lake St Clair National Park

Part of the Tasmanian Wilderness World Heritage Area, Cradle Mountain–Lake St Clair National Park is a rugged wilderness. It is one of the most popular places to visit in Tasmania and is known widely for its jagged terrain and icy lakes and streams.

The Aboriginal custodians of Lake St Clair, or Leeawuleena (meaning 'sleeping water'), were the Larmairremener of the Big River tribe, while Cradle Mountain and Lake Dove, or Weebonenetiner, were part of the traditional lands of the North tribe.

Plains of buttongrass (*Gymnoschoenus sphaerocephalus*) around Lake St Clair and in the Cradle Valley indicate where Aboriginal people used fire to manage grazing lands and attract a good supply of game animals. The relationship between Aboriginal Tasmanians, or Palawa, and their land is the inspiration behind the Lake St Clair Visitor Centre's natural fibre sculpture. Woven by three Indigenous artists using buttongrass, sedges and dodder vine from the Leeawuleena–Lake St Clair area, it pays respect to the nine Tasmanian Aboriginal tribes and complements the nearby Larmairremener Tabelti Walk.

Creative interpretation panels along this cultural heritage walk tell visitors about the life of the Larmairremener, the Indigenous people of this region who were part of the Big River clan. The walk goes through a wide variety of vegetation, such as banksias, buttongrass, tea-tree thickets, Tasmanian waratahs, rainforest ferns, and tall eucalypt stags. The track follows ancient ridges, called moraines, which were formed by retreating glaciers during the ice ages. It leads to a viewpoint above the Hugel River, then descends to a rainforest and joins the Watersmeet Track where the Hugel and Cuvier rivers meet.

Cradle Mountain–Lake St Clair National Park offers walking trails, skiing, camping, cabins, ranger-led activities, short walks (2 hours return), and overnight walks. For more information on activities, visit the Parks and Wildlife Tasmania website.

WHERE: Cradle Mountain is a 90-minute drive from Launceston. Vehicles weighing over 6.5 tonnes or over 8 m in length, such as caravans and campervans, are not permitted access to Cradle Mountain–Lake St Clair National Park.
CAMPING: Camping is available at Cynthia Bay. For further details contact the concessionaire: 03 6289 1137; frontdesk@lakestclairlodge.com.au
COST: Due to the popular nature of Cradle Mountain–Lake St Clair National Park and the vast array of activities on offer, there are various costs involved for visitors depending on the nature of their visit and length of stay. For more information, visit Parks and Wildlife Tasmania website.
CONTACT: 1300 827 727
www.parks.tas.gov.au/?base=3297

Mt Field National Park

The original custodians of the land where Mt Field National Park is located were the Pangerninghe people of the Big River tribe. Mt Field National Park supports a vast range of vegetation, from swamp-gum forests to rainforests, and even alpine moorlands at the higher elevations. The original custodians would hunt for wombat, platypus and Bennett's wallaby across this diverse landscape. They also traded with other groups for coastal resources and ochre. The park has several cultural sites with artefacts dating back 10 000 to 30 000 years. Scenic attractions include panoramic views, Russell Falls, Lake Dobson, bushwalks and skiing areas. Mt Field National Park is part of the Tasmanian Wilderness World Heritage Area.

WHERE: Mt Field National Park is just over an hour's drive from Hobart via New Norfolk. The park is also accessible by public transport.
CAMPING: There are 14 camping sites and government huts. Some sites are powered with electricity and gas. Bookings are not taken, camping is first come, first serve.
COST: Parks Pass required. The fees for camping and renting a government hut at Mt Field National Park are listed on Parks and Wildlife Tasmania website.
CONTACT: Mt Field Visitor Centre: 03 6288 1149
www.parks.tas.gov.au/index.aspx?base=412#mt

Rocky Cape National Park

Rocky Cape National Park lives up to its name, with colourful rock formations found along its coastline and inlets. Caves in the park contain Aboriginal middens, which are mounds made up of the ancient remains of shellfish, seals, scale fish, grass trees and ferns. These middens are evidence of the continuous occupation of this area over 8000 years. Rocky Cape National Park is a wonderful place for visitors who enjoy adventure and climbing and scrambling over rocks, as well as bushwalking, swimming, fishing and relaxing.

Rocky Cape National Park is only a day park, so camping is not permitted.

The Indigenous community continues its close spiritual and recreational connection with Rocky Cape. Visitors are requested respectfully not to enter North, South or Lee Archer caves.

Top: A rocky outlook over Mt Field National Park

Bottom: Lush green landscape on the Cradle Mountain Huts Walk, Cradle Mountain National Park

WHERE: Rocky Cape National Park is situated on the north-west coast of Tasmania about 2 hours drive west of Launceston.
CAMPING AND ACCOMMODATION: Limited private accommodation can be found at Sisters Beach and Boat Harbour, east of the park. West of the park there is camping with facilities at Rocky Cape township and Crayfish Creek, and camping at Peggs Beach Conservation Area.
COST: Parks Pass required.
CONTACT: Rocky Cape National Park Visitor Centre: 03 6458 1480
www.parks.tas.gov.au/index.aspx?base=3698

South Bruny National Park

South Bruny National Park is perfect for anyone who enjoys going for a bushwalk accompanied by the sound of crashing waves and a wide variety of birdsong. With its abundant wildlife, the area was an important hunting ground for the Traditional Owners; Bennett's wallabies, Tasmanian pademelons, brushtail possums and echidnas are just some of the animals that roam the forests here. The ocean surrounding Bruny Island is home to fur seals and whales, with occasional visits from leopard seals. Cloudy Bay, located in the park, is a popular spot for experienced surfers. Situated on the south-east coast of Tasmania, this national park can be reached by a 15-minute ferry ride that regularly departs from Kettering. For ferry times see: www.parks.tas.gov.au/index.aspx?base=3769

WHERE: Bruny Island is about 50 km south of Hobart. D'Entrecasteaux Channel separates the island from mainland Tasmania. A vehicular ferry departs from Kettering at regular intervals throughout the day, and the trip takes about 15 minutes. The ferry goes to Roberts Point, on north Bruny Island. From there, drive on sealed and unsealed roads to the southern part of the island.
CAMPING: Camping areas are located at Cloudy Bay and Jetty Beach. All have pit toilets, limited water and fireplaces. Firewood is not supplied so visitors should bring their own or use a fuel stove.

Top: Visitors enjoying the beautiful curved accommodation huts on the Wukalina Walk

Bottom: Dramatic scenery off the coast of South Bruny National Park

Campgrounds have no rubbish collection so please take your rubbish with you. There is also a campsite at the Bruny Island Neck Game Reserve. No bookings are taken. Campground sites are secured on a first come first served basis, but generally sites turn over regularly. Campers need to pay fees in cash on site.
COST: Parks Pass required. Camping fees are listed on Parks and Wildlife Tasmania website.
CONTACT: South Bruny National Park Visitor Centre: 03 6293 1419
www.parks.tas.gov.au/?base=3765

TOURS

Wukalina Walk

This is an Aboriginal-owned and operated guided walk that takes visitors on a 3-night, 4-day walk through the magnificent natural landscape of Larapuna (Bay of Fires) and Wukalina (Mt William) in north-east Tasmania, the cultural homeland of the Palawa people. The Palawa evolved in isolation for over 10 000 years, and their culture and heritage are different from mainland Aboriginal cultures, both in traditional times and since European occupation.

For visitors, the Wukalina Walk is a significant experience that will deepen your understanding of Lalawa (Tasmanian Aboriginal) culture and community history while you immerse yourself in the natural and rugged beauty of the area. Walk with Palawa guides in the footsteps of the Traditional Owners on the cultural homeland of Wukalina and Larapuna. The guide shares Palawa creation stories and invites visitors to participate in cultural practices that have been passed down for hundreds of generations.

Guests spend two nights staying in comfortable domed huts and one night in the meticulously renovated Lighthouse Keepers Cottage at Larapuna.

The magnificent natural landscape of north-east Tasmania is the perfect place for visitors to learn the Palawa story, as contemporary Palawa culture is most strongly tied to this part of Tasmania, as well as the Furneaux Islands.

WHERE: The walk starts at the Aboriginal Elders Council of Tasmania Centre, 163 St John St, Launceston.
WHEN: The walk departs from Launceston each Sunday at 8.45 am; for walks stating on certain Fridays throughout the year, check the *Wukalina Walk website.*
COST: Twin share: $2495 per person; single supplement: $1870.
CONTACT: 0447 244 727; www.wukalinawalk.com.au

ART GALLERIES, CULTURAL CENTRES AND MUSEUMS

Art Mob – Aboriginal Fine Art

Art Mob is a member of the Aboriginal Art Association of Australia. Located in Hobart, this art gallery gives visitors the opportunity to see and buy artworks by emerging Indigenous artists. Around 15 exhibitions are held each year. With more than 100 Indigenous artists from all over the country featured annually, the gallery displays a vast and diverse range of artworks and original pieces. Art Mob is a commercial gallery and visitors are able to purchase selected artworks, prints and jewellery. There is also an online shop. Details of the artist and the artwork, as well as authentication, are provided for all purchases.

WHERE: 29 Hunter St, Hobart.
OPEN: 10 am–6 pm daily; closed Christmas Day.
COST: Free admission.
CONTACT: 03 6236 9200
www.artmob.com.au

Tasmania Museum and Art Gallery

The Tasmania Museum and Art Gallery is the leading historical and cultural space for visitors to learn about the Indigenous and European histories of Tasmania. The art gallery hosts a permanent exhibition called *Ningina tunapri*, which means to 'give knowledge and understanding'. The exhibition showcases both a contemporary and historical displays of local Tasmanian Aboriginal art and culture. The museum and art gallery also provide educational tools and resources so visitors can learn about the history of Tasmania through an accessible platform.

THINGS TO DO: The Tasmania Museum and Art Gallery runs family Discovery Days five times a year, school-holiday programs and an annual children's festival, usually held in April. For more information visit: www.tmag.tas.gov.au/learning_and_discovery/families
WHERE: Dunn Pl, Hobart.
OPEN: 10am–4pm daily (26 December to 31 March); 10am–4pm Tuesday to Sunday (1 April to 24 December); 10am–4pm on Monday public holidays year-round.
COST: Free admission to the general galleries and most exhibitions. Some temporary exhibitions and events are ticketed; pension, student/concession and child discounts available.
CONTACT: 03 6165 7000
www.tmag.tas.gov.au

Tiagarra Aboriginal Culture and Art Centre

Tiagarra Aboriginal Culture and Art Centre is a space of great significance for Aboriginal people in Tasmania. It is a keeping place and museum that seeks to preserve and protect Tasmanian Aboriginal history. The cultural and art centre displays ancient petroglyphs (rock carvings) that reflect what life was like for the Aboriginal people in Tasmania many thousands of years before colonisation. On display are weapons and tools, as well as other artefacts. Tiagarra Aboriginal Culture and Art Centre protects these relics and uses them as a way to educate visitors and maintain traditional knowledge surrounding such tools and stories. Guided tours of the centre run every half an hour.

WHERE: Mersey Bluff, Devonport.
OPEN: 9 am–3 pm Monday to Friday; Saturdays by booking only.
COST: Guided tours: adult: $10; child: $5; concession: $8.
CONTACT: 03 6424 8250
www.aboriginalartdirectory.com/shop/museum/tiagarra-aboriginal-culture-centre-and-museum.php

8

AUSTRALIAN CAPITAL TERRITORY

NATIONAL PARKS

Namadgi National Park

A wide range of natural environments are found in the Namadgi National Park, which at 106 095 hectares covers almost 46 per cent of the ACT. The park is home to an abundance of wildlife with more than 700 plant species, 222 species of animals, 15 threatened species and more than 40 rare or uncommon species. It is also rich with Aboriginal history, with sites of cultural significance dating back 21000 years. The area was traditionally a meeting place, where neighbouring clans would meet for ceremonies and marriages. With 160 km of marked walking tracks that range in time from under 1 hour to 7 hours, the park is a stunning, diverse and fascinating destination for visitors who enjoy the outdoors.

WHERE: 3.5 km south of Tharwa.
WHEN: 9 am–4 pm weekdays; 9 am–4:30 pm weekends and public holidays; closed Christmas Day.
CAMPING: Honeysuckle, Orroral and Mt Clear campgrounds. Bookings are essential and can be made at the Namadgi Visitor Centre or online www.bookings.act.gov.au
COST: Admission to the park is free. See the website for camping fees.
CONTACT: Namadgi Visitor Centre: 02 6207 2900. Walking trail maps can be purchased at the visitor centre shop and the Canberra Regional Visitor Centre for $4.50.
www.environment.act.gov.au/parks-conservation/parks-and-reserves/find-a-park/namadgi-national-park

Huge granite boulders on Orroral Ridge, overlooking Namadji National Park

Tidbinbilla Nature Reserve

Located on the edge of Namadgi National Park, Tidbinbilla Nature Reserve is definitely worth visiting on the way to or from the park, or as a day trip on its own. The name *Tidbinbilla* is derived from the Ngunawal (the Traditional Owners of the Canberra region) word *Jedbinbilla*, which means 'a place where boys were made men'. The area is rich in Indigenous history, with artefacts and rock shelters dating back at least 21 000 years. The Birrigai Time Trail leads to the Birrigai rock shelter, one of the oldest rock shelters in Canberra and its surrounding regions. Visitors can learn about the natural and cultural history in the visitor centre or by joining a ranger-guided walk, held every weekend, school holidays and public holidays.

The reserve takes in wetlands, grasslands, wet forest and subalpine forests. With such diverse environments, it is home to a wide range of animals, including kangaroos, koalas, platypus, potoroos, wallaroos, wombats, echidnas and many other species. Tidbinbilla plays a vital role in wildlife management and protection, and runs breeding programs for the endangered Northern Corroboree frog and the Southern Brush-tailed rock wallaby. The Sanctuary at Tidbinbilla offers fabulous nature-based experiences and it is a great way for visitors to discover our natural world. It has wheelchair friendly footpaths so everyone can explore the wetlands of the nature reserve and see some of the many migratory birds and reptiles that are found there. The Sanctuary is also a lovely place for a picnic.

There are 22 walking trails throughout the reserve, which range from easy to moderate and hard, and span from 500 m to 19 km (the average walk is 4.5 km). A guide and map of the walking trails can be downloaded:

Top: Southern brush-tailed rock wallabies live in the sanctuary at Tidbinbilla Nature Reserve

Bottom: Some of the stunning rock formations to see in Tidbinbilla Nature Reserve

www.tidbinbilla.act.gov.au/experience/recreation/walking-trails

WHERE: Tidbinbilla Visitor Centre: 141 Paddys River Rd, Paddys River. Tidbinbilla is an easy 40-minute drive to the south of Canberra.
WHEN: 9 am–5 pm daily; closed Christmas Day.
COST: Private vehicle (8 seats max): $11.50; seniors: $9.50; concession: $7; motorcycle: $5.
CONTACT: Tidbinbilla Visitor Centre: 02 6205 1233
www.tidbinbilla.act.gov.au

TOURS

Dharwra Aboriginal Cultural Tours

Ngunawal man, Tyronne Bell, established the Thunderstone Cultural and Land Management Services Aboriginal Corporation in 2013. From this, the idea of providing informative services for visitors to Canberra resulted in the Dharwra Aboriginal Cultural Tours. The Nungawal people are the Traditional Owners of Canberra and surrounding areas of the Australian Capital Territory, which is where the tours operate.

There are three categories of tours: short, half-day and full-day. The short tours are the perfect way for visitors to view the Canberra scenery from up high, eat local bush food and become familiar with the local wildlife, including a few endangered species. The short tours take visitors to Mt Majura, standing at 888 m it is the highest peak in Canberra, or Mt Taylor, standing at 856 m, or Black Mountain, standing at 812 m.

The half-day driving tours take visitors to various cultural sites around Canberra, such as Red Hill and Theodore and Lanyon Homestead. The purpose of this tour is to showcase what life was like before colonisation, before Ngunawal country became the Australian Capital Territory. Half-day tours are recommended for those aged 12 years and above. Transport and morning tea are provided.

In the full-day tours visitors will be driven in a 4WD to some of Canberra's most scenic areas, such as Namadgi National Park and Flea Creek, located in the Brindabella Mountains region. There are many beautiful places of significance for Aboriginal people at Namadgi National Park, many dating back thousands of years, and Flea Creek is teeming with wildlife. In this tour there is the opportunity for a cool swim if the weather is fine.

WHEN: Namadgi National Park and Flea Creek tours operate from September to March. Dharwra Aboriginal Cultural Tours also operate kayak tours that run from October to March. All other tours are year round.
COST: Varies depending on the length of the tour. Short tours: $40 for adults; half-day tours: $85 for adults: full-day tours: $180 for adults; with prices for concession holders, children and families.
CONTACT: Enquiries: 0455 750 385; bookings, phone Canberra and Region Visitors Centre: 1300 554 114
www.thunderstone.net.au/index.php/tours

ART GALLERIES AND MUSEUMS

National Gallery of Australia

The National Gallery of Australia offers visitors the chance to immerse themselves in the work of iconic artists and artistic movements that span across time and continents. The gallery recognises that Aboriginal and Torres Strait Islander peoples have lived on the continent of Australia for tens of thousands of years, and their art and traditions are among the oldest and richest in human history. Its calendar of special exhibitions always includes work by

Indigenous artists. As well, it holds a rich and diverse permanent collection of Aboriginal and Torres Strait Islander art. The NGA also has an extensive library, study spaces, cafes, family-specific spaces and outdoor installations such as the Sculpture Garden, the Fern Garden and Skyspace.

WHERE: Parkes Place, Parkes, ACT. The NGA is located in the heart of Canberra, near Parliament House, the High Court of Australia and next door to the National Portrait Gallery. Visitors can walk through the Sculpture Garden to the NGA from the path around Lake Burley Griffin.
WHEN: 10 am–5 pm daily; closed Christmas Day
COST: Free admission to the general galleries. Some special exhibitions are ticketed.
CONTACT: 02 6240 6411
nga.gov.au

National Museum of Australia

The National Museum of Australia explores the land, nation and people of Australia. It is committed to its focus on Indigenous histories and cultures, European settlement and the Australian people's interaction with the environment. The museum undertakes many educational and archival programs to ensure that our knowledge of Australia will always be current and readily available to the public.

The museum holds one of Australia's largest collections of historical artefacts and the world's largest collections of bark paintings. As well as its exciting and educational permanent exhibitions, the museum calendar always features special exhibitions, with many that offer insights into Indigenous life, culture and history.

WHERE: Lawson Cres, Acton Peninsula, Canberra
WHEN: 9 am–5 pm daily; closed Christmas Day.
COST: Free general admission; admission fees for special exhibitions.
CONTACT: 1800 026 132
www.nma.gov.au

Top: Two hundred log coffins make up the Aboriginal Memorial at the National Gallery of Australia

Bottom: The Garden of Australian Dreams at the National Museum of Australia

PLACES

Aboriginal Tent Embassy

Embassies are known internationally as places of diplomatic representation of a country's government in another country. In 1972, four selected Aboriginal representatives erected the Tent Embassy in front of Parliament House, Canberra – now known as Old Parliament House. Today the Aboriginal Tent Embassy is still an extremely significant place for Indigenous Australians. It is an important physical place that represents the struggles for land rights that Aboriginal people have faced for more than 200 years, since colonisation in January 1788, and continue to experience today. Visitors to the Aboriginal Tent Embassy should treat it with respect.

WHERE: On the lawns of Old Parliament House on King George Terrace.

The Aboriginal Tent Embassy on the lawns opposite Old Parliament House, Canberra

9

TORRES STRAIT ISLANDS

The Torres Strait Islands stretch from Queensland's northernmost tip to Papua New Guinea's southern shores, and from the Coral Sea in the east to the Arafura Sea in the west. While the Torres Strait is made up of more than 200 islands, only 17 are inhabited.

Breathtaking in their diverse, unspoilt beauty, these islands sustain a unique culture, language and geography. Here you will find coral cays, mangrove swamps and rocky outcrops, and magnificent volcanic mountains, covered in thick rainforest, that rise majestically from the ocean.

Torres Strait Islander people are ethnically Melanesian and are distinct from Australian Aboriginal people, with small variations within each island community. Two traditional languages are spoken on the islands: Meriam Mir, spoken on the eastern islands and linguistically connected to Papuan languages; and Kala Lagaw Ya, spoken on the western islands and linguistically similar to mainland Aboriginal languages. There is also a Torres Strait Island Creole, which is spoken by most Islanders. It is a mixture of Standard Australian English and traditional languages.

The largest island is Muralug, but the administrative capital and most densely populated island is Thursday Island, also known as 'TI'.

The Torres Strait Islands have four seasons, which relate to the direction and type of wind that blows throughout the year. *Kuki*, January to April, is the Wet season, when the monsoons comes and there are strong north-west winds. *Sager*, May to December, is the Dry season, with south-east trade winds. Temperatures and humidity are at their highest in *Nay Gay*, October to December, when there are northerly winds. *Zey* are the cool, southerly winds that lightly blow from the south during the year.

There are regular ferry services and flights to the Torres Strait Islands.

QantasLink operates services twice daily from Cairns to Horn Island: www.qantas.com.au

Skytrans operates services on weekdays from Cairns: www.skytrans.com.au

Peddells Ferry Service runs regular ferries from the jetty at Seisia, at the tip of Cape York Peninsula in Queensland, to Thursday Island: www.peddellsferry.com.au

McDonald Charter Boats operate a ferry service between the islands. It also offers bus transfers between Horn Island airport, Horn Island jetty and Thursday Island: www.tiferry.com.au

Top: An orange dawn as the sun rises over the Torres Strait Islands

Bottom: Dance performance at the Torres Strait Cultural Festival

Top: Men wearing body paint at the Torres Strait Cultural Festival

Bottom: Friday Island offers idyllic scenery as well as a rich cultural heritage

TOURS

Peddells Thursday Island Tours

Learn about the culture and hidden past of Thursday Island with this locally guided historic tour. Visitors discover the military, maritime, pearling and cultural history of the Torres Strait with visits to the Thursday Island Museum and Japanese Pearl Divers Memorial. The 90-minute tour also includes a scenic drive around the island.

COST: For tour times and fares, visit the website.
CONTACT: 07 4069 1551
www.peddellsferry.com.au

ART CENTRES

Badu Art Centre

The work of artists from Badu Island is powerful, expressing strong cultural traditions and the love and dedication the Badu Island people show for the ocean, their island and all its inhabitants. The only Indigenous-owned casting foundry in Australia is located on the island. In addition to bronze and aluminium casting, artists use a range of techniques and mediums including carving, printmaking, textiles and jewellery. Some Badu Island artists are nationally and internationally acclaimed.

Visitors are welcome to the Badu Art Centre, however, permission must first be granted by the art centre Chair and the Chair of the Native Title Body. All requests must be emailed to the art centre: info@baduartcentre.com.au

WHERE: 274 Ahmat St, Badu Island.
CONTACT: 07 4090 0956
www.baduartcentre.com.au

Gab Titui Cultural Centre

The Gab Titui Cultural Centre is on Thursday Island, on the land of the Kaurareg nation. It was founded on the idea of a 'keeping place'; somewhere the community can feel safe and supported. It aims to preserve the vibrant Torres Strait Islander culture and promote the unique art of the islands.

The name 'Gab Titui' was recommended by the late Mr Ephraim Bani, who suggested the gallery could represent the eastern and western dialects of the Torres Strait by incorporating *gab*, meaning 'journey' from the eastern island, and *titui*, meaning 'stars', from the western island to form *Gab Titui*, which translates to 'Journey of the Stars'.

The centre includes the Wabunaw Geth Gallery of local contemporary and traditional art, and the Ephraim Bani Gallery of cultural and historical artefacts. The gallery's rotating exhibitions display paintings, sculpture, traditional headdresses, woodcarvings and lino prints, as well as locally made shell and pearl jewellery that represents the deep connection Torres Strait Islanders have to the sea and the land. New exhibitions are opened with traditional dances and song in an outdoor performance area, allowing visitors to experience the true spirit of the Torres Strait.

WHERE: Corner of Blackall St and Victoria Pde, Thursday Island.
OPEN: 9 am–4.30 pm Monday to Friday; 10 am–3 pm Saturday.
COST: Free entry; tours are available for a small fee.
CONTACT: 07 4069 0888
www.gabtitui.gov.au

INDEX

Note: Bold page numbers refer to illustrations.

A

Aboriginal and Torres Strait Islander people *see* Aboriginal peoples; Torres Strait Islander people
Aboriginal and Torres Strait Islander people and cultures
  lack of information for tourists about 49–50
  move for recognition in Australian Constitution 42
Aboriginal art 6–7, 20–8
  advice on buying authentic 23, 27–8
  authenticity 24, 27
  early collecting trips by explorers 20–3
  fraudulent 24
  sourcing 23–4
  styles 23
  see also art fairs; art galleries, cultural centres and museums; art sales
Aboriginal Art Association of Australia 27
Aboriginal artists 20–2, 24
  encounters with Europeans 22–3
  establish their own companies 23
  protection of rights 24, 27
  relationships with European artists 22
  themes 22
  traditional ownership of inherited styles 24–7
Aboriginal Blue Mountains Walkabout, NSW 158–60
Aboriginal children
  ask permission before photographing 68
  forced removal of 36–8, 43–7, 52
  see also Stolen Generations
Aboriginal Cultural Tours SA, Point Pearce, SA 188
Aboriginal English 14–15
Aboriginal Heritage Walk, Royal Botanic Gardens, Melbourne, Vic. 177
Aboriginal history 51–3
  no information available for tourists about 49–50
  readings and DVDs on 51
  suppression of by settlers 50–1
Aboriginal land management system 9–10
Aboriginal Land Rights Commission of Inquiry 52
Aboriginal-owned land 56
Aboriginal peoples 2, 72
  and the Australian Constitution 52
  in cities and towns 5, 172
  cultures and languages 11–15
  evidence of early occupation 2, 6, 7–9, 161–2
  frontier violence and deaths following colonisation 51, 205
  imprisonment rate 52–3
  kinship systems 16–19
  music and dance 12, 29–33
  and native title 38–41
  prehistory 2, 6–10, 161–2
  social and economic opportunities through RAPs 56–7
Aboriginal religion, and dance 33
Aboriginal reserves/settlements 34–6, 42, 52
Aboriginal rights 5, 38–42
  see also land rights
Aboriginal rights activists **39**, **40**
Aboriginal Tent Embassy, Old Parliament House, Canberra, ACT 221
Aboriginal tombs, Maria Island, Tas. **7**
Aboriginal words 14
Aboriginal Yarra River tour: Walkin' Country, Walkin' Birrarung, Melbourne, Vic. 5
Aborigines Protection Act 1909 (NSW) 46
acknowledgement of country 73
Adjahdura people 188
Adnyamathanha people 187, 188
Adnyamathanha Traditional Lands Association (ATLA) 188
Adventure North Australia, Cairns, Qld 200
Agalda clan 84
Agius, Quentin 188
Ah Chee, Marita **44**
Algaihgo (Fire Woman) 92
Allawara (language) 116
Almudj (Rainbow Serpent) 88
Altair Fine Art Gallery, Werribee South, Vic. 178–9
Alyawarre people 92, 93, 117
Amangu (language) 155
Amata people 194
Amurdak people 107
A<u>n</u>angu people 69–70, 100–4, 191
  art and artists 129, 136, 191–3
  ban on visitors climbing Ulu<u>r</u>u 104
A<u>n</u>angu Pitjantjatjara Yankunytjatjara (APY) Lands, SA 191–3
Anbangbang Billabong, Kakadu NP, NT 89
ancestors, regard for 11, 33
ancestral beings/spirits 7, 11, 12, 20, 69, 71, 99, 128, 153, 175
  Kakadu NP, NT 86–8, 89, 91, 92
  Yolŋu 16–17
ancestral stories 33, 63, 93, 96, 99, 100, 122, 204
  see also creation stories; Dreaming stories
Andrew, Brook 24
Anindilyakwa Art and Cultural Centre, Groote Eylandt, NT 11
Anmatyerr people 132
Anu, Christine **30**, 31
APY Lands, SA 191–3
Araluen Arts Centre, Alice Springs, NT 24, 121
archaeological evidence of early Aboriginal occupation 2, 6–9, 161–2
Arlpwe Art and Culture Centre, Ali Curung, NT 116–17
Arnhem Land
  early occupation 2
  tours and safaris 107–8, 109–10
Arnhem Land Plateau 88
Arnhemlander Cultural and Heritage Tour, NT 107, 108
Arrarrkbi people 84–5
Arrernte people 97, 99, 109, 112, 124, 127, 132, 136
  'skin' systems 19
art 6–7, 20–8
  authenticity 24
  see also Aboriginal art; rock art; Torres Strait Islander art and artists
art cooperatives/art organisations 23–4
art fairs 23, 24, 120, 121, 184, 195–6
art fraud 24–7
Art Galleries Association of Australia 27
art galleries, cultural centres and museums 116
  Australian Capital Territory 219–20
  New South Wales 24, 155, 169–70
  Northern Territory 21, 23, 26, 28, 66, 116–36
  Queensland 24, 210
  South Australia 184, 190–4
  Tasmania 215–16
  Torres Strait Islands 225
  Victoria 28, 178–82
  Western Australia 28, 137, 151–5
Art Gallery of New South Wales, Sydney, NSW 24, 155, 169
Art Gallery of South Australia, Adelaide, SA 184, 190
Art Gallery of Western Australia, Perth, WA 155
Art Mob – Aboriginal Fine Art, Hobart, Tas. 215
art sales
  Bathurst Island, NT 83–4
  Blak Markets, Sydney, NSW 169
art tours
  Ernabella Arts Tour – Longitude 131, NT 123
  Injalak Rock Art Tours, Gunbalanya, NT 126
  Tiwi Design Tours, Bathurst Island, NT 134
Arthur, Governor Sir George 49
Artists of Ampilatwatja, Ampilatwatja, NT 117
Arts Ceduna, Ceduna, SA 190
'assimilation' policy 34, 43
Association of Northern, Kimberley and Arnhem Aboriginal Artists 24, 28
auction houses 27
Australia Day 51
  protests **40**, **53**
Australian Commercial Galleries Association 27
Australian Constitution 52
  Aboriginal people given voting rights 52
  Indigenous Australians not classed as citizens 52
Australian history 51–3
  timelines 53
  see also Aboriginal history
Australian Indigenous Minority Supply Council 57
Australian Institute of Aboriginal and Torres Strait Islander Studies (AIATSIS) 12, 53, 73
Australian Memory of the World Register 23
Australian Museum 53
authenticity of art 24, 27
Ayal Aboriginal Tours Kakadu, NT 104
Ayers Rock *see* Ulu<u>r</u>u
Ayers Rock Resort, NT 115

B

Badimaya (language) 155
Badu Art Centre, Badu Island, Qld 225
Bamblett, Natarsha **55**
Bang Gerreng (season – April), Kakadu, NT 88
Bangarra Dance Theatre, Sydney, NSW 33, 170–2
Bani, Ephraim 225
Bannon-Harrison, Dwanye 165
Banuba (language) 152
Banumbirr ('morning star pole') 122
Barak, William 22
Baranbyatti Mirra Buuka (Dreamtime Southern Cross) 160
Bardi people 143, 144, 145, 146
Bardon, Geoffrey 23
bark paintings 20, 23, 119, 122, 123, 128, 130, 132, 134, 220
Barunga Festival, Barunga, NT 78
Bataluk Cultural Trail, East Gippsland, Vic. 178
Baudin, Nicholas 6
Baumann, Miriam 130

Bawaka Homeland Highlights, North-East Arnhem Land, NT 109
Be-lang-le-wool (Clark Island NP), Sydney, NSW 5, 169
Bell, Tyronne 219
Berndt, Catherine H. 22
Berndt, Ronald M. 22, 23
Bibbulman people 146
Bidawal people 157
Bininj/Mungguy people 86, 88
Birch, Tony, books by 36–7
Bird, Michael I. 9
birdwatching
  Bremer Island Banubanu Beach Retreat, Bremer Island, NT 104
  Coorong NP, SA 186
  Great Barrier Reef Marine Park, Qld 197
  Kakadu NP, NT 86, 88
  Litchfield NP, NT 94
  North Queensland 205
  Purnululu NP, WA 142–3
  Tjoritja (Western MacDonnell Ranges), NT 98–9
  Uluru–Kata Tjuta NP, NT 103
Birrarung Marr, Melbourne, Vic. 179
Birritjama, Dawidi 23
'Black Johnny' (artist) 22
Black Olive Catering 59
Black Point Cultural Centre, Garig Gunak Barlu NP, NT 85
Blair, Wayne 34
Blak Markets, Sydney, NSW 169
body painting **14**, **32**, 33
Bolung (Rainbow Serpent) 96
Bomaderry United Aboriginal Mission, Bomaderry, NSW 46
Booderee NP, JBT 161
Boonwurrung clan 173
Bowali Visitor Centre, Jabiru, NT 88, 90, 91
'Bradshaws' (rock paintings) 20
Brambuk – The National Park and Cultural Centre, Halls Gap, Vic. 62–3, 175, 177
Branagh, Kenneth 36
Bremer Island Banubanu Beach Retreat, Bremer Island, NT 104–7
Brian Lee Hunters Creek Tagalong Tours, Kooljaman at Cape Leveque, WA 143–4
Bringing them home: The 'Stolen Children' report 43, 52
British, establish settlements in Australia 49, 51
Broken (Torres Strait language) 14
Brown, Aunty Hazel 36
Bryant, Rob 33
Buku-Larrnggay Mulka Art Centre and Museum, Yirrkala, NT 23, **25**, 28, 117–18
Bula (Jawoyn Ancestor) 88
Bula'Bula Arts, Ramingining, NT 118–20
Bundjalung NP, NSW 157
Bundjalung people 59, 157
Bundy's Cultural Tours, Kooljaman at Cape Leveque, WA 144, 145
bunggul (ceremony) 123
Bunggul Dance, Garma Festival, NT **63**, 80
Bungle Bungle Range, WA 140–1, 142
Bungolee Tours, Fitzroy Crossing, WA 145
Bunjil (spiritual figure) 175
Bunjilaka Aboriginal Cultural Centre, Melbourne Museum, Carlton, Vic. 180
Bunurong clan 36
Burarra (language) 128
Burrungkuy (Nourlangie) area, Kakadu NP, NT 89
Burrungkuy (Nourlangie) Rock, Kakadu NP, NT 88, 89, 91–2
bushwalking/walking
  Bremer Island Banubanu Beach Retreat, Bremer Island, NT 104
  Chillagoe-Mungana Caves NP, Qld 198
  Coorong NP, SA 185–6
  Cradle Mountain-Lake St Clair NP, Tas. 212
  Ikara–Flinders Ranges NP, SA 187
  Judbarra-Gregory NP, NT 85
  Kakadu NP, NT 89, 90, 92
  Karijini NP, WA 139
  Karlu Karlu (Devils Marbles) Conservation Reserve, NT 93
  Larapinta Trail, West MacDonnells, NT 100
  Litchfield NP, NT 94
  Mount Field NP, Tas. 213
  Namadgi National Park, ACT 217
  Nitmiluk NP, NT 96–7
  Purnululu NP, WA 143
  Rocky Cape NP, Tas. 213
  South Bruny NP, Tas. 214
  Tjoritja (Western MacDonnell Ranges) 99, 100
  Uluru–Kata Tjuta NP, NT 103
business 48, 56–8
Butchulla people 199
buying authentic Indigenous art 23, 27

C
Cadi Jam Ora (First Encounters) walk, Sydney, NSW 166
Cairns Indigenous Art Fair, Cairns, Qld 24, **26**, 195–6
Campbell, Aunty Margaret 160
canoeing
  Coorong NP, SA 186
  Nitmiluk NP, NT 97
Capewell, Darren 149
Cassady, James 205
celebrations *see* festivals; NAIDOC Week
ceremonies 14, 33, 62, **63**, 64, **65**, **66**
  body painting **14**, **32**, 33
  dance performances 33
  'Welcome to Country' 11, **55**, 64
certificates of authenticity 24
Charcoal Lane (restaurant), Fitzroy, Vic. **60**, 61, 182
Charlie's Country (film) 119
Chief Protector of Aborigines 36
Chillagoe-Mungana Caves NP, Qld 198–9
clap sticks 29, 30
Clark Island NP, NSW 5, 169
Clarkson, Chris 7
clothing 69, 116, 123, 200, 212
Code of Ethics of the National Association for the Visual Arts 27
colonies, Federation of, to form Commonwealth of Australia 52
Colony of New South Wales 51
Commonwealth of Australia 52
community-based Aboriginal art centres 28
Community Development Program 58
convicts 51
Cook, Captain James 14, **49**
Cooper, Victor 104
Coorong NP, SA 184–7
Corn, Aaron 17, 18, 30
Council for Aboriginal Reconciliation 53
country, definition 72
Cradle Mountain-Lake St Clair NP, Tas. 212
creation stories 86, 88, 89, 96, 103, 122, 215
Creole (linguistic term) 14, 15
crocodiles *see* saltwater crocodiles
culinary tourism 59–62
cultural awareness for visitors 64
  dress standards 69, 116, 123
  language rules 67
  photographs and videos 68, **69**, 103, 116, 124
  questions may not be welcome 65–6, 67
  safety signs 70–1
  showing respect for your hosts 64–5
  signs and published cultural rules and protocols 68–71
  speaking local languages 64
  when to use names of people and places and when not to 66–7
cultural experiences *see* art galleries, cultural centres and museums; art tours; cultural heritage; cultural workshops; festivals; rock art; tours and stays
cultural heritage
  Bundjalung NP, NSW 157
  Coorong NP, SA 185
  Grampians NP, Vic. 175–7
  Great Sandy NP, Qld 199–200
  Ikara–Flinders Ranges NP, SA 187
  Judbarra-Gregory NP, NT 85
  Kakadu NP, NT 86–91, 107–8, 109
  Karijini NP, WA 138
  Karlu Karlu (Devils Marbles) Conservation Reserve, NT 92–3
  Kosciuszko NP, NSW 157–8
  Litchfield NP, NT 94
  Nitmiluk NP, NT 96
  Purnululu NP, WA 141
  Tjoritja (Western MacDonnell Ranges), NT 97
  Uluru–Kata Tjuta NP, NT 102
  see also tours and stays
cultural workshops
  Garma Festival, Gulkula, NT 80
  Godinymayin Yijard Rivers Arts & Cultural Centre, Katherine, NT **25**, 124
  Living Kaurna Cultural Centre, Adelaide, SA 191
  Maruka Arts, Uluru–Kata Tjuta Cultural Centre, NT 69
  Tasmanian Aboriginal Corporation for Women's Art and Craft, Launceston, Tas. 211
cultures and customs 11–12, 54–5
Currumbin Wildlife Sanctuary, Currumbin, Qld 200
cycling
  Ikara–Flinders Ranges NP, SA 187
  Tjoritja (Western MacDonnell Ranges) 99

D
DAAF Film Gala, Darwin, NT 120
Dagoman people 135
Daguragu, NT, recognition of Aboriginal land rights 52
Dan, Seaman 31
dance 29, 32–3
  Bangarra Dance Theatre, Sydney, NSW 33, 170–2
  Bunggul dance, Garma Festival, NT 80
  Laura Aboriginal Dance Festival, Cape York, Qld **32**, 195
  and traditional Aboriginal religion 33
  Yuggera Aboriginal Dancers, Brisbane, Qld 206
Darug people 158
Darwin Aboriginal Art Fair, NT 24, 120
Davidson's Arnhem Land Safaris, NT 107
deceased persons
  referring to 11, 66
  warnings at beginning of TV broadcasts 67, **67**
Demand and Supply Issues in Indigenous Tourism 58–9
Desart, Alice Springs, NT 23–4, 28
Desert Mob, Alice Springs, NT **22**, 24, 121
Devils Marbles, NT 92–3
Dhararawal people 162
Dharwra Aboriginal Cultural Tours, Canberra, ACT 219
dhäwu (stories) 123
Dhuwa clan 17, 19

Dickson, Dr Greg 14
didgeridoos *see yidarkis*
discrimination 48
diversity of Aboriginal populations 9
Dja Dja Wurrung clan 173
Djab Wurrung people 62
Djabugay people 206
Djabulukgu Association cultural 4WD and boat tours, Kakadu NP, NT 107, 108
Djadawitjibi people of the Djinang group 119
'Djapana: Sunset Dreaming' (song) 12
Djawa, Tom 23
Djinang (language) 128
Djirranganj Dreaming Tour, Narooma, NSW 165
Djómi Museum, at Maningrida Arts and Culture, Manigrida community, NT 128
Dodson, Prof Michael 43, 52
Dog Dreaming 136
Donovan, Clayton (Indigenous chef) 61
dot paintings 116, 129, 132
Dreaming stories 6, 11, 93, 96, 97, 99, 100, 140, 152, 155, 157, 190
  tours including 112, 126, 127, 136, 145, 146, 149, 160, 165, 200, 204
'Dreamtime' 11, 130, 204, 205
Dreamtime at the G (football), Melbourne Cricket Ground, Melbourne, Vic. 173–4, 179
Dreamtime Southern X (tours), Sydney 3, 4, 160
dress standards 69, 116, 123
Dunghutti-Ngaku Aboriginal Art Gallery, South Kempsey, NSW 170
Dunghutti people 160, 170

E
Eades, Dr Diane 15
East Alligator area, Kakadu NP, NT 88, 90
East Journey (band) 30
Eastern Kunwinjku (language) 128
Elcho Island Art and Craft, Galiwinku, NT 121–2
Elcho Island Arts Gallery, Darwin, NT 123
Elders 11, 36, 92, 118, 153, 156, 170, 174, 180
Electric Fields (band) 31
Ella, Tim 162
Ellery Creek Big Hole, Tjoritja (Western MacDonnell Ranges), NT 99
employment 58, 115, 116, 123, 178, 206
engravings on rock faces 6
Eora nation and people 51, 166, 169
Ernabella Arts Tour – Longitude 131, Yulara, NT 123
Erre people 124
Erub dialect (Torres Strait islands) 15
European artists
  collecting of Aboriginal art 23
  relationship with Aboriginal artists 22
European sociologists, documentation of Aboriginal society 22–3
Ewamian people 206
expeditions/exploration in Northern Australia 3, 20

F
fashion 120–1, 129–30
festivals
  Barunga Festival, Barunga, NT 78
  Garma Festival, Gulkula, NT **60**, 62, **63**, 68–9, 80–2
  Laura Dance Festival, Cape York, Qld **32**, 195
  Mahbilil Festival, Jabiru, NT 80
  Merrepen Arts and Music Festival, Nauiya, NT 130
  Mowanjum Festival, Derby, WA 137
  Nayri Niara Good Spirit Festival, Bruny Island, Tas. 211
  Survival Day Festival, Adelaide, SA 184
  Tanderrum, Melbourne, Vic. 173
  Tarnanthi Festival of Contemporary Aboriginal and Torres Strait Islander Art and Art Fair, Adelaide, SA 184
  Yabun Festival, Sydney, NSW 51, 156, 172
fibre art 119, 122, 123, 128, 130, 132, 134–5
film 12, 34–6, 119, 120
fire use in management 9–10
First Australians *see* Aboriginal peoples; Aboriginal and Torres Strait Islander peoples and cultures; Torres Strait Islander people
First Australians (DVDs) 51
First Nations peoples 72
First People 72
fishing
  Bremer Island Banubanu Beach Retreat, Bremer Island, NT 104
  Coorong NP, SA 186
  Garig Gunak Baru NP, NT 85
  Judbarra-Gregory NP, NT 85, 86
  protocols 71
  Rocky Cape NP, Tas. 213
  tours 113, 144, 203
Fogarty, Lionel 37
Follow The Rabbit Proof Fence (film) 34–5
forests 10
Forrest, Andrew 58
Fortescue Metals 57, 58
fraudulent art 24–7
fresh water sources, avoid contaminating 71
From Country to Couture: The DAAF Fashion Show, Darwin, NT 120–1
funeral ceremonies 33
funerary sculptures 20

G
Gab Titui Cultural Centre, Thursday Island, Qld 225
Gadigal people of the Eora nation 5, 162, 166, 169
Gagudju (people and language) 86, 88
Galamban Extraordinary Aboriginal Experiences (Booderee NP), Wreck Bay Village, JBT 161
Gammage, Bill 9–10
Gammeraigal people 5, 169
Ganalbingu (language) 12
Gapan Gallery, Garma Festival, Gulkula, NT 82
Gapuwiyak Culture and Arts Aboriginal Corporation, Gapuwiyak, NT 123
Garden Point Mission, Melville Island, NT 44
Garig Gunak Barlu NP, NT 84–5
Gariwerd *see* Grampians NP, Vic.
Garma Festival, Gulkula, NT **60**, 62, **63**, 80–2, 120
  'Behaviour protocols' 68–9
'Garma Statement on Indigenous Music and Dance' 29
Gawurra (musician) 31
genocide 43–4
geological history 62, 88, 93, 96, 142, 187
Gija people 155
giritjirri (dance) 123
Giro Giro (Kimberley rock figures) 20
Godinymayin Yijard Rivers Arts & Cultural Centre, Katherine, NT **25**, 123–4
Gooniyandi (language) 152
Gostelow, Tia 31
gourmet food and culinary tourism 59–62
Grampians NP, Vic. 175–7
grasslands 10
Great Barrier Reef Marine Park, Qld 196–8
Great Sandy NP, Qld 199–200
Grey, Sir George 20
Gudjewg (season – December to March), Kakadu, NT 88
Guerard, Eugene von 22
Gulpilil, David 12, 36
Gululu Day Tour, North-East Arnhem Land, NT 110
Guluyambi Cultural Cruise, Kakadu NP, NT 107, 109–10
Gumatj (people and language) 12
Gumbula, Dr Joe 17, 30
Gun-nartpa (language) 128
Gunai-Kurnai people 178
Gunditjmara Nation 178
Gundjeihmi (language) 86, 88
Gunitjmara clan 174
Gunumeleng (season – mid-October to late December), Kakadu, NT 88
Gupapuyngu (clan and language) 23, 123, 128
Gurindji people 52
Guringai people 5, 169
Gurrgoni (language) 128
Gurrung (season – mid-August to mid-October), Kakadu, NT 88
gurruṯu (Yolŋu kinship) 16, 17–19
Gutharraguda (Shark Bay) 151
Gwion Gwion (Kimberley rock figures) 20

H
hand stencils 6
Harrow Discovery Centre and Johnny Mullagh Interpretive Centre, Harrow, Vic. 174, 175
Harry Nanya Tours, Lake Mungo, NSW 161–2
Harvey Norman Rugby League All Stars Match, The, NSW 156
Hawk Dreaming Wilderness Lodge, Kakadu NP, NT 108
Hayden, Mick 149
Healing Foundation 46
Heiss, Dr Anita 37
Hermannsburg mission, NT **50**, **53**
Hermannsburg Potters, NT 124
Hermannsburg school (of painting) 131
High Court of Australia
  Mabo No 2 (Mabo decision) 40, 41
  overturns *terra nullius* 40
  Yorta Yorta case 41
Holt, Yvette 37
Horton, David 12
Howard, John 44
Hudson, David 206
Hughes, Robert, *The Fatal Shore: The Epic of Australia's Founding* 51
human migration out of Africa 7
Human Rights and Equal Opportunity Commission 53

I
Ikara–Flinders Ranges NP, SA 187–8
Ikuntji Artists, Haasts Bluff, NT 126
Ilbijerri Theatre Company 173
Imintji Campground and Art Centre, Gibb River Rd, Kimberley, WA 145
imprisonment rate 52–3
Indigenous art and artists *see* Aboriginal art; Aboriginal artists; Torres Strait Islander art and artists
Indigenous Art Code 27
Indigenous art market 20, 23
Indigenous business 48, 56–8, 59
  attitudes towards 56
  government procurement from 57–8
  provision of goods and services through Supply Nation 57
  and RAPs 56–7
Indigenous Business Australia (IBA) 58, 59, 188
Indigenous Business Month 58
Indigenous chefs 59–61
Indigenous goods and services, corporate and government procurement of 57
Indigenous Land Corporation 61, 115
Indigenous language groups 12, **13**
Indigenous languages 12–15, 64

grammars and dictionaries 64
rules of use in Aboriginal society 67
speaking 64–5
Indigenous musicians 12, 29–31
Indigenous people *see* Aboriginal peoples; Aboriginal and Torres Strait Islander people and cultures; Torres Strait Islander people
Indigenous rangers 5, 10, 65
Indigenous systems of law 42
Indigenous tour guides
not all questions are welcome 65–6, 67
showing respect for 48, 64–5
see also Indigenous rangers
Indigenous Tourism Champions Program 59
Indigenous tourism sector 58–9
Indigenous writers 36–7
Ingan Tour, Tully, Qld 202
Injalak Arts and Crafts, Gunbalanya, NT 124–6
Injalak Rock Art Tours, Gunbalanya, NT 126
injuries and illnesses 69
international collecting institutions 23
international galleries and exhibitions 23, 24, 118
Iwaidja (language) 84
Iwantja Arts, Indulkana, SA 193, 194

J
Jabiru area, Kakadu NP, NT 88, 90
Jadawadjali clan 174
Jaminjung people 85
Janbal Gallery, Mossman, Qld 210
Janbanbarra Jirrbal people 202
Jardwadjali people 62
Jaru (people and language) 141, 154
Jawi people 146
Jawoyn (people and language) 86, 88, 89, 95, 135
Jibbon Aboriginal Carvings Tour – Sydney Coast Walks, NSW 162
Jilamara Arts and Crafts, Milikapiti, Melville Island, NT 126–7, 131
Jilamara Arts and Crafts Association 83
Jilji (sand-hill country of the Great Sandy Desert) 152
jin-Merdewa (female water spirit) 128
Johnny Mullagh Interpretive Centre, Harrow, Vic. 174, 175
Johnson, Carole J. 33
Jones, Mark 206
Jose, Ellen 24
Journey into Olkola Country, Cairns, Qld 202–3
Judbarra-Gregory NP, NT 85–6
Jukurrpa (Dreaming) 152

K
Kadoo Indigenous and Historical Tours, Sydney, NSW 162
Kahau, Mahealani 48
Kakadu Animal Tracks Safari, Kakadu NP, NT 107
Kakadu Cultural Tours, Kakadu NP, NT 107–8
Kakadu NP, NT 48, 86–93
Mahbili Festival, Jabiru 82
saltwater crocodiles **71**, 89, 91
six seasons of Kakadu 88
tours 104, 107–8, 110, 115
see also Noulangie Rock; Ubirr
Kakadu Tourism Adventure Tours, Kakadu NP, NT 108
Kakadu Tours, NT 107
Kala Lagaw Ya (Torres Strait Islands dialect) 15, 222
Kalaw Kawaw Ya (Torres Strait Islands dialect) 15
kangaroos 14
Karijini NP, WA 138–40
Karijini Visitor Centre, Karijini NP, WA 140
Karlu Karlu (Devil Marbles) Conservation Reserve, NT 92–3
Karrangpurra people 85
Karrke Aboriginal Cultural Experiences, Wanmarra community, NT 109
Katherine Gorge, NT 96
Kattipul, Kieren 130
Kaurareg nation 225
Kaurna people 190, 191
Kawrareg (Torres Strait Islands dialect) 15
kayaking, Coorong NP, SA 186
Kaytetye people 92, 116
Keating, Paul
on the Mabo decision 40
Redfern Park Speech 172
Keneally, Thomas, *The Commonwealth of Thieves: The Story of the Founding of Australia* 51
Kepa Kurl Art Gallery and Gift Shop, Esperance, WA 151
Kepa Kurl Tours, Esperance, WA 145
Keringke Arts, Santa Teresa, NT 127–8
Keringke Style 128
Kija (people and language) 140, 141
Kimberley Coastal Adventure, Broome, WA 145
kinship 16–19
Kooljaman at Cape Leveque, WA 146
Koomal Dreaming Tours, Yallingup, WA 61–2, 146
Koongurrukun clan 94
Koori Heritage Trust, Melbourne, Vic. 182
Kosciuszko NP, NSW 157–8
Kow Swamp people, Vic. (13,000–9,000 years ago) 9
Kriol (language) 14
Kuju Aboriginal Arts, Port Lincoln, SA 191
Kukatja (language) 154
Kuki (season – January to April), Torres Strait Islands 222
Kuku Yalanji (people and language) 203, 204, 208, 210
Kuku Yalanji Cultural Habitat Tour, Mossman, Qld 203
Kulin nation 173, 177
Kulkalgai Ya (Torres Strait Islands dialect) 15
Kumbi, Gracie 130
Kunbarlang (language) 128
Kunibidji (people and language) 128
Kunwinijku (people and language) 86, 88, 124
Kupka, Karel 23
Kwartatuma 100

L
Lake Mungo, NSW
human occupation from 60,000 years ago 9, 161
tours 161–2
land rights **39**, 52, 73, 102, 118, 172, 182, 221
languages 72
see also Indigenous languages
Larapinta Trail, West MacDonnells, NT 100
Larmairremener of the Big River tribe 212
larrakitj (painted ceremonial poles) 123
Laura Aboriginal Dance Festival, Cape York, Qld **32**, 195
Lee, Brian 143
Liberto, Pamela Yvonne and Ivan, sell fraudulent art 24–7
Limilngan (language) 88
Limilngan-Wuna Cultural Tour, NT 110
Limilngan-Wuna people 110
Lirrwi Tourism, NT 109–10
Litchfield NP, NT 94–5
Living Kaurna Cultural Centre, Adelaide, SA 190–1
Lombadina community, WA 146–8
Loos, Noel 38
Lord's Kakadu and Arnhem Land Safaris, Kakadu, NT 110
lorrkons (hollow logs) 124
Ltyentye Apurte (Santa Teresa) 127
Lulydjudjan (Rainbow Serpent) 88
Luritja (people and language) 109, 112, 132, 136

M
Maalinup Aboriginal Gallery, Henley Brook, WA 151
Mabo, Eddie Koiki 38, 40
Mabo No 2 (Mabo decision) 40, 41
Mabuyag (Torres Strait Island dialect) 15
MacDonnell Ranges, NT 97–100
McKenzie, Queenie 142
McRae, Tommy 22
McTaggart, Aaron 130
Madjunbalmi clan 84
Magela Cultural and Heritage Tour, Kakadu NP, NT 107
Mahbilil Festival, Jabiru, NT 80
Mailman, Deborah **35**
Maku Tjukurpa (song line) 193
Malak Malak (language and people) 129
Malgana people 149
Mamukala wetlands, Kakadu NP, NT 89
Mangkaja Arts Resource Agency, Fitzroy Crossing, WA 152
manikay (singing style) 30, 123
Maningrida Arts and Culture, Maningrida, NT 128
Manupi Art Centre, Garden Point, Melville Island, NT 131
Mari Nawi (Big Canoe) 5, 169
Marika family 118
marine parks 196–8
Marranunggu clan 94
Marrawuddi Gallery, Jabiru, NT 91
Martu people 152
Martumili Artists, Newman, WA 152
Martutjarra people 34–6
Martuwarra (river country) 152
Maruku Arts, Uluṟu–Kata Tjuṯa Cultural Centre, NT 21, 28, **65**, 129
Mary River area, Kakadu NP, NT 89
Mary River Wetlands, NT 112
Mauboy, Jessica 34, **35**, 83
Maymuru family 118
Melbourne, Vic.
Aboriginal peoples 5, 182
Aboriginal tours 5, 177
Mengerrdji people 124
Mer Island people and dialect 15, 38, 40
Meriam Mir (language) 15, 222
Merrepen Arts Centre, Nauiya, NT 130
Merrepen Arts and Music Festival, Nauiya, NT 130
Methodist Overseas Mission, Milingimbi, NT 23
Mickey of Uladulla (artist) 22
migration routes, to Australia 7, 9, **10**
Milingimbi Art and Craft Centre, Milingimbi, NT 23, 130
Mimi Aboriginal Arts and Crafts, Katherine, NT 130–1
Mimi Spirits 131
Mimili Maku Art Centre, Mimili, SA 193–4
miners and mining 56, 57
Minjungbal Aboriginal Cultural Centre, Tweed Heads, NSW 170
miny'tji (sacred designs) 123
Miriam people of Mer Island 38, 40
Miriwoong people 154
miscegenation 43
Mission Australia 61
missionaries 52
missions 23, 44, 46, **50**, 52, **53**, 188
Moffatt, Tracey 24
Moore River Native Settlement, WA 34–6
Mossman Gorge Centre and Ngadiku Dreamtime Walks, Mossman, Qld 203–4
Mount Borradaile, NT, rock art **7**, **21**, 107
Mount Field NP, Tas. 212–13

Mowanjum Art and Cultural Centre, Derby, WA 28, 137, 152–3
Mowanjum Festival, Derby, WA 137
Mungalla Aboriginal Tours, Ingham, Qld 204–5
Mungkuri, Peter 193
Mungo National Park, NSW **8**, 66
Muran clan 84
Murray Island, land ownership and inheritance system 38
Museum and Art Gallery of the Northern Territory (MAGNT), Darwin, NT 133
music 12, 29–31
  Garma Festival, NT 80
  Merrepen Arts and Music Festival, Nauiya, NT 130
  National Indigenous Music Awards, Darwin **30**, 31, 83
Mutawintji Eco Tours, NSW 165
Mutawintji NP, NSW 165

N
Naaguja (language) 155
Nabilil (dragon-like creation-time figure) 96
NAIDOC Week 54–5
NAISDA (National Aboriginal Islander Skills Development Association) 33
Najombolmi (artist) 91
Nakkara (language) 128
Namadgi NP, ACT 217, 218
Nama'rdeedjurr (Rainbow Serpent) 88
Namarrgon (Lightning Man) 88
Namatjira, Albert 8, 131
Namatjira Project (film) 120
names of people and places
  attempting pronunciation 6
  names of people which cannot be spoken 11, 66
  place names 67
Namorrorddo (spirit being) 128
Nanguluwur (art site), Kakadu NP, NT 91–2
Narana Aboriginal Cultural Centre, Geelong, Vic. 28, 180
Narlijia Cultural Tours, Broome, WA 148
National Aboriginal and Torres Strait Island Art Awards 120, 130, 133, 136, 193
National Gallery of Australia, Canberra, ACT 24, 27, 155, 193, 219–20
  hollow-log memorial **22**, 119
National Gallery of Victoria, Melbourne, Vic. 155
National Indigenous Constitutional Convention 42
National Indigenous Music Awards, Darwin, NT **30**, 31, 83, 120
National Indigenous Television 48
National Museum of Australia, Canberra, ACT 53, 220
national parks
  Australian Capital Territory 217–19
  Jervis Bay Territory 161
  New South Wales 5, 66, 157–8, 165, 169
  Northern Territory 48, 69–70, 84–104
  Queensland 196–200
  South Australia 184–8
  Tasmania 211–15
  Victoria 62, 175–7
  Western Australia 138–43
National Reconciliation Convention 52
National Recording Project for Indigenous Performance in Australia 29
National Sorry Day 44, 46
native title 38–42, 57, 73, 157
  and bitter debate over Australian land tenure 40
  Canada and New Zealand 42
  claims through Native Title Tribunal 41–2
  and Mabo No 2 (Mabo decision) 40, 41
  and need to prove connection to land through unbroken line of descent 41
  successful claims 42
  Yorta Yorta case 41
Native Title Act of 1993 40
Native Title Tribunal 41–2
Nay Gay (season – October to December), Torres Strait Islands 222
Ngaanyatjarra people 153, 191
Ngaanyatjarra Pitjantjatjara Yankunytjatjara Women's Council 134
Ngadiku (stories and legends) 204
Ngadiku Dreamtime Walks, Mossman, Qld 203–4
Ngadjuri people 188
Ngaindjagar clan 84
Ngaliwurri people 85
Ngalyod (Rainbow Serpent) 88, 128
Ngan'gi language group 129
Ngan'gikurrungurr (language) 129
Ngaran Ngaran Cultural Awareness, Narooma, NSW 163
Ngargee to Nerm Cultural tour, The: from Ancient Tree to Ancient Sea, Melbourne, Vic. 5
Ngarigo people 157
Ngariman people 85
Ngarinyin (people and language) 137, 152, 153
Ngarluma people 149
Ngarranggarni (Dreaming) 154
Ngarrindjeri people 187
Ngarti (language) 15
Ngen'giwumirri (language) 129
Ngunawal people 218, 219
Ngurra 126
Ngurrangga Tours, Roebourne, WA 148–9
Ngurratjuta Iltja Ntjarra Many Hands Art Centre, Alice Springs, NT 131–2
Nhanagardi (language) 155
Nhanda people 149
Nitmiluk NP, NT 95–7
Njaki Njaki Tours, Merredin, WA 149
No Fixed Address (band) 31
non-Indigenous guides 48–53
  ignore Aboriginal history and culture 48
  racist statements/jokes about Aboriginal people 48
Noongar people 36, 145, 146, 149
North tribe 212
Nugul-bulok. Ngarra. Nurru-nurru. Yinga – 'Stories. Dance. Ochre. Song' 173
Numbulwar Red Flag Dancers 31
Nungali people 85
Nura Diya – Taronga's Aboriginal Discovery Tour, Mosman, NSW 165–6
Nyinkka Nyunyu Art and Culture Centre, Tennant Creek, NT 132
Nywaigi people 204–5

O
ochre pits 99
O'Dowd, Chris 34
'Old People', idea of 11
Olgas, The *see* Kata Tjuṯa
Olive, Mark (Indigenous chef) 59–61, **60**
Olkola people 202–3
Olsen, Christine 36
Ormiston Gorge and Pound, Tjoritja (Western MacDonnell Ranges), NT 100
Orr, Ricky 112
Outstation Art, Darwin, NT 132

P
Paakantyi people 161
Page, Stephen 33
painting, 19th and 20th century 22–3
Palawa people 215
Pamagirri Aboriginal Experience at the Woodward Family RainForeStation, Kuranda, Qld 205–6
Pamagirri people 205
Pangerninghe people of the Big River tribe 212
Papunya style of art 23, 133
Papunya Tjupi Aboriginal Arts, Papunya, NT 132–3
Papunya Tula Artists Pty Ltd, Alice Springs, NT 23, 28, 132, 133
Parks and Wildlife Commission of the Northern Territory 85, 93, 96
Pascoe, Bruce, books by 36
Passi, Fr Dave 38, 40
Peddells Thursday Island Tours, Thursday Island, Qld 225
penal colonies 51
permits
  art centres on Aboriginal land 116, 118, 120, 126, 127, 128, 130, 131, 134, 136, 155, 193
  festivals 80, 82
  national parks 85, 86, 90, 97, 100, 104
  tours and stays 107, 110
Pertame Southern Arrernte (people and language) 109, 112
Phillip, Captain Arthur **49**, 51
Phillip Creek Native Settlement, Manga Marda Waterhole, Tennant Creek, NT 46
photography 102, 112, 139, 143
  unauthorised 68, **69**, 103, 116, 124
Pilkington Garimara, Doris 34, 36
Pintupi (people and language) 132, 154
Pitjantjatjara people 100, 191
place names 67
playwrights 37
poets 37
Point Pearce Aboriginal Mission, Point Pearce, SA 188
Poornarti Aboriginal Tours, Denmark, WA 149
pottery 116, 124, 131
prehistory 2, 6–10, 161–2
printmaking 193, 225
Pudakul Aboriginal Cultural Tours, NT 110
Pukatja people 123
Purcell, Leah, books by **35**, 37
Purnululu NP, WA 140–3

Q
Queensland
  annexation of traditional land 38
  and native title rights 38–40
Queensland Art Gallery and Gallery of Modern Art (QAGOMA), Brisbane, Qld 24, 210
Queensland Coast Islands Declaratory Act 1985 38, 40
questions which may not be welcome 65–6, 67

R
Racial Discrimination Act 1975 (Cth) 38
racism 48
Rain Maker spirit 20
Rainbow Serpent 86, 88, 96, 128
Rainbow Valley Cultural Tours, NT 112
reconciliation 44, 48
Reconciliation Action Plans (RAPs) 56–7
Reconciliation Australia 56
Redbank Gorge, Tjoritja (Western MacDonnell Ranges), NT 100
Redfern, NSW, Aboriginal community 172
Reef 2050 Plan 197–8
Reef islands, Great Barrier Reef Marine Park, Qld 198
Rembarrnga (language) 128
remote Aboriginal communities, protest against forced closure of **39**
Retta Dixon Home, Darwin, NT 46
Reynolds, Henry 38
Rice, James 38, 40
Rio Tinto 57
Riverlife Mirrabooka, Brisbane, Qld 206

Roach, Archie 61, 83
Robinson, Brian 24
rock art 6–7, 11, 20, 127
Burrungkuy (Nourlangie) Rock, Kakadu NP, NT 88, 89, 91–2
Chillagoe-Mungana Caves NP, Qld 198–9
European interpretation 67
Flinders Ranges, SA **26**
Grampians NP, Vic. 62, 175
Ikara–Flinders Ranges NP, SA 187
Injalak Hill, NT 126
Judbarra-Gregory NP, NT 85
Kakadu NP, NT 86, 88, 89, 90, 91–2
Kimberley, WA 151
Mt Borradaile, NT **7**, **21**, 107
Pilbara, WA 149
Purnululu NP, WA 142
Ubirr, Kakadu NP, NT 88, 90, 91
Uluru–Kata Tjuta NP, NT 102
rock music 31
Rocky Cape NP, Tas. 213–14
Roelands Village, Roelands, WA (property) 61, 155
Royal Botanic Gardens, Aboriginal Cultural Walk, Melbourne, Vic. 177
Royal Botanic Gardens Sydney Aboriginal Heritage Experiences, Sydney, NSW 166
Royal Commission into Aboriginal Deaths in Custody 52–3
Rrengetyirpe (Simpsons Gap) 99
RT Tours Australia 112–13
Rudd, Kevin, National Apology to Stolen Generations 36, 44–5, **47**
Ruhanen, Dr Lisa 58, 59
Ryan, Lyndall 51

S
sacred in everyday life 11, 12–14
sacred sites 69, 70, 127
Karlu Karlu (Devils Marbles) Conservation Reserve, NT 93
Mt Borradaile, NT 107
Nitmiluk NP, NT 96
Tjoritja (Western MacDonnell Ranges), NT 97, 100
Uluru–Kata Tjuta NP, NT 100, 102, 103–4
safety signs 70–1
Sager (season – May to December), Torres Strait Islands 222
Salee, Mrs Celuia Mapo 38, 40
saltwater crocodiles
Judbarra-Gregory NP, NT 85
Kakadu NP 71, 89, 91
Litchfield NP, NT 94
Nitmiluk NP, NT 96
warning signs **71**
Sambono, Marita 129
Sand Dune Adventures, Port Stephens, NSW 166
Sandra Bardas Art Gallery, Healesville, Vic. 180
Sapphires, The (film) 34, **35**
Sayers, Andrew 22
scenic touring
Ikara–Flinders Ranges NP, SA 187
Nitmiluk NP, NT 97
Purnululu NP, WA 143
Tjoritja (Western MacDonnell Ranges), NT 99
scenic views
Coorong NP, SA 186
Karijini NP, WA 139–40
Uluru–Kata Tjuta NP, NT 103
Scott, Kim, books by 36
screen-printed fabrics 124, 129, 134
seasons 88, 222
Sebbens, Shari **35**
SEIT Outback Australia 113
Serpentine Gorge, Tjoritja (Western MacDonnell Ranges), NT 99
settlers 3, 9, 52
and Aboriginal history 50–1
conflict with Aboriginal people 51, 205
Sharp, Naomi 124
showing respect
for Aboriginal and Torres Strait Islander hosts and guides 64–5
for protocols of the first Australians 67
signs and published cultural rules and protocols 68–71
Simpsons Gap, Tjoritja (Western MacDonnell Ranges), NT 99
singing styles 30, 123
'skin systems' 16, 19
smoking ceremonies 11, **14**, 64, **65**, **66**
Soft Sands (band) 30–1
songs and song cycles 6, 12, 29, 30
South Alligator area, Kakadu NP, NT 89
South Australian Museum, Adelaide, SA 193
South Bruny NP, Tas. 214–15
Southern Arrernte language 112
souvenir shops 24
spiritual beings/spiritual presence 11, 20, 69, 71, 175, 213
see also ancestral beings/spirits
sport
Dreamtime at the G, Melbourne Cricket Ground, Melbourne, Vic. 173–4
Harrow Discovery Centre and Johnny Mullagh Interpretive Centre, Harrow, Vic. 174, 175
The Harvey Norman Rugby League All Stars Match, NSW 156
Tiwi Islands Grand Final and Art Sale, Bathurst Island, NT 83–4
Stewart, Dean 5
Stolen Generations 43–7
compensation claims 44
definition 43
demonstrations **47**
John Howard refuses to apologise to 44
Memorials and plaques 46–7
National Apology to, by Kevin Rudd 36, 44–5, **47**
national inquiry and report 43–4, 52
numbers of children forcibly removed 43
significance of the Apology 45–6
story of (in film) 34–6
Stolen Generations Memorial
Phillip Creek Native Settlement, Manga Marda Waterhole, Tennant Creet, NT 46
Reilly Lane, Sydenham Green, Sydney 46
Stolen Generations Memorial Garden, Beinda Street, Bomaderry, NSW 46–7
Stone, Cheryl 33
storytelling 7, 34–7
Straddle Adventures, One Mile, Stradbroke Island, Qld 206
sunset 12–13
Supply Nation 57
Survival Day Festival, Adelaide, SA 184, 191
sustainable land management 9
swimming
Bremer Island Banubanu Beach Retreat, Bremer Island, NT 104
Kakadu NP, NT 89
Karijini NP, WA 140
Litchfield NP, NT 94
Nitmiluk NP, NT 97
Rocky Cape NP, Tas. 213
Tjoritja (Western MacDonnell Ranges), NT 99
Swindley, Brian 'Binna' 210
Sydney, NSW
Aboriginal peoples 5, 166, 169, 172
tours 3, 4, 5, 162, 165–9
Sydney Harbour 5

T
taboos, on saying the name of deceased persons 11
Tandanya National Aboriginal Cultural Institute, Adelaide, SA 184, 191
Tanderrum, Melbourne, Vic. 173
Tangentyere Artists, Alice Springs, NT 133
Tapsell, Miranda **35**
Tasmania
Black Wars 49
British attempt to eliminate Indigenous population 49
Indigenous people **50**
no information about Aboriginal people and culture for tourists 49–50
suppression of Aboriginal history 50
Tasmanian Aboriginal Corporation for Women's Art and Craft, Launceston, Tas. 211
Tasmanian Museum and Art Gallery, Hobart, Tas. 216
Tasmanian Wilderness World Heritage Area 212, 213
Taungurung clan 173
Taylor, Bob 112
Telstra's National Aboriginal and Torres Strait Island Art Awards 120, 130, 133, 136, 193
Ten Canoes (film) 12, 119
terra nullius 38, 40
Thaiday, Ken, Sr 24
The Olgas *see* Kata Tjuta
The Sapphires (film) 34, **35**
Thomas, Rover 27, 142
Thornton, Warwick 24
Thursday Island, Qld 222, 225
Tiagarra Aboriginal Culture and Art Centre, Devonport, Tas. 216
Tidbinbilla Nature Reserve, ACT 218–19
Tiwi Design Tours, Bathurst Island, NT 134
Tiwi Designs, Wurrumiyanga, Bathurst Island, NT 28, 134
Tiwi Island art 126–7, 131, 134
Tiwi Islands Grand Final and Art Sale, Bathurst Island, NT 83–4
Tjala Arts, Amata community, SA 194
Tjanpi Desert Weavers, Alice Springs, NT 134–5
Tjapukai, Cairns, Qld 206–8
Tjatu Gallery, Marla, SA 194
Tjoritija (Western MacDonnell Ranges), NT 97–100
Tjukurpa (ancient laws and traditions) 102, 126, 153, 194
Tjungu Palya, Nyapari community, SA 194
Top Didj Cultural Experience & Art Gallery, Katherine, NT 66, 135
Torres Strait Island Creole (language) 14, 15, 222
Torres Strait Islander art and artists 24, 225
Torres Strait Islander music 31
Torres Strait Islander people 2, 72
kinship rules 16
languages 14, 15, 222
and native title 38–41
social and economic opportunities through RAPs 56–7
Torres Strait Islands 222–3
seasons 222
tours 225
tour guides
Indigenous 64–5
what if your guide is not Indigenous? 48–53
tourism 3, 56
gourmet food and culinary tourism 59–62
immersive cultural experiences 62
outback: landscapes of Indigenous Australia 62–3
tourists, what are they looking for? 59
tours and stays

Australian Capital Territory 219
New South Wales 3, 4, 158–69
Northern Territory 104–15
Queensland 200–9
South Australia 188
Tasmania 215
Torres Strait Islands 225
Victoria 5, 177–8
Western Australia 61–2, 143–51
see also art tours; cultural heritage; scenic tours
Tower Hill Visitor Centre, Warrnambool, Vic. 178
Traditional Owners
joint management schemes at national parks 48
knowledge of the world 2
performance of welcome ceremonies 11
protocols for visitors 68–70
traditional ownership of inherited styles (art) 24–7
Trevorrow, Bruce 44
'Tribal Voice' (song) 12
Tribal Warrior Cultural Cruises, Sydney, NSW 5, 169
Truganini (Tasmanian Aboriginal woman) **50**
Tumut Brungle Gundagai Area Aboriginal community 158

U
Ubirr, Kakadu NP, NT **4**, 88, 90, 91, 92
Udepata (Ellery Creek Big Hole) 99
Ulpma (Serpentine Gorge) 99
Uluṟu 100, 102
Aṉangu people's views on climbing of 69–70, 104
ban on tourists climbing on 70
National Indigenous Constitutional Convention 42
sacred nature of 69, 70, 104
Uluṟu Statement from the Heart 42
Uluṟu–Kata Tjuṯa NP, NT 48, 69–70, 100–4, 113
Uptuyu Aboriginal Adventures, Kimberley, WA **65**
Us Mob (band) 31

V
van Neerven, Ellen 37
vegetation management 9–10
Venture North Safaris, NT 113–15
videos 68, **69**
Voyages Indigenous Tourism Australia – Ayers Rock Resort, NT 115

W
Waanyi nation of the Gulf of Carpentaria 37
Wadandi people 61, 146
Wagal people 5
Wajarri (language) 155
Walk for Reconciliation 44
Walkabout Cultural Adventures, Mossman, Qld 208
Walkatjara Art Centre, Cultural Centre, Uluṟu–Kata Tjuṯa NP, NT 103, 135–6
Walker, Clinton 149
Walker, Juan 208
Wallace, Kathleen 127
Wallumedegal people 5, 169
Walmajarri (language) 152, 154
Wandjina paintings/spirit 7, 20, 153
Wangal people 169
Wangkajunga (language) 152, 154
Warakurna Artists, Warakurna, WA 153–4
Waray clan 94
Wardaman people 85
Waringarri Aboriginal Arts, Kununurra, WA 28, 154
Warlayitri Artists Aboriginal Corporation, Wirrimanu (Balgo), WA 28, 154–5
Warlpiri (people and language) 92, 116, 132, 135, 136, 154
marriage and descent in Warlpiri 'skin system' 19
Warlukurlangu Artists Aboriginal Corporation, Yuendumu, NT 136
Warlukurlangu (Fire Dreaming) 136
Warmun Art Centre, Warmun, WA 28, 155
Warmun artists 27, 142, 155
Warradjan Cultural Centre, Kakadu NP, NT 88, 90
Warramurrungundji (Earth Mother) 88
Warumungu (people and language) 92, 116
water blessings 11, 64
waterfalls
Kakadu NP, NT 89
Litchfield NP, NT 94
Nitmiluk NP, NT 95, 97
Wathaurung clan 173
'Welcome to Country' 72
ceremonies 11, **55**, 64
Wemba Wemba-Wergaia people 5
Werat clan 94
West MacDonnell NP, NT 97
Western Desert art movement 132, 133
Western MacDonnell Ranges, NT 97–100
Wetland Discovery Tour, Corroboree Billabong, NT 110
Whiteland, Josh 'Koomal' **60**, 61, 146
Whitlam, Gough 52
wildflowers
Karijini NP, WA 139
Tjoritja (Western MacDonnell Ranges), NT 98, 99
Uluṟu–Kata Tjuṯa NP, NT 102
wildlife
Currumbin Wildlife Sanctuary, Currumbin, Qld 200
Great Barrier Reef Marine Park, Qld 197
Kakadu NP, NT 88, 89, 90, 91, 115
Karijini NP, WA 139
Mary River Wetlands, NT 110
Nitmiluk NP, NT 95
Nura Diya – Taronga's Aboriginal Discovery Tour, Mosman, NSW 165–6
Purnululu NP, WA 142
South Bruny NP, Tas. 24
Tidbinbilla Nature Reserve, ACT 218
Tjoritja (Western MacDonnell Ranges), NT 98, 99
Uluṟu–Kata Tjuṯa NP, NT 102–3
Wilkens, Sir George Hubert 3
Willandra Lakes, NSW 161–2
Williams, Joey 149
Wilpena Pound Resort, Ikara–Flinders Ranges NP, SA 188
Wilson, Sir Ronald 43, 52
Wilson, Sammy 70
Wilunyu (language) 155
Winch, Tara Jane 37
Woiwurrung clan 173
Woolagoodja, Donny 153
Woolkabunning Kiaka Incorporated 61
Worimi Local Aboriginal Land Council 166
work-for-the-dole scheme 58
World Heritage sites
Kakadu NP, NT 86
Purnululu NP, WA 140
Uluṟu–Kata Tjuṯa NP, NT 102
Willandra Lakes, NSW 161–2
Worrorra (people and language) 137, 152, 153
Wotjobaluk clan 174
Wright, Alexis, novels by 37
writers 36–7
Wuddi Cultural Tours and Cultural Centre, Dumbleyung, WA 149
Wukalina Walk, Launceston, Tas. **214**, 215
Wula Guda Nyinda Eco Adventures, Shark Bay, WA 149–51
Wundargoodie Aboriginal Safaris, Wyndham, WA 151
Wunumbal (people and language) 137, 152, 153
Wurlaki (language) 128
Wurramara, Emily 31
Wurre 112
Wurrgeng (season – mid-June to mid-August), Kakadu, NT 88
Wurumpi Band 31
Wurundjeri people 174

X
X-ray paintings 91

Y
Yabun Festival, Sydney, NSW 51, 156, 172
Yalkarriwuy, Gali 122
Yamaji Art, Geraldton, WA 155
Yamaji people 155
Yankunytjatjara people 100, 102, 191
Yarrenyty Arltere Artists, Alice Springs, NT 136
Yarretyeke 100
Yawkyawk (female water spirit) 128
Yegge (season – May to mid-June), Kakadu, NT 88
Yellow Water area, Kakadu NP, NT 90
Yellow Water Cruise, Kakadu NP, NT 115
yidarkis (didgeridoos) 29, 116, 118, 122, 123
Yindjibarndi people 149
Yirbana Gallery, Art Gallery of New South Wales, Sydney, NSW 169
Yirritja clan 17, 19
Yirrkala artworks 22–3, 117–18
Yirrkala Bark Petition 118
Yirrmal (musician) 31
Yolŋu people 12, 104, 109
artworks and artists 22–3, 117–20, 123, 130
ceremonies and culture 62
clan groupings 17
classified as Dhuwa or Yirritja 17, 19
cultural experiences 109–10
Garma Festival 62, 68–9, 80–2
kinship and classification system 16–19
marriage rules 17
musicians 29
yothu–yindi (child–mother) relationships between clans 18
Yolŋu society, *manikay* role in 30
Yolŋu-Matha languages 12, 16
Yorta Yorta Aboriginal Community v State of Victoria and Others 41
Yothu Yindi (band) 12, 30, 31, **31**, 83
Yothu Yindi Foundation (YYF) 62, 68
Yuggera Aboriginal Dancers 206
Yuin-Dharawal nation 162
Yuin people 163
Yunupingu, Dr M. 12, 83
Yunupingu family 118

Z
Zey (season), Torres Strait Islands 222

ABOUT THE AUTHOR

Professor Marcia Langton AM PhD Macq U, BA (Hons) ANU, FASSA is one of Australia's most important voices for Indigenous Australia. She first became an Indigenous rights activist as a student at the University of Queensland, before spending time in Papua New Guinea, Japan and North America learning about those countries' peoples and cultures. On her return to Australia Marcia Langton graduated in Anthropology at ANU. Since then, she has worked with the Central Land Council, the Cape York Land Council, and for the 1989 Royal Commission into Aboriginal Deaths in Custody.

Professor Langton has received many accolades, including an Order of Australia. She has held the Foundation Chair of Australian Indigenous Studies at The University of Melbourne since February 2000. As an anthropologist and geographer, she has made a significant contribution to government and non-government policy as well as to Indigenous studies. Professor Langton has written several books, both academic and popular, including *First Australians* (MUP, 2009), co-authored with Rachel Perkins, which was written in conjunction with an SBS documentary by the same name. She is also regularly asked to comment on issues related to Indigenous rights and art. In 2016 she was honoured as a University of Melbourne Redmond Barry Distinguished Professor. The following year, Professor Marcia Langton was appointed as the first Associate Provost at the University of Melbourne.

Acknowledgements

This book is the work of many, most of all those people who own and manage places and attractions in Indigenous Australia and enable visitors to enjoy our beautiful country and cultures. The need for a practical guide to Indigenous Australia has been raised by many, but it was the publisher at Hardie Grant, Melissa Kayser, who took the initiative and approached me to make it happen. Melissa understood the complexity of this project and the need for Indigenous authorship. She asked Nina Fitzgerald and Amba-Rose Atkinson, two Aboriginal students at The University of Melbourne, to write the place and event entries, and I am grateful to them and to staff at Hardie Grant for detailing these attractions. My own writing for this guide was improved immensely by Bernadette Foley, whose editing is greatly appreciated.

My friend and colleague Professor Aaron Corn of Adelaide University helped by providing a lucid account of how two Aboriginal kinship systems work – Yolŋu and Warlpiri – accompanied by the artwork and maps he produced with the late Dr Joe Gumbula and Steven Jampijinpa Patrick.

All of those people who gave permission for information, photographs, diagrams and maps to be included are also important contributors to this guide. I am especially grateful to the Australian Institute of Aboriginal and Torres Strait Islander Studies for giving permission to Hardie Grant to reproduce the AIATSIS map of Indigenous Australia. The maps and illustrations are a special feature of this book, and I thank all who assisted.

Published in 2018 by Hardie Grant Travel, a division of Hardie Grant Publishing

Hardie Grant Travel (Melbourne)

Building 1, 658 Church Street
Richmond, Victoria 3121

Hardie Grant Travel (Sydney)
Level 7, 45 Jones Street
Ultimo, NSW 2007

www.hardiegrant.com/au/travel

A catalogue record for this
book is available from the
National Library of Australia

Marcia Langton: Welcome to Country
ISBN 9781741175431

Publisher
Melissa Kayser
Editor
Bernadette Foley
Researchers
Nina Fitzgerald, Amba-Rose Atkinson
Proofreader
Ellen van Neerven
Editorial assistance
Aimee Barrett, Serena Thompson
Design
Hamish Freeman
Typesetting
Patrick Cannon, Kerry Cooke
Index
Max McMaster
Prepress
Splitting Image Colour Studio

Printed in China by 1010 Printing International Limited

Publisher's note: Every effort has been made to ensure that the information in this book is accurate at the time of going to press. The publisher welcomes information and suggestions for correction, addition or improvement.

Aboriginal and Torres Strait Islander readers are advised that this book may contain images and names of people who have died.

Cover artwork
Kuru Ala © Spinifex Women's Collaborative (Estelle Hogan, Myrtle Pennington, Ngalpingka Simms, Lorraine Davies, Debbie Hansen, Tjaruwa Woods)/Licensed by Viscopy, 2018/Image courtesy of Spinifex Arts Project and Outstation Gallery

Photography credits

Title page: Eunice Napanangka Jack in the studio at Ikuntji Artists, Northern Territory (courtesy of Dr Chrischona Schmidt)

Images (left to right, top to bottom where more than one image appears on a page): Page 3 (a)Wayne Quilliam/TA, (b) Mary Evans/Natural History Museum/imagefolk; 4 (a) Kakadu Cultural Tours/TA, (b) Dreamtime Southern X/TA; 7 (a) James Fisher/TA, (b) Science & Society Picture Library/Getty Images; 8 (a) Roberto Seba/TA/Time Out Australia, (b) Central Land Council; 14 (a) Shaana McNaught/TNT, (b) Kristi O'Brien/TA; 21 (a) James Fisher/TA, (b) Shaana McNaught/TNT; 22 (a) Adrian Brown/TA, (b) Steve Strike/TA/TNT; 25 (a) Shaana McNaught/TNT, (b) Godinymayin Yijard Rivers Arts & Cultural Centre; 26 (a) Chris McLennan/TEQ, (b) LOOK Die Bildagentur der Fotografen GmbH/Alamy Stock Photo; 28 Rob Blackburn/TA; 30 (a) Pacific Press/LightRocket/Getty Images, (b) East Journey Music/TA; 31 Steve Eichner/WireImage/Getty Images; 32 (a) Cathy Finch/TEQ, (b) Andrew Watson/imagefolk; 35 (a) Don Arnold/WireImage/Getty Images, (b) Bridget Wood, (c) Taylor Hill/FilmMagic/Getty Images; 39 (a) Tim Graham/Robert Harding/imagefolk, (b) Anadolu Agency/Getty Images; 40 Anadolu Agency/Getty Images; 44 (a) John van Hasselt/Sygma/Getty Images, (b) Lisa Maree Williams/Stringer/Getty Images News/Getty Images; 47 (a) Jack Picone/Alamy Stock Photo, (b) Pool/Getty Images News/Getty Images; 49 (a) Hulton Archive/Stringer/Getty Images, (b) Time Life Pictures/ The LIFE Picture Collection/Getty Images; 50 (a) Paul Fearn/Alamy Stock Photo, (b) Ullstein bild/Getty Images; 52 (a) Bill Bachman/Alamy Stock Photo, (b) Scott Barbour/Stringer/Getty Images News/Getty Images; 55 (a) Darrian Traynor/Stringer/Getty Images News/Getty images, (b) Top Photo Corporation/Alamy Stock Photo; 60 (a) Lynton Crabb/TV, (b) Walk Into Luxury/TA, (c) Valarc Films/Richard Grey/TA; 63 (a&b) Valarc Films/Richard Grey/TA, (c) Robert Blackburn/TV; 65 (a) James Fisher/TA, (b) Shaana McNaught/TNT; 66 (a) Top Didj Cultural Experience & Art Gallery, (b) Harrow Discovery Centre; 67 Jeff Greenberg/Universal Images Group/Getty Images; 69 (a) Jason Edwards/National Geographic/Getty Images, (b) Wim Wiskerke/Alamy Stock Photo; 71 David Wall/Alamy Stock Photo; 73 Pudakul Aboriginal Cultural Tours/TA; 77 Daniel Boud/Bangarra Dance Theatre Australia; 81 (a) Peter Eve/TNT, (b) Valarc Films/Richard Grey/TA; 83 (a) East Journey Music/TA, (b) Peter Eve/TNT; 84 (a) Nick Rains/TNT, (b) Peter Eve/TNT; 87 (a) Johan Lolos/TNT, (b) Jane Burhop/Common Ventures/TNT; 90 (a) Peter Eve/TNT, (b) Shaana McNaught/TNT; 93 Nick Rains/TA; 95 (a) Allan Dixon/TA, (b)Ellenor Argyropoulos/TA; 98 Paddy Palin/TNT; 101 Shaana McNaught/TNT; 105 (a) Bremer Island Banubanu Beach Retreat, (b) James Fisher/TA; 106 (a) Ellenor Argyropoulos/TA, (b) Shaana McNaught/TNT, (c) Peter Eve/TNT; 109 Warwick Thornton/Brendan Fletcher/TA; 111 (a) Shaana McNaught/Pudakul Aboriginal Cultural Tours/TA, (b) Lords Kakadu and Arnhem Land Safaris, (c) Shaana McNaught/TNT; 112 (a) James Fisher/TA, (b) Shaana McNaught/TNT; 113 SEIT Outback Australia; 114 Venture North Safaris; 115 Voyagers Indigenous Tourism Australia; 117 Shaana McNaught/TNT; 119 (a) Roy Burnyila, (b) Robyn Djunginy Malibirr; 121 Steve Strike/TA/TNT; 122 (a) Baillie Lodges, (b) Elise Guittet; 125 (a&b) Godinymayin Yijard Rivers Arts & Cultural Centre, (c) Tamara Penniket; 127 (a) Jilamara Arts and Crafts, (b) David Hancock Photo; 129 NTBC/TA; 135 (a) Rhett Hammerton/Tjanpi Desert Weavers, (b) Top Didj Cultural Experience & Art Gallery; 137 Matt Scurfield Photography; 138 (a) TWA/TA, (b) Lincoln Fowler/TA; 141 (a) Rich Keam/TA, (b) TWA/TA; 144 (a) Kristi O'Brien/TA, (b) James Fisher/TA; 147 (a) James Fisher/TA, (b) Koomal Dreaming; 148 James Fisher/TA; 150 (a) Rich Keam/TA, (b) Anson Smart/TA, (c) Rich Keam/TA; 153 PA Images/Alamy Stock Photo; 159 (a) Paul Blackmore/DNSW, (b) Paddy Pallin/TA; 160 Dreamtime Southern X; 161 (a) Parks Australia, (b) Don Fuchs/DNSW; 163 (a) James Pipino/DNSW, (b) Kadoo Tours, (c) Tony Yeates/DNSW; 164 (a&b) Ngaran Ngaran Cultural Awareness, (c) Hamilton Lund/DNSW; 167 (a) Kristi O'Brien/TA, (b&c) Courtesy of the Royal Botanic Garden Sydney; 168 (a) Ethan Rohloff/DNSW, (b)Belinda Pratten, (c) Pierre Toussiant/DNSW; 171 (a) Mabel Ritchie, (b) Keith McInnes/DNSW; 174-175 Harrow Discovery Centre; 176 Brambuk National Park & Cultural Centre; 179 (a) Mark Chew/TV, (b) Roberto Seba/TV; 181 (a) Lynton Crabb/TV; (b&c) Narana Aboriginal Cultural Centre; 183 Lynton Crabb/TV; 185 (a) Craig Ingram/SATC, (b) Mike Haines/SATC; 186 (a) Adam Bruzzone/SATC, (b) Mike Haines/SATC; 189 (a) Wilpena Pound Resort, (b) James Fisher/TA; 190 Adam Bruzzone/SATC; 192 Andre Castellucci/SATC; 196 Chris McLennan/TEQ; 197 (a) Elizabeth Carlson/TEQ, (b) Underwater Earth/TEQ; 199 (a) Tony Gwynn-Jones/TEQ, (b) Alan Jensen/TEQ; 201 (a) Currumbin Wildlife Sanctuary, (b&c) Adventure North Australia; 202 (a) Wayne Quilliam/TA, (b) James Fisher/TA; 204 (a) Mungalla Aboriginal Tours, (b) Kristi O'Brien/TA; 205 Supplied by the CaPTA Group; 207 (a) Amber Toms/TA, (b &c) Straddie Adventures; 208-209 Walkabout Cultural Adventures; 210 TA; 213 (a) Graham Freeman/TA, (b) Cradle Mountain Huts/TA; 214 Rob Burnett/TT; 217-220 Visit Canberra; 221 CulturalEyes-AusSoc2/Alamy Stock Photo; 223 Peter Lik/TEQ; 224 (a) Peter Lik/TEQ, (b) Mark Fitz/TEQ

Abbreviations

DNSW Destination New South Wales
TA Tourism Australia
TEQ Tourism and Events Queensland
TNT Tourism Northern Territory
TT Tourism Tasmania
TV Tourism Victoria
TWA Tourism Western Australia